INTRODUCTION TO COMPUTATIONAL
CULTURAL PSYCHOLOGY

Human psychology is deeply rooted in the cultures in which people live. *Introduction to Computational Cultural Psychology* introduces a revolutionary approach to studying cultural psychology. Drawing on novel computational tools and in-depth case studies, Professor Yair Neuman offers thought-provoking answers to questions such as: How are thought and language deeply related? How can computers help us to understand different cultures? How can computers assist military intelligence in identifying vengeful intentions? And how is our concept of "love" rooted in our basic embodied experience? Written by a leading interdisciplinary researcher, this book is a tour de force that will be of interest to a variety of researchers, students, and practitioners in psychology, as well as an interdisciplinary audience with an interest in the intricate web woven between the human psyche and its cultural context.

Yair Neuman is a Professor in the Department of Education at Ben-Gurion University of the Negev in Israel, a researcher at the Homeland Security Institute (Ben-Gurion University of the Negev), and a Senior Fellow at the Brain Sciences Foundation (USA). He was the chief algorithm developer at the IARPA Metaphor Project (ADAMA Group), where novel algorithms have been developed for the identification of metaphorical language. His work has been published extensively in leading journals for various disciplines including psychology, psychoanalysis, theoretical biology, mathematical modeling, semiotics, and information sciences. His most recent book, *Reviving the Living: Meaning Making in Living Systems*, was published in 2008.

CULTURE AND PSYCHOLOGY

Series Editor
David Matsumoto, *San Francisco State University*

As an increasing number of social scientists come to recognize the pervasive influence of culture on individual human behavior, it has become imperative for culture to be included as an important variable in all aspects of psychological research, theory, and practice. *Culture and Psychology* is an evolving series of works that brings the study of culture and psychology into a single, unified concept.

Ute Schönpflug, *Cultural Transmission: Psychological, Developmental, Social, and Methodological Aspects*

Evert van de Vliert, *Climate, Affluence, and Culture*

David Matsumoto and Fons J. R. van de Vijver, *Cross-Cultural Research Methods in Psychology*

Angela K.-y. Leung, Chi-yue Chiu and Ying-yi Hong, *Cultural Processes: A Social Psychological Perspective*

Romin W. Tafarodi, *Subjectivity in the Twenty-First Century: Psychological, Sociological, and Political Perspectives*

Introduction to Computational Cultural Psychology

Yair Neuman

Ben-Gurion University of the Negev, Be'er-Sheva, Israel

CAMBRIDGE
UNIVERSITY PRESS

CAMBRIDGE
UNIVERSITY PRESS

University Printing House, Cambridge CB2 8BS, United Kingdom

Published in the United States of America by Cambridge University Press, New York

Cambridge University Press is part of the University of Cambridge.

It furthers the University's mission by disseminating knowledge in the pursuit of education, learning, and research at the highest international levels of excellence.

www.cambridge.org
Information on this title: www.cambridge.org/9781107661585

First published 2014

Printed in the United Kingdom by Clays, St Ives plc

A catalog record for this publication is available from the British Library

Library of Congress Cataloging in Publication Data
Neuman, Yair, 1968–
Introduction to computational cultural psychology / Yair Neuman.
     pages   cm. – (Culture and psychology)
Includes bibliographical references and index.
ISBN 978-1-107-02584-4 (hardback) – ISBN 978-1-107-66158-5 (paperback)
1. Ethnopsychology.   2. Social psychology.   3. Culture–Psychological aspects.   I. Title.
GN502.N474   2014
155.8–dc23
2013032797

ISBN 978-1-107-02584-4 Hardback
ISBN 978-1-107-66158-5 Paperback

Dedicated to the memory of my late grandmother, Bracha (Berta) Lifshitz (1926–2008): "Let her soul be weaved in the bundle of life."

"There is a pleasure in the pathless woods."

(Lord Byron)

CONTENTS

FIGURES

TABLES

PREFACE

For Lord Byron, who was an adventurer and probably a thrill seeker, the pleasure in the "pathless woods" may have been the result of the thrill associated with the uncertainty, promise, and danger of traveling in an unknown territory. I am neither an adventurer nor a thrill seeker. However, from a very young age, I have found great pleasure in traveling the pathless woods of knowledge. A kind of a wimpy adventurer, you may call me. These travels have led me to very varied territories of human knowledge, from experimental psychology (Neuman and Weitzman 2003) and psychoanalysis (Neuman 2009a) to mathematical modeling (Neuman *et al.* 2012); from theoretical biology (Neuman 2008) to semiotics (Neuman 2009b); and from discourse analysis (Neuman *et al.* 2001) to innovative information technologies (Neuman *et al.* 2013b). What is interpreted by some of my colleagues as a symptom of an academic multiple personality disorder is for me a natural and legitimate expression of a deep intellectual passion.

Knowledge is not naturally demarcated by borders, and wherever borders exist in our minds they indicate our tendency to force order in a simplistic way and to follow the social power relations of academic politics. Physicists who study the semantic networks of language are not linguists, but their contribution to our understanding of human language is indispensable. Should this work be appreciated despite the fact that it transcends disciplinary boundaries? My answer is: yes!

My passion knows no borders and this book is the expression of this passion and an attempt to introduce a new path of inquiry for cultural psychology. It is not a prototypical text in any of the disciplines on which it draws, from cultural psychology to computational science, and those who seek their academic heroes and secure niches in this book might be disappointed. By analogy: anyone who has practiced a traditional martial art such as karate might be disappointed to find how limited their rigid schemes are in real-life situations. To successfully mess your hands in real-life situations a more flexible attitude is necessary, an attitude that is interdisciplinary in nature. Following the previous fighting analogy, a real-world fighter should be competent in kicking, punching, grappling, biting, and perhaps even chewing, and I have said nothing yet about the psychology of a real fight and how to "read" conflict situations.

This book follows the same general attitude. However, while interdisciplinary in nature, it backs its thesis with a heavy theoretical and empirical arsenal of justifications and evidence from the relevant disciplines. Various chapters have already been published in academic journals and were warmly accepted. Therefore, my hope is that readers will find in this book a serious and well-grounded visionary thesis, and that at the same time they will be patient with its interdisciplinary nature and the free play of ideas, which is what science is all about.

I have chosen to introduce the idea of computational cultural psychology through several case studies. As the field of computational cultural psychology is not yet established as a discipline, some of the case studies present in-depth elaboration of research questions, some provide minimal examination, and some wild thoughts for the future to come. It is time to enter the pathless woods.

ACKNOWLEDGMENTS

My grandmother and my grandfather used to eat fish as a part of the traditional Jewish Friday dinner. After the dinner, they used to share the fish remains with the neighborhood's cats. My grandmother used to look at the cats feasting on their food and say: "They are hungry." As a child, this repeated statement sounded to me like the most trivial thing a living being could utter. However, on an unconscious level, I noticed that when my grandmother uttered this statement her face expressed deep sorrow. It took me years of growth and studying psychology to recall this repeated incidence and in retrospect to understand that, when my grandmother looked at the hungry cats, she actually saw a mirroring of herself and her people starving to death in Bergen-Belsen, the same concentration camp where the famous Anne Frank's life ended.

A Hassidic proverb says, "All the darkness of the world cannot extinguish the light of a single candle, yet one candle can illuminate all the darkness." For me, the famous question of whether poetry can exist after Auschwitz is of minor importance. The real question is whether human beings who experienced the deep darkness of the world may still want to illuminate it with their almost invisible light.

My grandmother's empathy for living creatures gave me the answer. She used to feed the hungry, whether human beings or animals, with humility and respect. One Saturday, when I was a very young child, she and my grandfather invited one of the city's poor people for dinner. When I opened the door for the guest, I was shocked by the appearance of a dwarf with a hunchback. My only acquaintance with a person with such a grotesque appearance was from the novel *The Hunchback of Notre-Dame*, and therefore I fled with horror. To my surprise my grandparents were indifferent to the grotesque appearance of their guest and hosted him with great respect.

If there is a lesson to be learned from the above stories it is a lesson about the ability of human beings, like my grandmother, to illuminate the darkness of the world with their almost unnoticeable and daily grace, with a single candle.

When I was a graduate student it was Zvi Bekerman who first introduced me to the field of cultural psychology. Following his advice I started reading Bakhtin, Bateson, Billig, Cole, Valsiner, and many others who have opened up for me the cultural semiotic sphere. This book could not have been written without Zvi Bekerman's trust and continuous encouragement over the years. Doron Havazelet was the first to support my information-technology projects despite the fact that I was an outsider to the field and that my ideas have been considered nonconventional to say the least. He was found to be correct. Peter Turney was and still is my expert field guide for natural language processing, and our research collaborations have been not only highly successful but also a major source of professional growth. Jaan Valsiner hosted me warmly in Clark University's "kitchen" and supported my interdisciplinary efforts with great enthusiasm. He is a model intellectual who is both a radical thinker and open minded. My research assistant, Dan Assaf, and my programmer, Yochai Cohen, both of whom worked with me on all of my computational projects, provide me with many examples of what it means to be an "A team." My friend Saadia Gozlan has been a continuous source of support, and his insightful understanding of systems encouraged me to believe that my creative ideas may finally gain recognition. Finally, I would like to thank the book series editor, David Matsumoto, for his trust and warm support in my book venture, and Hazel Harris for her excellent editorial work. The chaotic nature of life is such that trust and encouragement are necessary at the bifurcation points that inevitably pop up along the road. The aforementioned people have proved it beyond any reasonable doubt.

Some of the book's chapters draw heavily on my previous publications. I would like to thank the following publishers for their permission to use these copyright materials: Palgrave Macmillan for Yair Neuman. 2012. "On revenge." *Psychoanalysis, Culture & Society* 17: 1–15. Springer for their permission to use Yair Neuman, Peter Turney, and Yochai Cohen. 2012. "How language enables abstraction: a case study in computational cultural psychology." *Integrative Psychological and Behavioral Sciences* 46.2: 129–45. De Gruyter for their permission to use Yair Neuman. 2009. "Peter Pan's shadow and the relational matrix of the 'I.'" *Semiotica* 176: 15–27; Yair Neuman, Norbert Marwan, and Daniel Unger. In press. "Dinner is ready!

Studying the dynamics and semiotics of dinner." *Semiotica*. Guilford Press for their permission to use Yair Neuman, D. Assaf, and Yochai Cohen. 2012. "Automatic identification of themes in small group dynamics through the analysis of network motifs." *Bulletin of the Menninger Clinic* 76: 53–68. IEEE for their permission to use Danny Livshits, Howard Newton, and Yair Neuman. 2012. "Can computers help us to better understand different cultures? Toward computer-based CULINT." Paper presented at the *2012 European Intelligence and Security Informatics Conference* (EISIC 2012), August 22–24, University of Southern Denmark, Odense, Denmark.

1

What is computational cultural psychology?

Dr. Samuel Johnson is known for refuting Berkeley's idealism by stomping his thumb against a solid stone. Whether this anecdote is historically grounded or not is of minor importance. The lesson, however, is extremely important. Some arguments and ideas are refutable or clearly confirmed when they come up against the solid rock of reality. While a naive materialist would consider stones as the hallmark of reality testing, cultural encounters may provide us with a painful experience that confirms the reality of "culture" no less than the reality of stones.

At this point you may intuitively sense my pragmatic approach: it is pain that defines our boundary in encountering reality. To say it differently, let me recall Terry Eagleton, a nonrepresentative of pragmatism, who in his book *How to Read a Poem* writes (2006, 8): "Reality is what turns its back upon us, resisting our infantile demand that the world should serve as our looking glass." Well, as the following example teaches us, the world is not the looking glass of our fantasies.

An ultimate example of coming into the reality of culture appears in a wonderful literary piece: H. G. Wells's *The Country of the Blind* (1947). The story's plot is simple and illuminating. During travel in South America an explorer by the name of Nuñez accidently arrives in a valley exclusively populated by blind people. The valley is geographically cut off from the rest of the world and therefore inhabited by an isolated community that, due to a disease, has over the generations become blind. The community and its habitat are perfectly adjusted to the blindness. Nuñez, however, sees the opportunity in this situation and reminds himself that "In the country of the blind the one-eyed man is king."

To recall Lacan (cited in Žižek 2006), the madman is not only the beggar who considers himself a king but also the king who considers himself a king. While Lacan gained his justified reputation through cryptic writing, in this case his observation is perfectly clear: there is always a difference between our representation of reality and reality itself; between the map and the territory. The beggar who considers himself a king is a madman because his self-image is diagrammatically opposed to his public symbolic status. However, the king who identifies himself with the king fails too in understanding the gap between his symbolic status and his real existence as an individual nullified of any symbolic meaning. *The Prince and the Pauper*, by the great American writer Mark Twain, is a wonderful illustration of Lacan's thesis.

In Nuñez's case, the fantasy of being a king through the superiority of sight is blind to the gap between different symbolic systems, between different cultures. As Nuñez quickly and painfully realizes, the otherness of the blind men's culture is not necessarily a source of weakness. The inhabitants have designed a culture perfectly adjusted to their blindness and the one who turns out to be maladjusted is Nuñez, who fails to function and whose talk of sight seems to the blind men a kind of mental disturbance.

The village doctor suggests that Nuñez's eyes be removed, claiming that they are diseased and are affecting his brain. Thus, as we can see, stomping into another culture may be no less painful than stomping into a stone. I will leave the curious reader who is not familiar with the story with the pleasure of reading it and finding for himself whether Nuñez accepted the physician's advice.

The story teaches us a lesson not only on the danger of patronizing a different culture but also on *the reality of culture as a theoretical construct*. The reality of culture is evident precisely at the point where our unconscious and automatic habits of interaction, practice, and communication fail to function as a result of a changing context characterized by a different group's symbolic organization.

Let me explain this idea by providing a personal example. Years ago, I was invited to participate in an Israeli delegation organized by the Israel Ministry of Science. The aim of the delegation was to establish new guidelines for the cooperation of young Israeli and German scientists through the German–Israeli Foundation for Scientific Research and Development, equally sponsored by the governments of both countries.

A week before the planned departure to Germany we participated in a meeting that aimed to plan the delegation. A *week* before our travel … Here you can sense a first feature of Israeli culture: the preference for improvisation over careful planning. It is not that Israeli culture avoids or dismisses the importance of careful planning. However, through experiencing the chaotic nature of the world, specifically on the battlefield, Israelis have acknowledged and praised the importance of improvisation in attempts to find practical and creative solutions to a problem, given the absence of conventional solutions and available resources.

As can be expected, the meeting was a total catastrophe and quickly slipped into arguments and quarrels among the participants. As the only social scientist in the delegation, I was trying to do my best to constructively manage the group's dynamics but unfortunately with no success. That evening, I got an urgent call from the chief scientist of the ministry. She explained that the person who was in charge of the delegation had decided to quit her job a week before the planned departure. However, the chief scientist had heard from the participants in the meeting that I was probably the only one who could handle this chaos, as a result of my psychological background, and she asked me to travel as the head of the delegation. This was how I became the head of the delegation and an ad hoc cultural psychologist.

I traveled with a group of brilliant people who belonged to one of the most informal, nonhierarchical, and impolite cultures in the world. We traveled to Germany, which was relatively very formal, hierarchical, and polite. The world may be a global village but within this village there are huge differences in the ways in which groups of people think and interact.

In one of our working sessions, we were introduced to a top manager in one of the prestigious Max Plank Institutes. The man was in his sixties, well dressed with an expensive suit, and self-assured in his position and in his attitudes (he didn't like the social sciences and the humanities). After presenting his guidelines for cooperation, time was given for comments and questions. Our young German colleagues avoided any criticism of their professors. They usually came to their Israeli colleagues, presented their concerns, and asked the Israelis to present them instead. Therefore, it was not a surprise that the first to raise his hand was a young Israeli Ph.D. student in electrical engineering. He was dressed in tattered jeans and a T-shirt. His hair was in a long, hippy style, and after a couple of days of not shaving his stubble could be seen from afar. "I don't agree with you," he said. The Max Plank professor was shocked – not only that the young man who challenged him looked like a hippy but also that he was brutally and directly challenging an authority!

Israeli culture is proud of its direct and frank style of speaking, known as *dugri* (Katriel 1986). This is quite similar to the American style of "don't bullshit me." Do you remember the martial-art analogy I presented in the preface? Using the same analogy, it is Krav Maga, the Israeli combat system, that best represents this approach. No ancient rituals, unnecessary sophistication, or codes of honor. It is about getting straight to business without wasting too much energy. The Israeli *dugri* style of discourse is considered mere rudeness in most cultures. In fact, it is the same kind of impoliteness Americans are sometimes accused of by their European colleagues.

Back to the story. While the young Israeli student presented his criticism, I examined with great concern the facial expressions of the German professor, who was probably fantasizing about the various possible techniques he might use to discipline this young churl.

While I did my best to neutralize these kinds of cultural mines, they popped up throughout all the interactions, reminding us, to paraphrase Mark Twain, that the report of culture's death by some postmodernist thinkers is an exaggeration.

Culture is a concept that is still alive and kicking. It is the construct we use to explain stone-stumbling intergroup interactions like that described above. Culture does not exist objectively as a metaphysical structure. It is an invented concept that has an "objective" status no less than the existence of a stone. This idea is not new.

The idea that concepts are constructed in an attempt to explain a dissonance clearly appears in the writing of Charles Sanders Peirce, one of the greatest American thinkers. For instance, Peirce considers the emergence of the self as a psychological explanatory construct. His example is of a child who touches a hot oven. The pain may be experienced as it is, but the Western culture that approaches the child as an individual causes him to attribute the pain to an internal agency: "*I* am in pain."

This form of cultural mediation is only one way of conceptualizing this experience, and there are various alternative forms of conceptualization. The pain is not necessarily "mine." It is not necessarily a part of myself and I am not necessarily "in" pain. The pain may be conceived as a temporary experience that has nothing to do with my subjective agency. It does not mean that the pain is not painful but rather that it is experienced or conceptualized in a different way.

One of my students, a clinical psychologist, experienced this logic first-hand when she traveled in the jungles of the Amazon. She and her husband traveled with a group of natives, both adults and children. To move through the jungle the natives used machetes: big, sharp knives. As the motor ability of children is far from perfect, my student saw some accidents in which a child mistakenly sliced another one. In our Western and modern culture a slice to a child would probably result in a hysterical reaction by the child and his or her parents. However, my student was shocked by the indifference with which the child and the surrounding people responded to these injuries. No agency, no hysteria, and no blame. After brief medical treatment the group kept moving in the jungle.

According to Peirce, the self is the invented construct that aims to integrate a variety of experiences. It is not a transcendental agency à la Kant, nor a natural hardwired organization of the brain, a reductionist explanation that is the mirror picture of the metaphysical one. The self is a construct we *pragmatically* build for making sense of our experience. It is evident in tragic brain catastrophes, such as Alzheimer's disease, when the self is fragmented.

The same logic holds for the concept of culture. Culture does not exist in Plato's ideals, nor can it be reduced to our genes. Therefore, when we try to understand a culture we attempt to understand the way we conceptualize otherness as it emerges from the failure of our habits to function in a given symbolic environment.

Otherness is not necessarily the otherness of an exotic culture. The culture in which we live is usually opaque to our own reflection because we lack the view from within or, saying it differently, we are blind to our own environment.

Talented novelists are probably those who are the most sensitive in providing us with the ability to mirror our own culture, albeit in an intuitive manner. In his great novel *The Possibility of an Island*, Michel Houellebecq (2007) provides us with a critical reflection on the current European culture in which pets have replaced children and in which, under the influence of pornography and liberalism, sex has turned into an alienated form of entertainment.

To what extent can we consider Houellebecq's novel as validly representing the current "European culture"? And in what sense?

Following Bakhtin (1990) and Kundera's (1988) insightful work, one should remember that the novel is a unique form of consciousness that does not aim to introduce arguments but rather aims to provide a mirroring function in its complex, aesthetic form. Indeed, texts, whether novels or newspapers, are an important source for understanding culture as a form of "collective consciousness" (Volosinov 1986) – whether a distant culture or our own.

One can better understand European culture by reading Houellebecq in the same way as one can better understand American culture, with its superheroes and apocalyptic anxiety, by reading *Watchmen* (Moore and Gibbons 1995) and better understand the life of American Jews of Eastern European origin by reading Philip Roth's *Portnoy's Complaint* (Roth 1967). The reason is simple. A text, in its most general sense, is a gateway to the understanding of a culture because culture is semiotically mediated (Valsiner 2007). According to this proposal, culture as a distant text should be approached through a careful semiotic analysis of various texts.

As argued by the linguistic anthropologist Alton Becker:

> In reading a distant text, one tries to project oneself not into another mind – at least at first – but into another language, which held grip on that other mind, that other person, who inherited with his language, choicelessly, the greater part of the ideas by which and from which he or she loves, without thinking about them at all.
>
> (Becker 2000, 371–2)

This wonderful insight will be repeatedly echoed in this book. It means that understanding a culture entails understanding the semiotic systems and processes that mediate the "mind" of its members. What do we actually mean by "semiotically mediated"? To address this question, I would like to present the semiotic perspective, at least according to my own modest understanding.

RELATIONAL HENS AND SEMIOTIC MINDS

Philosophers have bothering questions that cannot be easily addressed. For example, Leibniz (1646–1716) asked the famous question: "Why is there something rather than nothing?" A simple pragmatic answer is that if there were nothing instead of something then Leibniz could not have asked his sophisticated question. However, such a simple answer is a wit that might be dismissed by the philosopher and therefore a better answer should be given.

Surprisingly, an experiment conducted by the Gestalt psychologist Wolfgang Köhler (1887–1967) provides an answer, albeit to a slightly different question. In the age of fMRI and other sophisticated toys of the behavioral sciences, we may have lost the sensitivity for simple and brilliant experiments such as those used by some of the pioneers of psychology. This experiment (described in Luria 1976) is an example of such brilliance.

The experiment involved a hen, grains, and two sheets of paper. While hens have never been the psychologist's favorite experimental pet, Köhler seems to wisely use his animalistic repertoire.

The hen was presented with grain on two sheets of paper, one *light gray* and the other *dark gray*. On the light gray sheet, the grains simply rested on the surface of the paper so that the chicken could peck at them and joyfully eat them. In contrast, the grains on the dark gray sheet of paper were glued in place so that the chicken could not eat them.

After being exposed to the sheets in several trials, the chicken learned the logic of the experiment. It pecked at the light gray sheet and avoided the dark gray sheet. In this phase, Köhler turned to the crucial test stage of the experiment and presented the hen with a new pair of sheets, one of which was the same light gray sheet and the other a new white sheet that was lighter than the light gray one.

Now the interesting question was how the chicken would behave in this case and to which of the sheets she would positively react. When reading about this experiment I imagined three possible hypotheses corresponding to three different epistemological stances. The first hypothesis and stance is that the chicken would peck the same light gray paper from which she had previously gained her nutrition. This hypothesis adheres to a Platonic absolutist stance in which the absolute brightness of the sheet is the one determining the hen's behavior. The second hypothesis is a caricaturist version of the Darwinist stance. It suggests that at the individual level of analysis the hen's behavior is of no importance. Some hens are intelligent enough to understand the change, some are not, and let the best man or hen win. The third epistemological stance will be introduced through the experiment's result. In most of the cases, the chicken pecked at the new white sheet.

Köhler explained this result by arguing that the hen had been directed not to the absolute darkness or lightness but to the *relative* darkness. In other words, what triggered the hen's response was a relation, and the most basic of them all: a difference.

In this context, we may amuse ourselves by imagining Köhler's hen answering Leibniz by explaining to him that only an intelligent being can ask a question such as, "Why is there something rather than nothing?" And, for such a creature, the nature of the world cannot be artificially demarcated from the nature of his or her contemplating mind.

In this context, the "why" question should be replaced with a "how" question: how does the mind come into being? The hen could also have answered this question, by explaining that the basic unit of the mind – whether the mind of a chicken, the mind of the immune system, or the mind of a human being – is as explained by Gregory Bateson (2000, 318) a "difference which makes a difference."

The hen's response has been triggered by a difference. However, in itself, a difference (or a bit of information) is meaningless. A difference may exist at the physical level of analysis as a characteristic of the "objective" reality, whatever it is. However, the difference turns into a difference that makes a difference (i.e., a unit of meaning) only if it is mapped into another difference. For instance, the difference between the light gray sheet and the dark gray sheet is mapped into the difference between the pleasure of eating the grains and the "pain" of pecking the glued grains.

What we see is that the mapping function between the differences involves a similarity of differences that establishes a correspondence between two different realms: the physical realm of colors and the "mental" realm of pleasure and pain.

In this context, the difference between the two sheets functions as a *sign*, "something which stands to somebody for something in some respect or capacity" (Peirce 1931–1966, vol. II, 228). This generic definition of the sign was introduced by Peirce and is applicable to various systems, from natural language to the immune system (Neuman 2008).

Signs, as units of meaning, exist in every complex biological system. We may therefore define the "mind" as the general term for a *meaning-making system*. In this sense, there is a common denominator shared by the human mind interpreting a text, a chicken looking for grain, the immune system seeking to differentiate between self and nonself, and fungi seeking the optimal path to a source of energy.

There is of course a difference in the way different systems are involved in meaning making. Human language and its written representation create a sharp demarcation between human beings and the rest of the animal kingdom. Despite similarities with other signaling systems, human semiotic systems are complex and abstract in a unique way.

The idea of studying the human mind through a semiotic perspective is not new. It was Valentine Volosinov (1986), probably the greatest theoretician of this thesis, who made the statement that "outside the material of signs there is not psyche" (1986, 26). The following statement identifies mental activity with semiotic activity: "Psychic experience is the semiotic expression of the contact between the organism and the outside environment" (1986, 26). According to this thesis, the interface between the individual and the environment, whether the external environment or the internal environment, is mediated by signs – differences that are transformed into differences that make differences.

The mind is therefore a *relational* and *social* process as *signs exist only at the level of a communicating collective*. Therefore, our subjective mental experience is grounded in social interactions and, in contrast with the Cartesian solipsistic approach, the social-material has precedence over the metaphysical, transcendental, and individual self.

Even our ability to reflect on our thoughts is, according to this thesis, possibly only an internalization of external dialogues. Indeed, there is an accumulating body of evidence that self-consciousness is mediated by inner speech, and there are good reasons to explain this mediation in scientific terms (Neuman and Nave 2009a).

Cultural psychology is therefore, in the broadest sense, the study of mediation or the way signs that are formed in the social context frame our process of meaning making. Schweder and Sullivan (1990) suggest that the "semiotic subject" is the core concept of cultural psychology. It is the subject for whom the "meaning of the situation is the major determinant of his or her response to it" (1990, 402).

In sum, we have presented the semiotic perspective and have adopted the idea that the mind is the generic term for meaning making and that cultural psychology is the field that studies the unique processes through which human beings make sense of their environment through the mediation of signs emerging in their social contexts. The methodology through which we may study cultural psychology is discussed in the next sections.

FROM DR. JOHNSON TO WISŁAWA SZYMBORSKA

Let us return to the stone-stomping anecdote. We must admit that Dr. Johnson's aggressive form of refuting a thesis looks like a typical caricature of masculine behavior. In fact, it was precisely the same approach introduced by Galileo to the study of nature. There is, however, an alternative. The poet and Nobel laureate Wisława Szymborska (1995, 30), who I deeply admire, has a poem titled "Conversation with a Stone." The poem's opening is as follows:

> I knock at the stone's front door.
> "It's only me, let me come in.
> I want to enter your insides,
> Have a look round.
> Breathe my fill of you."

Szymborska's conversation with the stone (or reality) presents an alternative idea of how to understand it. Politely and with great respect she asks to come in and experience the stone from within. This "feminine" style of understanding is of course not the sole property of females and it has been described by Henry Bergson (1946, 161) in terms of intuition: "We call intuition here the sympathy by which one is transported into the interior of an object in order to coincide with what there is unique and consequently inexpressible in it. Analysis, on the contrary is the operation which reduces the object to elements already known."

This definition of intuition precisely captures the essence of Szymborska's conversation with the stone and the alternative she portrays in understanding reality. If we examine the research in cultural psychology, not to be mistaken for cross-cultural psychology, we can see that to a large extent it has followed this methodological path. Instead of forcing reality to answer our questions, cultural psychology has usually adopted a more intuitive interpretative stance. Adopting this methodological position is far from simple, as it requires extreme sensitivity to the most delicate nuances of the studied realm. Let me illustrate this point using another personal example.

Following a grant I received from the Israeli Ministry of Defense, I traveled to the USA to participate in a conference dealing with information technology and intelligence. During one of the conference's boring dinners, I met a very nice academic, with a background in political science, who makes his living by advising the intelligence community.

During this time, the American troops were up to their necks in the Iraqi mud, and we were discussing the difficulties faced by American intelligence in understanding other cultures in general and Iraqi culture in particular.

My argument was somehow provocative. Until you know the *smell* and the *sense of humor* of a different culture, you don't understand it at all. How many American intelligence officers know what makes the Iraqis laugh? How many of them know the unique smell of the Iraqi people? Do the Shia have a different smell from the Sunni Muslims?

My colleague was shocked by my rather provocative thesis, but I remembered my experience of getting into an Arab house with a detective team in an attempt to "bust" a suspect. It was dark and quiet and no resistance was evident as the sleeping residents were not aware of our entrance. As my sight and hearing were limited, my olfactory system became more sensitive. It was the smell that shocked me. For the first time, I became aware of the unique smell of the house, and in a deep and integrative way I felt that I better understood the otherness of this culture.

An intelligence officer can be an Ivy League graduate. He or she can master the language and read a wealth of academic books about a culture but never ever understand this otherness unless he or she experiences it with the most material, micro, and interactional particularities of the target group. He or she must be able to read the cultural text in its most petite nuances from *within*. This is probably the reason why the Israeli Shabak was much more accurate than the prestigious Mossad in warning the Israeli government against cooperation with the Lebanese Maroons during the First Lebanon War (Shiff and Ya'ari 1985). Shabak people are primarily field people who work with the target population and know their language, habits, smell, and sense of humor down to the micro level. They are within the stone. In the Lebanese case they were found to be right in their warning, as the Maroons were shown to be a broken reed, and the price of the wrong decision to cooperate with them still echoes in the Israeli borders.

Culture is not only the construct we use to explain "otherness" that cannot be attributed to universal or biological variance. It is the field where the psychology of individuals is "mediated." By that I mean that human psychology cannot simply be explained by universal mechanisms alone. Otherness is constituted by a variety of semiotic processes, of which the most important is human language. From an evolutionary perspective (and I'm quite suspicious about the simplicity with which this perspective is sometimes presented), language probably evolved as a tool of communication but turned into a tool of reflection. As such, the way members of different cultures communicate their different experiences has turned into different ways of reflection and self-understanding. This sounds like a very complex idea, but what does it actually mean?

THE BORROMEAN RINGS OF CULTURE

To explain the above thesis we have to return and present in a nutshell a thesis introduced by Luria and Vygotsky in their seminal work *Ape, Primitive Man and Child* (Luria and Vygotsky 1992). This book is excluded from some academic circles as drawing an analogy between "primitive" people, apes, and children is considered insulting. However, Luria and Vygotsky were not arrogant and colonialist Westerners. They belonged to a certain zeitgeist that might have failed to understand the complexity and otherness of cultures but they were also sensitive and insightful researchers.

Luria and Vygotsky suggest that the human mind is the synergetic and, to use a modern term, "emerging" product of three threads: the biological-evolutionary, the ontogenetic, and the cultural. According to this thesis the human mind is like the Borromean rings, which cannot lose a single ring without disintegrating as a whole. Figure 1.1 illustrates the rings. This integrative approach advises us to see the mind from three converging perspectives.

FIGURE 1.1 Borromean rings.

The evolutionary perspective makes the rather trivial claim that human beings are part of a wider biological-historical context. We share some similarities with other nonhuman organisms, and examining these similarities as well as differences is crucial for understanding the mind as a construct grounded in the biological realm. The fact that we are descendants of less complex life forms and share family resemblance with other creatures is not enough to explain our mind. We are an emerging product of a complex ontogenetic process through which we are formed from a sperm and an egg, mature as a fetus, are born as babies, grow as children, turn into mature adults, and finally decline as old people when the second law of thermodynamics wins over life.

This developmental process is of major importance, but again it is not enough. Our life, growth, maintenance, and decline take place in a cultural context, the context in which sign-communities (Volosinov 1986) use signs for mediating their encounters with the world, with others, and with themselves. As suggested by Hegel (2004) in his *Aesthetics*, the first man who carved the shape of a bison and created a symbolic distance from reality is the one who launched human civilization. Indeed, the psychoanalyst Donald Winnicott (1971) described culture as a "potential space," a space in which we use signs that paradoxically exist in between the reality they signify and the fantasy we share. The carved bison is a cultural artifact precisely because it is a "real" bison, a fantastic one, and neither of them at the same time.

While we arrogantly attribute play in the potential space to human beings, it is clearly evident albeit in different forms in other nonhuman organisms.

For instance, in his observation of animals' play, Gregory Bateson identified the "semiotic" aspect that is actually the potential space of their play. When two dogs play together they use the same behavior as in a real fight; for instance, they bite each other. How do they know whether a bite signals "play" or "fight"?

This process of communication is not a mechanical one, as is evident from the fact that play may sometimes slip into a fight. What Bateson identified was *meta-signals* that frame and make sense out of the basic signal. These meta-signals are actually the context of the play. *Context is meta-signals*. The bow position is one of these meta-signals that creates the context of play. A bite is sometimes just a bite, in the same way as a cigar is sometimes just a cigar. However, for understanding and communicating the meaning of a sign there is always a built-in ambiguity in the sign and an accompanying context that aims to interpret it.

These signal–context relations oblige us to adopt a multilevel perspective on semiotic systems to include culture. Dogs' culture may be less complex than that of human beings, but one cannot deny its semiotic nature. From now on the idea that "culture" is semiotically mediated will be taken as an axiom.

The importance of "context" for understanding semiotic mediation is a cornerstone in cultural psychology, but what is a context? What is the meaning of meta-signals? Volosinov presents the following scenario:

> A couple is sitting in a room. They are silent. One says, "Well!" The other says nothing in reply. For us who were not present in the room at the time of the exchange, this "conversation" is completely inexplicable. Taken in isolation, the utterance "well" is void and quite meaningless. Nevertheless, the couple's peculiar exchange, consisting of only one word, though one to be sure is expressively inflected, is full of meaning and significance and quite complete.
>
> (Volosinov cited in Shukman 1983, 10)

According to Volosinov, context involves a *spatial purview* shared by the speakers, *common knowledge* and circumstances, and the *common evaluation* of these circumstances. Understanding a different culture in context involves our understanding of cultural situations as trivial as that described above. It involves our ability to grasp the material environment with its symbolic value as well as the common knowledge of the participants and their evaluation of the situation from within, their set of values.

This idea of meaning as embedded in patterns of material objects, knowledge, and values is highly important. John Barwise has attempted to mathematize the notion of situation, but this venture led nowhere. Situations are patterns of cultural information. A dinner, a birthday, playing a game, or going to school are all culturally embedded situations. As such they are packets of information used for practical inference in daily life.

A computational approach drawing on huge data repositories and on novel fields such as textual entailment may be highly important for understanding situational knowledge and practical inference. Let us take for instance the situation of "dinner." Dinner, a term that denotes the main meal of the day, is a cultural construct whose meaning emerges along the lines set forth by Volosinov.

Let us use the Corpus of Contemporary American English (COCA) (Davies 2008) and examine the concrete objects/nouns associated with "dinner." We find table, wine, plates, dishes, and so on. These material objects constitute both the spatial context of "dinner" and the declarative factual knowledge involving these objects (e.g., that a common drink at dinner is wine rather than milk or beer).

We may extend this logic for identifying the procedural common knowledge associated with the situation of dinner through verbs and the objects on which they operate. The evaluation of this expectation in terms of emotions may be identified through sentiment analysis, and the beliefs associated with dinner by tracing the appearance of objects, actions, and emotions at different phases of the situation. Moreover, we may use the advancement in textual entailment to statistically infer relevant information from textual data. For instance, it is culturally dependent whether dinner describes the first, second, third, or even fourth meal of the day. In North America, dinner is eaten around 6 p.m. Now, let's have a look at the following sentences:

1. Danny ate dinner.
2. After he ate, Danny went to sleep.

For a member of North American culture the second sentence reasonably entails the first one. However, if the first sentence were "Danny ate breakfast" then the second sentence would be inferred with less confidence. It is of course possible that Danny is an infant who went to sleep after breakfast, that he is a mature man who was on a vacation, or even a high-school student who went to sleep after a sleepless Sunday night. There are many potential qualifications and pieces of contextual information that may make the second sentence "true" or highly likely. However, it is our habitual knowledge that if dinner usually takes place around 6 p.m. then it is more likely that a person will go to sleep after dinner than after breakfast.

This simple reasoning or practical semantic inference concerning a daily situation is highly complex and loaded with knowledge, expectations, and qualifications. We may use the above conceptualization not only to characterize situations or other cultural practices (e.g., dinner, lunch, breakfast) but also to examine the similarities and differences across cultures. For instance, is there a difference between American and English dinner? Is there a difference between the representation of dinner in fiction and newspapers?

While there is no news in understanding cultures and the way they interact with the psychology of the individual, there is news in the way I propose to address this challenge. Cultural psychology has gained insights from close ethnographic analysis of other cultures as well as from some quantitative studies. However, in recent years we have been experiencing a change that cannot be ignored or dismissed by cultural psychologists. The emergence of the Web, the establishment of huge data repositories unprecedented in human history, and the development of powerful information-technology tools for text processing and data analysis have changed the scope of our research. Whether such a changing landscape is an opportunity or a fashion is still an open question, but my aim is to introduce a new field and some preliminary evidence that this is indeed an opportunity.

This book, however, has no revolutionary pretensions but only the modest aim of enriching the toolkit of cultural psychology. To understand a culture we must understand its smell and sense of humor. I doubt whether information technology can currently contain this hiatus of embodiment but, as I hope to show, it has plenty of new ways of addressing the challenge of understanding otherness for a variety of aims.

2

The digital psychologist: information technology and cultural psychology

In 2008, during the great fall of the stock market, I was on my way to my university coffee shop. One of my colleagues, a graduate of an Ivy League university and an internationally recognized economist, met me and we started talking (how surprisingly) about the stock market and the failure of economic models to predict its chaotic behavior. "Everyone would like to predict whether a stock price is going to increase or decrease," he said, "but unfortunately it is impossible. You cannot beat the system."

As a researcher deeply interested in the psychology of human beings in their complex sociocultural context, I was not surprised by this pessimistic conclusion. Complex systems, specifically complex interactive psychocultural systems, are difficult to understand and to predict. The question is what constructive and optimistic vision we may provide for those who mess their hands while trying to understand these systems.

Several months later, in June 2009, an Israeli economics newspaper revealed to the public that a trading company by the name of Final earned $60 billion during 2005 and reached $100 billion in profit two years later. The company's meteoric success in automatically trading stocks had been achieved through sophisticated algorithms and powerful computers. Moreover, I learned that current stock-market trading is largely governed by algo-trading companies and that a disproportionate number of these successful companies are run by young veterans of the Israel Defense Forces' technological and intelligence units.

These young people are not experienced or well-educated economists, and it seems that one key to their success is that they have not been indoctrinated to believe that "you cannot beat the system." On the contrary – they have been educated and encouraged to beat the system. The algo-trading

16

companies have become a reality and a very disturbing one. However, my aim is not to judge the danger in the emergence of the money machines but to make a point. Here we get into the next section.

ON "UNDERSTANDING" HUSBANDS AND THE LIMITS OF THEORIES

How can we explain the gap between the theoretically well-grounded pessimistic argument of my expert colleague and the incredible and both encouraging and disturbing success of Final and other algo-trading companies?

There are two possible explanations that I would like to introduce. The first concerns the limits imposed on our understanding of complex systems by some academic scientific theories. The second explanation concerns the way technology extends the limits of our understanding.

Let us start with the first explanation. Scientific theories, as modeled by Newtonian physics, have been cherished as the sacred maps that must guide our understanding and rational activity in the world. An amusing study, whose source I cannot recall, questions this dogma.

This psychological study found that men who try to understand their wives divorce in significantly greater proportion than men who do not try to understand their wives. We should recall, though, that even Freud, the great observer into the secrets of mental life, summarized his attempt to understand women via the desperate question/cry, "What does a woman want?"

Men who try to understand their wives would probably use simple conscious theories – naive or academic – that include a limited number of variables and the functions associating them. As we learned from the famous three-body problem in physics, our ability to provide analytic solutions is very limited.

There is no reason to assume that women are less complex than the stock market (or vice versa) and therefore it is most probable that the men who try to understand their wives, by using classical models, will fail in the same way as the classical economists who try to understand the complexity of the stock market.

This conclusion may sound cynical, but not to those who are familiar with complex systems: biological, economic, political, or psychological. In contrast to the understanding husbands, men who *don't* try to understand their wives may be more attentive to minor, almost unnoticed, and numerous informative cues and will use these cues to *adjust* themselves to their spouses. Like dancing with one's spouse, what is really important is not a simple conscious and predictive theory but the adaptive adjustments and the ongoing, real-time corrections that prevent one from stepping on one's partner's toes.

In complex realms a theory is not judged only by its simplicity and direct correspondence with reality but also through its ability to conceptualize our ignorance and to handle the messy realm in an adaptive way. In this context, technology functions as an indispensable tool for extending the limit line of our understanding and for dealing with complex systems. This point has been realized by researchers in physics, biology, and ecology who use computer simulations as a natural part of their toolkit. Here we get into the second explanation of the success of algo-trading. Algo-trading, as a natural implementation of the complexity zeitgeist, would not have been possible without the use of powerful computers that harvest the information landscape, identify predictive cues, and conduct an enormous number of transactions at a rapid pace.

While technology has traditionally been underestimated by theoretically oriented science, it has been brought to the forefront by recognizing the complexity of our world and the power of technology in studying this complexity.

It is reasonable to assume that powerful information technologies may also improve our way of managing the complexity of the social and the psychological realms. The Music Genome Project uses 400 factors in order to characterize a song. Is a human being less complex than a song? Probably not, and therefore it seems natural that the recognition of the complex psychological realm plus the introduction of novel information technology would revolutionize psychology. As the next section illustrates, things are far from simple.

THE PSYCHOLOGIST AND THE MATH BRAINS

Psychology seems to "suffer" from the same difficulties as economics. In both cases, the researcher faces a complex realm. Therefore, it could have been expected that psychology would be inspired by ventures such as those of the algo-trading companies. However, as a practice rather than as an academic discipline, psychology seems to be largely indifferent to the new opportunities introduced by emerging information technology.

This argument should be qualified. Latent semantic analysis (LSA) and its practical applications have been developed by psychologists. One may argue that the use of computational tools, simulations, and neuroimaging by researchers in psychology and cognitive sciences completely refutes my argument. However, one may find it difficult to identify even a single analogy to the success of the Israeli algo-trading company in psychological practice. Is anyone familiar with a single team of psychologists who earned $100 billion by incorporating information technology into their practice to address *real-world problems*? Let us exclude research grants from our analysis. Are you familiar with such a team that earned even $10 billion in a venture similar to algo-trading? To the best of my knowledge the answer is negative, although a couple of years ago there seemed to be hope.

Netflix is a leading American movie rental company that uses a recommendation system for its clients. For instance, if you enjoyed an action movie with Steven Seagal you will probably get a recommendation to watch the latest movie with Jet Li.

Netflix encountered a limit while trying to improve its recommendation system. Therefore, in October 2006 the company announced a challenging competition. Netflix offered a $1 billion prize for an algorithm that would improve the performance of its recommendation system by 10%. This competition attracted great interest and a thousand programs were offered a month after the competition was announced.

It could have been expected that researchers from the data-mining community would lead this race. However, an interesting competitor broke into the scene, questioning the hegemony of the "math brains."

The mysterious competitor – who went by the name "Just a guy in the garage" – outperformed some of the sure-bet horses in the race and created great curiosity and interest. His story was enthusiastically described in a 2008 article in *Wired* magazine: "This psychologist might outsmart the math brains competing for the Netflix prize" (Ellenberg 2008).

It was found that the guy in the garage was a 48-year-old English man by the name of Gavin Potter, who was a former IBM employee with a background in operations research and psychology.

Potter was enthusiastically portrayed in the article as the "great white hope" of psychology because he tried to implement psychological knowledge as an essential component of his strategy. As described by the author of the article, who is a leading Princeton mathematician, "A deeper part of Potter's strategy is based on the work of Amos Tversky and Nobel Prize winner Daniel Kahneman, pioneers of the science now called behavioral economics" (Ellenberg 2008).

In retrospect I understand the enthusiasm that a psychologist created in this mathematician. Maybe the mathematician thought that finally pure, simple, and beautiful theory could overcome the dirty and theory-free mess of the computer guys who, to tell the truth, are not "real mathematicians" but rather wise guys meddling with a complex reality.

The *Wired* article was published in February 2008. The reader who is not familiar with the end of the story must be curious to know whether the psychologist finally "outsmart[ed] the math brains competing for the Netflix prize."

In July 2009 Netflix awarded the prize to … an international group of "math brains" headed by a young researcher – Yehuda Koren – from Yahoo's research center in Israel. The paper in which Koren describes the winning strategy is titled "Matrix factorization technique for recommender systems." No psychology. No "science" of "behavioral economics." Just a "matrix factorization technique." This title is so unsexy that it is almost painful to believe that it outperformed the "science" of "behavioral economics."

The Netflix case is not the only case in which math brains using computational power have outperformed social sciences. Here is another example. The study of attitudes has been the bread and butter of social psychology, but, as we all know, the relationship between attitudes measured by social psychologists and behavior has been practically nonexistent.

This is a shocking conclusion for a field pretending to be scientific. If the attitudes one measures, regarding cheating for instance, cannot predict behavior (e.g., actual cheating) *in vivo*, why do we need social psychology? After all, most scientists don't accept with respect other fields (such as graphology) that fail in prediction.

Surprising as it may sound, the behavior of people may be powerfully predicted by the math brains. Epagogix is a UK-based company that presents itself as follows on its website:

> Advanced Artificial Intelligence in combination with proprietary expert process enables Epagogix to provide studios, independent producers and investors with early analysis and forecasts of the Box Office potential of a script. Clients then make evidenced decisions about whether or not to spend their scarce capital, adjust budgets, or to increase the Box Office value of the property.

The company actually advises Hollywood on the commercial potential of movie scripts, and has earned several billion dollars due to success in prediction.

While Epagogix's algorithm is not public, another algorithm, developed by Bernardo Huberman, has gained incredible success in predicting box-office revenues. Huberman, a physicist from Stanford University and HP

Labs, has shown that the rate of tweeting about a movie can successfully predict box-office revenues (Asur and Huberman 2010).

Twitter is a rich source of information, and various applications have been used to search it (e.g., Reips and Garaizar 2011). As argued by Bollen *et al.* (2011), Twitter mood may even be used to predict the stock market. Mood or general sentiment (positive vs. negative) seems to be a powerful predictor despite its apparent simplicity.

By using huge repositories of news, Leetaru (2011) argued that sentiment mining in the news may provide valuable information on mass behavior, including the uprising in Egypt in 2011. He examined the average tone in 52,438 news articles mentioning Egypt from January 1979 to March 2011. Leetaru found that "only twice in the last 30 years has the global tone about Egypt dropped more than three standard deviations below average." The most recent drop overlapped with the recent uprising. Leetaru, however, did not a priori examine situations identified by experts as describing a crisis in Egypt. Therefore, while his approach represents an interesting thread, the predictive power of his methodology is far from clear.

Leetaru's methodology is an instance of an overall project of developing automatic crisis early-warning systems. It is no surprise that such systems are developed by the US government. As argued by O'Brien (2010, 87): "For more than 40 years, the U.S. government has invested in research to develop crisis early warning systems."

The system he describes – the Integrated Crisis Early Warning System – is an interesting venture in extending the limit of our understanding to issues that were considered up to now the results of chaos only. Whether the results of this system and others currently justify the buzz is something that should be critically examined.

In addition, O'Brien presents a new paradigm described as "computational social science," which involves the application of "social science knowledge to complex highly nuanced issues" (2010, 100) through the tools of computational science. The major difference between general "computational social sciences" and computational cultural psychology is the focus of the latter on the semiotically mediated nature of the human mind and the attempt to understand it as a meaning-making system.

How can we explain the fact that social psychologists (who are supposed to be experts in attitudes and behavior), cognitive psychologists (who are supposed to be experts in thinking), and psychoanalysts (who are supposed to dig deeply into our unconscious motives) are absent from the gold rush of predicting behavior for practical means?

My conclusion is that we are experiencing a quantum leap in our culture and that academic psychology is lagging behind. Information technology has introduced powerful tools that did not exist for my professors of psychology. Some of these tools and resources have reached maturity only in recent years. This changing context invites new innovations, as described in the next section.

However, before moving on, an important qualification should be added. I am not a technology geek who believes that technology is the ultimate solution to the world's problems in general and to cultural psychology in particular. Technology is a power indifferent to ethical consequences. It is also a "drug" necessarily accompanied with side effects that we are well aware of. In this book I propose a realistic approach to the use of technology in cultural psychology with no messianic inspirations in my mind. Admiring a novel tool is idol-worshiping but ignoring it is stupidity.

CULTURAL PSYCHOLOGY AND THE DIGITAL PSYCHOLOGIST

What is the lesson we may learn so far? My suggestion is that in order to be relevant to the study of complex systems and to cultural psychology in particular, psychology should undergo a change, becoming interdisciplinary in nature by relying on enormous resources of digital information through the platforms provided by modern information technology and by adopting powerful computational tools for the analysis and simulation of real-world data.

At this point another qualification should be added. My criticism should not be confused with a passionate urge against a discipline. Personally, I find great joy and importance in theorizing, experimenting, and speculating in psychology, and my publications in hardcore journals of psychology may save me from a possible ad hominem argument questioning my personal stance against the discipline. In addition, I don't believe in throwing away all of our old theories and tools.

Our intuition and our ability to provide in-depth analysis of psychological and cultural phenomena are indispensable and irreplaceable. Nevertheless, I truly believe that, in addition to its classical theories and methodologies, psychology and specifically cultural psychology, which is the focus of this book, should also adopt a different perspective in order to be more relevant for a changing world.

In this context the idea of computational cultural psychology may be of great relevance. Culture – as a theoretical construct describing the shared collective representations, signs, and practices of a given group – exists for the first time in human history *in silico*. It would be absurd to ignore this potential for better understanding the way humans think and behave. By using computational tools for inquiring into cultures, we may have a better grasp of culture and psychology – from the way a given culture represents other groups to the dynamics according to which a given culture establishes its code of honor. It is the aim of this book to inquire into this promising venture.

Let me sum up the thesis so far: *"computational cultural psychology" is the field that studies the semiotic mediation of the human mind through computational tools and digital data repositories.* In contrast with the general idea of "computational social science," computational cultural psychology focuses on the way the human mind is mediated through sign systems, and the way this mediation may be studied through computational tools and new data repositories. In this sense, the venture of computational cultural psychology goes hand in hand with the vision of "Web 3.0."

While Web 2.0 was a neologism used to describe the emergence of shared content (e.g., Wikipedia, YouTube) through collaborative work and the appearance of novel social media platforms (e.g., Facebook, Twitter), Web 3.0 is a term used to describe the efforts of "meaning making" out of this new content and platforms.

The emergence of "collective intelligence" out of the social web is a defining characteristic of Web 2.0 (O'Reilly 2005). However, it was quickly realized that the title "intelligence" should not be easily granted to systems such as Wikipedia or YouTube, and that the transformation from "collected intelligence" to "collective intelligence" is far from trivial. In other words, Web 3.0 is a venture that urges us to see the forest rather than the trees.

Meaning making is the challenge facing many companies dealing with semantic technologies, and social computing is one of the hot topics in current scientific activity. The development of social computing systems is impressive but should be critically examined. It has been argued that it is "premature to apply the term collective intelligence to these systems because there is no emergence of truly new levels of understanding" (Gruber 2008, 4). It has been further argued that "true collective intelligence can emerge if the data collected from all those people is aggregated and recombined to create *new knowledge* and new ways of learning that individual humans cannot do by themselves" (Gruber 2008, 5, my emphasis).

In other words, in order to move from *collected* intelligence to *collective* intelligence, the system should "enable computation and inference over the collected information leading to answers, discoveries, or other results that are not found in the human contributions" (Gruber 2008, 6). This challenge, usually discussed under the heading "Web 3.0" (Markoff 2006), is that of "representing meaning" (Gruber 2008). However, few technologies have gone beyond "summarizing or sorting the data" (Gruber 2008, 7). In the context of cultural psychology the challenge is even more demanding, since the meaning of "representing meaning" is far from clear, and proving that the computational tools can address long-lasting questions of the field, such as the relation between language and thought, is far from trivial.

From a broad intellectual perspective, the subject matter of cultural psychology is the human dynamic and humanity's elusive existence. In his insightful novel *Gould's Book of Fish*, Richard Flanagan reflects on human existence from a poetic perspective. He writes:

> Men's lives are not progressions, as conventionally rendered in history paintings, nor are they a series of facts that may be enumerated & in their proper order understood. Rather they are a series of transformations, some immediate & shocking, some so slow as to be imperceptible, yet so complete & horrifying that at the end of his life a man may search his memory in vain for a moment of correspondence between his self in his dotage & him in his youth.
>
> (Flanagan 2001, 305)

Indeed, men's and women's lives cannot be summarized as a series of facts describing a linear progression. Our lives are a series of transformations through which we recognize the emerging "objects" that populate our environment, from the series of transformations that constitute our emerging *self* to the series of transformations that constitute our collective consciousness. If there is any stability in this Heraclitean river it is the stability or forced order created by the sign systems through which we collectively force order on this chaos. In the following chapters I will try to delve deeply into these sign systems and the way they turn our world into a meaningful experience.

3

Why don't primates have God? Language and the abstraction of thought

"EAT YOUR LASAGNA!"

In 2010 I was invited to participate in a joint seminar for Israeli and American researchers. During the opening dinner, as the only social scientist in the group, I was seated near an old professor of linguistics from the hosting university, who was almost immediately proud to introduce herself as one of Chomsky's students.

After positioning herself as a direct descendant of the guru, she asked about my field of expertise. I humorously apologized for not having one but expressed my long-lasting interest in issues of language and thought. "Of course," she said. "Sapir–Whorf hypothesis regarding the influence of language on thought." I explained that neither Sapir not Whorf ever presented such a "hypothesis" and never ever presented any simple causal link between "language" and "thought." "It doesn't matter," she said. "This hypothesis has been experimentally refuted." I tried to explain that the "hypothesis" is really a theoretical assumption and to support my argument made the mistake of bringing to my help several (dead) soviet colleagues such as Lev Vygotsky and Valentine Volosinov.

The lady did not accept doubt as an answer. For some reason she considered the idea that "language" and "thought" are deeply related as an iconoclastic statement challenging her religious dogma. "Eat your lasagna," she said and angrily turned her back to speak with the person who sat to her right.

Sharing this incident with a colleague who is an American, albeit a non-Chomskyan linguist, I learned that the jealousness and tyranny of the Chomskyans are established as well-known facts in academia, with a wide scope of influence to a level that almost extinguished any alternative ideas in linguistics in the USA, the same country where two giants such as

Sapir and Whorf formulated their ideas. So what was Sapir actually arguing and why should we reject the straw man known as the Sapir–Whorf
hypothesis?

Sapir insightfully realized that once a language is established it can "discover" meanings for its speakers that are not simply traceable to the given
quality of experience itself, but must be explained to a large extent as the
projection of potential meaning into the raw material of experience (Sapir
1949, 7). Thought is "hardly possible in any sustained sense without the
symbolic organization brought by language" (1949, 15).

To explain this idea let's think about the abstract idea of "potential
energy." Pretheoretically, people were probably familiar with this concept,
when building and manipulating bows or stoning their enemies from the
top of a hill, long before potential energy was scientifically formulated in
the nineteenth century. In other words, people were familiar with the *experience* of potential energy through *patterns of activities*.

Our first encounter with the world is intuitive, not in the sense that it
isn't mediated by "symbolic" structures but rather in the sense that acting
in the world and being in the world have precedence over reflecting on the
world and on our thoughts.

Intuitively we are familiar with potential energy in the same way as a
monkey is familiar with it. When a monkey uses a stone to break the shell
of a coconut, it is using energy in a sophisticated way. However, one may
hardly imagine a situation in which the monkey is mathematically formu-
lating the idea of potential energy and developing it further without the
symbolic power of language. In other words, our ability to transcend the
concrete operations that are the atoms of experience and to turn the *abstract*
mental operations into an object of reflection is heavily dependent on the
use of language.

The primitive hunter, who used bows, unconsciously discovered a pattern in which the elastic potential energy of the bow played a crucial role.
However, without symbolizing this pattern in an abstract manner and turning it into an object of contemplation and communication it could not have
been further developed beyond a limited practical context.

In this context, we should remember that Whorf greatly appreciated
Gestalt psychology (Whorf 1956, 14), and through the idea of Gestalt – a
whole that is different from the sum of its parts – we may better understand
the patterning of symbolic activity and conceptual structures.

To identify a general pattern – a Gestalt, which is an abstraction of concrete operations – we need some kind of powerful tool that may help us
to conduct the quantum leap from one level of operating in this world to

another level of operating in this world. Bees, for instance, create a wonderful geometrical pattern when building their beehive. A spider weaving its web was a source of amazement for the old geometricians. Neither the bee nor the spider have ever developed the mathematical field known as Group Theory, which is the abstract formulation of "group transformations" and that can point at the deep level of similarity between different geometrical patterns.

In sum, language as an organized form of symbolic activity is not sharply distinguished from the activity we describe as "thinking." While conceptual patterning can take place without the significant mediation of a social and complex system of signification, this system may leverage the conceptual activity.

As argued by Penny Lee (1996) in her extensive analysis of Whorf's theory, Whorf never formulated a "hypothesis" regarding the influence of language on thought, as the dichotomy between language and thought was alien to his thinking. Experience and the meaning we attribute to experience was the context of Whorf's "linguistic relativity principle" (Lee 1996, 86). In this context, the naive idea that different languages created different thoughts is meaningless.

Lee suggests that, according to Whorf, "What varies as a function of particular languages … is not thought in general … but conceptual processing" (1996, 87). This is to say that the human mind as a web of signs and signification provides the *worldview through which people experience the world and act on it*. It is not the grammatical structure of American English versus Russian, for instance, that creates the different worldviews of Americans and Russians. It is the web of signs with their associations, connotations, and metaphors that produces a difference that makes a difference.

The way in which patterns and activities of signification explain cultural psychology is a major theme that will be deeply elaborated in this book. However, I would like to return to the way language enables abstract thought.

It goes without saying that the ability to abstract patterns of experience is the landmark of intelligent systems, whether human or nonhuman. In a paper published in *Science*, the Japanese researcher Toshiyuki Nakagaki and his colleagues demonstrated the way in which a slime mold known as *Physarum polycephalum* expresses "intelligent behavior."

The researchers grew the mold on an outline map of Tokyo with oat flakes placed on the locations of thirty-six cities in the greater Tokyo area. In an attempt to consume the food, the mold created a network of paths between the cities that almost exactly matched Tokyo's real transportation network. In fact, *Physarum* came up with a slightly better solution – "Not bad for a creature without a brain" (Bohanon 2010).

It seems therefore that a brain, not to say language, is not a necessary condition for what we may describe as intelligent behavior. The mold's ability to form an optimal network is the expression of an intelligent behavior of patterning. Finding an optimal solution for a problem is a cognitively demanding task, and the mold deserves to be described as intelligent, at least in this specific sense, which is crucial for its survival.

However, in contrast with the mold, the human mind has the ability to represent patterns of experience through symbolic devices and even to invent new patterns of experience by using this symbolic power. The scientists and engineers who planned Tokyo's transportation network may have achieved a poorer performance than the mold in terms of optimization, but the mold cannot reflect on its patterning intelligence while the scientists can.

This unique ability to use language as a tool of *reflection* cannot be considered from a simple evolutionary perspective but as an indication of emerging complexity only. The human mind, with its linguistic capacity and complex culturally laden semiotic networks, has no advantage whatsoever over the other forms of natural intelligence. Human beings may be proud of their ability to write poetry, to SMS, to read the signs of symptoms, and to wisely reflect on the political situation. However, this incredible complexity doesn't guarantee their survival as a species.

As insightfully commented by Irun Cohen ("Dancing with the wolf of entropy," in preparation), this emerging complexity even has the seeds of destruction. Cohen is not an apocalyptic thinker but a leading immunologist who invented a vaccine against type 2 diabetes that is in advanced phases of confirmation by the US Food and Drug Administration. His argument is that explaining biological mechanisms and activities through the naive Darwinist perspective is wrong.

Regardless of the clarifications, elaborations, and studies of the Sapir–Whorf hypothesis, or what is known as the linguistic relativity principle, this hot topic fails to relax for reasons that are themselves an interesting object for scholarly analysis.

Along the same line, in August 2010 the *New York Times* published an article titled "Does your language shape how you think?" (Deutscher 2010). The article, written by Guy Deutscher, a professor of linguistics, urges us to reexamine our "prejudice" against the notion that "language shapes the way we think." By using the term "prejudice" Deutscher exposes the academic cultural bias that I mentioned at the beginning of this chapter.

"Thought" and "language" are not ontological categories. They don't exist in the world in the same way as apples, clouds, and trees. And, even in the case of apples, clouds, and trees, it is doubtful whether categories can exist without a mediating mind. In the case of thought and language the issue is much more complicated, so how can it be that a death sentence was given to the relation between language and thought without even clearly understanding what these entities are all about? The answer probably resides in a specific academic culture that conquered the West and specifically American academia. However, let us return to Deutscher's thesis.

Deutscher starts with a very specific sense of Whorf's "hypothesis," according to which different languages impose on their speakers' thoughts in the sense that the *lack* of certain signs entails the lack of corresponding mental structures. Deutscher rejects this "hypothesis," but argues that on the positive side different languages oblige us to think differently. He points to the fact that, while the English language does not compel you to describe the gender of a third party (e.g., "I was speaking with a friend"), German does. That is, different languages may oblige you to specify different types of "information." Nice example. But what does it mean?

The implication of these different specifications to the understanding of different minds is not clear, at least for me. I learned a lot from some academic mentors who used to listen patiently to the ideas I presented to them (mine and others) just to ask at the end "So what?" The "So what?" question is very important because it forces us to reflectively evaluate our theses, ideas, or findings by adopting a clear criterion. The criterion may vary from context to context. An idea may be evaluated by its novelty or the unique aesthetic way in which it is presented. A thesis may be evaluated by its pragmatic consequences, such as improving prediction or lowering computational load. However, a criterion is a must.

Returning to Deutscher's thesis, we should ask the "So what?" question. What does it mean that English and German are different in terms of specifying the gender of a third party or even an object? The fact that the German language forces you to specify gender is a matter of fact, but a matter of fact has informative value only when the difference, such as the one between German and English, turns into a difference that makes a difference. As a young graduate student I learned a lot from one of my brilliant professors, Sorel Cahan, who was an expert in psychological and educational measurement. One day we were talking about the diagnostic and predictive power of graphology (null). He pointed out that graphology is totally meaningless as a method of diagnosis. My reply was that he can't deny that a person's handwriting means something. "It may definitely mean something," he poignantly replied. "The question is what."

The German language may force you to convey information about the gender of your friend but Hebrew does too. Does this mean that the German and the Hebrew "minds" share similar properties? And in what sense? As there are no clear answers to these questions, the soft version of the Sapir–Whorf "hypothesis" presented by Deutscher seems to lead to amusing linguistic-anthropological anecdotes and no more. Given the role of mass media in academic life, amusing anecdotes have turned some of their users into stars of the academic world. However, a critical mind should differentiate between the rhetorical power of anecdotes and their scientific value.

THOUGHT AND LANGUAGE

As I argued before, the problem is deeper (as one may guess), and it relies on the general theoretical framework we choose in order to define and examine the meaning of "thought" and "language," and their relation.

It was Lev Vygotsky (1962), the great Jewish Russian psychologist, who considered the fact that, despite their different roots, thought and speech interact in their ontogenetic development as two "intersecting circles." A better synergetic metaphor is the Borromean rings, but let us continue with Vygotksy's thesis. Vygotksy located this point of intersection/interaction in "word meaning." As he insightfully suggests:

> A word without meaning is an empty sound; meaning, therefore, is a criterion of "word," its indispensable component ... But from the point of view of psychology, *the meaning of every word is a generalization or a concept.* And since generalizations and concepts are undeniably acts of thought, we may regard meaning as a phenomenon of thinking. It does not follow, however, that meaning formally belongs in two different spheres of psychic life. Word meaning is a phenomenon of thought only in so far as thought is embodied in speech, and of speech only in so far as speech is connected with thought and illumined by it. It is a phenomenon of verbal thought, or meaningful speech – *a union of word and thought.*
> (Chapter 7, 1, my emphasis)

The idea of *word meaning* as the unit of interaction is very important for the thesis presented here and it will be used as our own unit of analysis. While it is Vygotsky's name that popped into our mind while discussing the relation between "thought" and "language," and while Sapir and

Whorf are the two people who are usually associated with the linguistic relativity "hypothesis," the most important essay written about the subject is probably Volosinov's *Marxism and the Philosophy of Language* (1986). This remarkable essay proposed a totally different approach to the study of language and thought.

According to Volosinov: "Outside the material of signs there is no psyche" (1986, 26). In other words, the sharp and artificial differentiation between the realm of signs (i.e., language) and the realm of "psyche" (i.e., thought) should be replaced by a semiotic perspective according to which "psychic experience is the semiotic expression of the contact between the organism and the outside [and the inside] environment" (1986, 26).

According to this perspective, the simple Newtonian causal relationship between "language" and "thought" is meaningless, and the mind should be studied as a "semiotic interface" (Neuman 2003) that human beings, as well as other intelligent systems, use to make sense of their world (Neuman 2008). This perspective is in line with the Whorfian theory, according to which:

> There is little point in arguing about whether language influences thought or thought influences language for the two are functionally entwined to such a degree in the course of individual development that they form a highly complex, but nevertheless systematically coherent, mode of cognitive activity which is not usefully described in conventionally dichotomizing terms as either "thought" or "language."
>
> (Lee 1996, xiv)

Given this unique synergy of "language" and "thought," an interesting question is how abstract thought that uniquely characterizes the human mind is possible through the mediation of natural language. More specifically, we may ask how language, in the Saussurean sense of a sign system (Saussure 1972), may become more and more "abstract."

The *Online Etymology Dictionary* (www.etymonline.com) teaches us that "abstract" as an adjective means "withdrawn or separated from material objects or practical matters." Another sense, "'difficult to understand, abstruse' is from *c.* 1400."

"Abstract" therefore entails withdrawing something from concrete objects or practical activities, turning the product into something difficult to understand. Indeed, even a child can understand the geometrical pattern of the beehive, but discussing the beehive in abstract mathematical terms is extremely difficult to grasp, even for intelligent people.

In the context of natural language, the enigmatic notion of abstraction may be explained in psychological terms as follows. We know that certain signs have a concrete denotational sense that is grounded in our senso-rimotor experience: the sign "dark" concerns a certain visual experience shared by people across cultures, as do "sweet" and "bitter" concerning taste experiences.

At the most basic level of our existence we share universal forms of experience resulting from our concrete physical form of being in the world. We have no access to the way other creatures perceive the world. Except for King Solomon or Doctor Doolittle, who were known for their ability to converse with animals, ordinary human beings can only observe other creatures as outsiders.

We know though that other creatures live in different habitats and exist in the world through different biophysical bodies. A dog is extremely sensi-tive to smells. For the dog the universe is to a large extent a universe of signs embodied in the olfactory system.

Human beings have a universal embodiment of signs. Sweet is sweet, dark is dark, and hot is hot. It must be noted that I don't present a simple reductionist perspective. The fact that our mind is embodied in our basic sensorimotor experience doesn't mean that the complexity of the mind can be simply reduced to sensorimotor experience. This is an important point. *Embodiment doesn't entail reductionism.* We are all stardust, or the mat-ter dreams are made of, as proposed by Shakespeare, but trying to explain human beings by reducing them to the physics of stardust would probably lead nowhere.

Signs are basically embodied in our sensorimotor experience. However, there are other signs that are more abstract in the sense that we cannot eas-ily trace their embodied origin – "God," for instance, or even the connota-tion of "dark" in the word pair "dark thoughts."

While people may share the basic experience of being in the world due to their shared physiology, the more abstract our sign system becomes the more evident are cultural differences that load our abstract signs with meaning. In other words, a higher level of abstraction is evident when the concrete reference of the sign cannot be easily traced and when it is loaded with connotations or metaphors that increase its variance across speech communities.

Abstract signs may expose cultural, historical, or national differences through which the abstract notion of our sign system is constituted. How does the mind, as a social interactive and dynamic semiotic system, support us in performing this transformation?

At the most basic level, one interesting suggestion comes from C. S. Peirce, who is seldom if ever mentioned in this context despite his clear relevance to "embodied cognitive science" (Clark 2006). Let me move on to the next section to discuss Peirce's interesting hypothesis and the way it can explain how language "influences" our thoughts and their abstraction.

PEIRCE ON HYPOSTATIC ABSTRACTION

Peirce's concept of "hypostatic abstraction" may explain the abstraction of signs and thoughts. To understand Peirce's notion of hypostatic abstraction, we should be familiar with his theory of relations. I plan to draw on this theory in several chapters of this book and therefore it will be repeatedly presented and elaborated.

According to Peirce there are three basic relational types that correspond to his three categories of being: firstness, secondness, and thirdness. Peirce describes these categories as "modes of being." In what sense are these categories "modes of being"? Peirce answers this question by saying:

> Therefore, we do not ask what really is, but only what *appears to every one of us* in every minute of our lives. I analyze experience, which is the cognitive resultant of our past lives, and find in it three elements. I call them Categories.
>
> (Peirce 1931–1966, vol. II, 84, my emphasis)

In other words, the categories discussed by Peirce are *forms of experience* as it is evident to human beings. These are not ontological categories concerning the state of the world as it "really" is but psychological categories according to which human experience can be analyzed.

Firstness is the "mode of being of that which is such as it is, positively and without reference to anything else" (Peirce 1931–1966, vol. VIII, 328); it is the "qualities of feeling" (Peirce 1931–1966, vol. VIII, 329).

Firstness is therefore a category of experience that is nonrelational or paradoxical in nature as it concerns a kind of "monadic" or isolated experience. Peirce explains elsewhere that firstness cannot exist in itself – that even the most monadic form of existence is relational.

To explain the meaning of firstness let us consider the basic experience of sweet taste. Tasting a cherry or a chocolate cake may result in a very basic experience that leads to our description of the cherry or cake as sweet. The sweetness of the cake has no reference to anything else. The cake is simply sweet. Firstness is the category of being that is the closest to our embodied experience: the cake is sweet, the night is dark, the oven is hot, and the lawn is wet.

In contrast, secondness "consists in one thing acting upon another" (Peirce 1931–1966, vol. VIII, 330). It is "the mode of being of that which is such as it is, with respect to a second but regardless of any third" (Peirce 1931–1966, vol. VIII, 328). Secondness is a category that introduces to our world of experience dyadic relations, relations between two objects.

For example, the category of *causality* actually involves secondness, as one variable (e.g., infection) influences another variable (e.g., body temperature). Even a simple association between two signs is an example of secondness. The concept of the sign emerged from the Greek *semion*, indicating a kind of symptom. The Greek physicians, such as Hippocrates, noticed that there is an association between certain physical indicators and illness. The indicators are signs associated with illness. For instance, beyond a certain threshold, body temperature is an indication/sign/symptom that our body is fighting a certain pathology, whether a vicious virus or a vicious bacterium. Therefore, secondness is a category in which our mind associates two things with no need for more complexity.

This category is evident in other species as well. For the deer, the green color of bushes is associated with a source of water. For the meerkat, a sign of alarm produced by the group's guard is associated with an approaching enemy.

Secondness cannot exhaust the complexity of experience and therefore Peirce introduced thirdness. Thirdness is the "mental or quasi-mental influence of one subject on another relative to a third" (Peirce 1931–1966, vol. V, 469). It is the "mode of being of that which is such as it is, in bringing a second and third into relation to each other" (Peirce 1931–1966, vol. VIII, 328).

Peirce is making an important point by introducing thirdness. The point is that some interactions between two elements are necessarily "mediated" by a third component. For instance, sign activity is the expression of thirdness as it involves the sign, the signified (i.e., object), and the mind it affects – namely the "interpretant." It means that when I hear the word "dog" I associate in my mind the physical acoustic pattern of the word "dog" as interpreted in my mind with an object it denotes as well as with the general concept "dog."

In sum, Peirce's categories involve the level of basic qualities (firstness), a dyadic relation between two objects, and a triadic form in which each element cannot be considered separately from the triadic whole of which it is a part.

With this typology in mind, we may turn to Peirce's theory of relations (Peirce 1931–1966, vol. V, 119). What is the difference between the categories and relations? Peirce's typology of relations is isomorphic to his categories but seems to emphasize another aspect. While his categories, as influenced by Kant, aim to represent universal forms of "experience," his relations seem to represent the "valence" of the categories.

In chemistry, "valence" is a term used to indicate the number of chemical bonds formed by the atoms of a given element. Peirce's typology of relations emphasizes the three general forms of "bonding" that constitute our forms of experience. In other words, while the categories demarcate our experience according to three abstract forms, the typology of relations characterizes the nature of the forms through the "bond" they create between the basic elements of our experience.

A monadic relation is a fact about a single object. Saying that the "cat is black" or that "I'm afraid" (or, more accurately, the feeling of being frightened) is an expression of a monadic relation. A monadic relation is thus not really a relation but a basic quality of feeling that may be expressed linguistically through an adjective or adverb. It is a "relation" between the object and itself.

A dyadic relation is a fact about two things or objects. "Honey possesses sweetness" is an example of a dyadic relation of "possession" between two objects: honey and sweetness.

A triadic relation is a relation between three objects, such as "A gave B to C." A triadic relation cannot be reduced to two dyadic relations and still preserve its meaning as a whole. For instance, the meaning of the utterance "Danny sold the book to Jerry" cannot be reduced to "Danny sold the book" and "Book to Jerry." That is, the triadic relation of *selling* involves the seller, the buyer, and the object sold. The activity of selling and buying cannot therefore be reduced to dyadic relations without losing its unique meaning. It is triadic in nature, meaning that breaking the triad apart is like breaking the triad of the Borromean rings.

The Borromean rings are an incredible structure. If you remove just one ring from the structure it falls apart. They are the best visual representation of Peirce's idea of triadic relations. One may then ask about higher-level relations – a tetradic relation, for instance, that has four arguments (e.g., Danny [ARG1] sold the book [ARG2] to Harry [ARG3] for a hundred dollars [ARG4]).

Pierce suggested that any higher-order relations can be reduced to triads. For instance, the sentence "Danny sold the book to Harry for a hundred dollars" can be reduced to "Danny sold the book to Harry" and "Danny sold the book for a hundred dollars" with no loss of information. Peirce's reduction thesis is interesting and deserves further discussion in later parts of this book.

At this point we may move forward to "hypostatic abstraction." Peirce proposed hypostatic abstraction to be a crucial mechanism in abstraction: "the simplest mathematics" (Peirce 1931–1966, vol. IV, 235, 227–323). The idea of hypostatic abstraction is that there is a procedure that *converts a quality expressed as an adjective or predicate into an additional object*. That is, the mechanism transforms a basic quality into an object. For example, the expression "honey is sweet" may be converted to "honey possesses sweetness." The transformation is actually a transformation from a monadic relation characterizing honey to a dyadic relation between one object, which is honey, and a new invented concept by the name of "sweetness."

The Smiths, one of the favorite bands of my youth, had a song titled "Bigmouth strikes again" (on the album *The Queen Is Dead*, 1986). In the song Morrissey sings:

> Oh … sweetness, sweetness, I was only joking
> When I said by rights you should be
> Bludgeoned in your bed.

One may question the limited mind of teenagers, but teenagers who listen to The Smiths illustrate hypostatic abstraction in action. While writing these words, I amuse myself by imagining a time machine transporting Peirce – the troubled Harvard genius – to the 1980s to find himself at a rock concert of The Smiths. If Peirce could have overcome the cultural shock and the levels of noise, he would have enjoyed seeing the "sweetness" he used to illustrate hypostatic abstraction being instantiated in a rock concert.

The transformation from a predicate into an argument results in a "reification" of the basic quality, as in the transformation from "sweet" to "sweetness." Reification is a term used to describe the way a thing turns into an object. The transformation described by Peirce involves abstraction as the predicate "sweet" turns from a quality into an "object-in-relation."

The unique ability of human beings to manipulate objects through orchestrated and sign-mediated social activity (Vauclair 2003) makes it clear why the mechanism of hypostatic abstraction is necessary for transcending embodied experience. For instance, while the predicate "sweet" is firmly grounded and constrained by our experience, "sweetness" as an object may be linked with a variety of associated senses, connotations, and metaphors.

Honey is definitely sweet. Just taste it. When a man describes his lover as a "sweetheart" he doesn't use the predicate "sweet" in the same literal sense, unless he is a cannibal. The idea of describing your lover as a sweetheart is possible only if the predicate "sweet" can somehow be abstracted from the

concrete context of honey. Winnie the Pooh, like other bears,
the way we do. The less-human-like members of Winnie the Po
family would never imagine that a "heart" could be sweet.

Hypostatic abstraction therefore makes the predicate functionally i.
pendent of its embodied experience and a sign arbitrarily associated with . ,
origin and material cloth, a property that uniquely characterizes the human
language (Saussure 1972).

In sum, turning a quality into an object involves its abstraction and
relocation in a relational network of signs. This mechanism helps us to
better understand the way "language" mediates "thought." The idea is that
through the mechanism of linguistic abstraction one may convert a basic
quality embodied in a sensorimotor activity and turn it into a noun, an
object, which is less constrained by the concrete context of its original use.

Imagine the power of a concept such as God. Through history rivers of
blood have been shed and are still shed in the name of God. But what is
God? When using the name of God religious fundamentalists actually use
it in a *reified sense* as if God were an object. For some interesting psychological reasons people are more ready to kill or be killed when fighting over
reified and obscure concepts. No war will be launched over DNA, the Higgs
boson particle, or Group Theory in mathematics.

My argument doesn't represent a naive form of atheism à la Richard
Dawkins. God has a sacred status that cannot be crystallized by simple-
minded preachers. The deep and profound religious traditions, from Judaism
to Zen Buddhism, have noticed the danger of reification and warned against
this reification and its use. I would like to illustrate this point by drawing on
The Zohar, which is the most central text of the Kabbalah (and please don't
confuse this text with the "honey bunny" style of Kabbalah propagated by
the pop star Madonna).

Rabbi Shlomo Carlebach (1925–1994), known as the "Singing Rabbi,"
was a Jewish musician, teacher, and singer. In one of his lessons (undated)
Rabbi Carlebach said that there are two questions one may ask oneself. The
first is "What are you?" and the second is "Who are you?"

Rabbi Carlebach associated the first question with some kind of evil and
the second with some kind of goodness. This teaching draws on *The Zohar*,
the most important Jewish mystical text, albeit in a very unique sense.

The Zohar (Matt 2004) says: "Who created this (Isaiah 40:26) … *Lift
your eyes on high* … There you will discover that the concealed ancient one,
susceptible to questioning, *created these*. Who is that? *Who?*" (1:1b). In foot-
note 27 the commentary explains that "the mystical name *Who* becomes a
focus of meditation, as question turns into quest."

In contrast with the "Who", there is another thing called "*What*." (1:1b):

> What distinguishes the two? The first concealed one – called *Who* – can be questioned. Once a human being questions and searches, contemplating and knowing rung after rung to the very last rung – once one reaches there: *What?* What do you know? What have you contemplated? For what have you searched? All is concealed as before. (1:1b)

Rabbi Carlebach's psychotheological reading of *The Zohar* takes the above questions originally addressed to God and turns them inward as questions addressed to the human being. This move might be interpreted as a form of naive psychologism but may also be interpreted from a psychotheological perspective as an inquiry into *God's image within humanity*.

In other words, as the human being has been created in God's image, whatever that may mean, asking oneself "Who are you?" or "What are you?" are two different ways of inquiring into God's image within us.

What is the difference between the aforementioned questions? The first question "What are you?" is a question of *reification* (Neuman 2003). It is a question that invites an answer in terms of an *object*: "I am a ..." For instance, "I am a Jew." This answer grasps only a superficial aspect of a human being created in God's image.

The second question – "Who are you?" – is a question opening a quest. It is not a question leading to an answer but a question that opens an inquiry that cannot be simply answered by stipulating an abstract and fragmented category of language: "I am a ..."

Back to Peirce. At this point, the reader is probably convinced that Peirce's idea of hypostatic abstraction is an interesting idea. Nevertheless, the "So what?" question immediately pops into the discussion. Can we better understand the human mind by adopting this idea? And in what sense?

First, we have to examine whether Peirce's idea is empirically grounded. Whether this idea is empirically grounded is an open question. In other words, it is not clear whether Peirce's idea can be supported through empirical evidence as collected and analyzed by using well-established scientific methods. In this sense, Peirce's notion of hypostatic abstraction is an "abduction," an "open question" or hypothesis that should be tested empirically. Here the idea of computational cultural psychology comes into the picture. Can we use computational methodology to empirically test Peirce's hypothesis? This is a challenge that I have addressed with two of my colleagues – a challenge that I would like to describe in the following sections. It is an illustration of computational cultural psychology, as it is an attempt to address a basic question in cultural psychology by using modern computational tools.

TESTING THE HYPOTHESIS

The hypothesis we have produced is as follows: if Peirce's idea is empirically grounded, we should expect that when examining word pairs of the type X–Xness (e.g., sweet–sweetness) we should find that the right-hand term, the "reified noun," is more "abstract" than the left-hand term – the predicate/adjective.

This test doesn't provide the ultimate confirmation or refutation of Pierce's idea. In contrast with Pooper's criterion of refutation, psychology doesn't work along the same lines. Science too doesn't work along the same lines but this is another story. What we can provide here is just a novel approach that may further increase or decrease our trust in the psychological existence of the hypothetical concept of hypostatic abstraction.

To test this hypothesis, together with my colleague Peter Turney and my programmer Yochai Cohen, I have used recent advancements in computational linguistics for measuring the abstractness/concreteness of a word. In the next section, "Measuring abstractness and concreteness," I describe our algorithm for rating words according to their degree of abstractness. The algorithm developed by Peter Turney draws on a methodology for measuring the semantic similarity of words and involves the comparison of a given word to paradigmatic abstract and concrete words.

I must emphasize that the next sections get into technicalities and particularities that might be far beyond the knowledge of the average educated reader. This is fine. The reader can just skip the technical stuff and get a general picture of what has been done.

MEASURING ABSTRACTNESS AND CONCRETENESS

Concrete words refer to things, events, and properties that we can perceive directly with our senses, such as "trees," "walking," and "red." Abstract words refer to ideas and concepts that are distant from immediate perception, such as "economics," "calculating," and "disputable." Concrete objects can be tasted, smelled, heard, touched, or seen. A lemon can be touched, smelled, and seen. An economy cannot be touched or seen although its real presence cannot be denied.

In this section, I describe an algorithm that can automatically calculate a numerical rating of the degree of abstractness of a word on a scale from

0 (highly concrete) to 1 (highly abstract). For example, the algorithm rates "purvey" as 1, "donut" as 0, and "immodestly" as 0.5.

An algorithm is a kind of a recipe for an ordered set of actions used to produce some kind of output from an input. If you are a talented baker preparing a cake you know that whipping the egg whites should be done before some other actions. Preparing a cake works along the lines of a well-defined algorithm. The algorithm, however, doesn't necessarily guarantee a complete solution. In some cases, the solution is a good-enough solution and no more. That is, an algorithm doesn't necessarily lead us to the best solution. It is just a recipe materialized *in silico*.

The algorithm that we used for measuring abstractness is a variation on Turney and Littman's (2003) algorithm that rates words according to their semantic orientation. Let me explain it briefly.

Positive semantic orientation indicates praise ("honest," "intrepid") and negative semantic orientation indicates criticism ("disturbing," "superfluous"). The algorithm developed by Turney and Littman calculates the semantic orientation of a given target word by comparing it to seven positive words and seven negative words that are used as paradigms of positive and negative semantic orientation:

> Positive paradigm words: "good," "nice," "excellent," "positive," "fortunate," "correct," and "superior."
> Negative paradigm words: "bad," "nasty," "poor," "negative," "unfortunate," "wrong," and "inferior."

Turney and Littman (2003) chose these paradigm words manually, using their personal intuition about which words best convey positive and negative semantic orientation. The idea is both simple and appealing. If you are interested in the semantic orientation of a word just check how similar it is to negative or positive words. This idea follows the common wisdom of "tell me who your friends are and I will tell you who are you."

The same logic is applied to the semantic orientation of words. Like human beings, words are clustered in groups. They appear together and the regularity of their co-appearance teaches us an important lesson about the words themselves. If we would like to determine the semantic orientation of a target word such as "dog," we should see whether the word appears in the context of more positive or more negative words. Context of course is culturally determined. In the context of modern Western societies "dog" may mean a pet and therefore be associated with positive words. In the context of Arab Muslim societies, "dog" is used as a curse word that is associated with negative words. Mohammad didn't like dogs and some of his disciples continue his tradition.

How do we calculate the semantic similarity between words? How do we know whether two words are close to or far from each other? This question is far from trivial, and many papers in natural language processing have been dedicated to testing the semantic similarity between words.

Turney and Littman (2003) experimented with two measures of semantic similarity: pointwise mutual information (Church and Hanks 1989) and LSA (Landauer and Dumais 1997).

Pointwise mutual information is a common measure of association between words. For illustration, let's assume that we would like to know how far the word "dog" is from the negative word "bad" and from the positive word "good."

To answer this question, I used COCA with "dog" as my target word and searched the corpus for cases in which "good" or "bad" appeared in the context of my target. By context I simply mean the immediate lexical neighborhood of "dog," four words to the left and four words to the right. Surprisingly, I found that "dog" is associated more with bad (mutual information [MI] = 0.49) than with good (MI = 0.23) words.

LSA is a sophisticated method for statistically constructing a semantic space. In this case, and I'm oversimplifying things for the sake of clarity, the measurement is based on vector space models of semantics. In physics a vector is a magnitude with a direction. Figure 3.1 shows a vector in a two-dimensional space.

In semantics a vector space is created by using words as vectors. For instance, let's assume a simple world with three words only: "dog," "cat," and "fish." This is a low-dimensional world that can be represented in terms of the distance between "dog," "cat," and "fish." The extent to which these words are close to each other is measured by calculating the cosine between the vectors representing them. The more they appear together, the closer they are. Again, the core idea is to represent words with vectors and to calculate the similarity of two words using the cosine of the angle between the two corresponding vectors. The values of the elements in the vectors are derived from the frequencies of the words in a large corpus of text. This general approach is known as a vector space model of semantics (Turney and Pantel 2010).

The semantic orientation of a word is calculated as the sum of its similarity with the positive paradigm words minus the sum of its similarity with the negative paradigm words. That is, if we want to know how positive or negative the word "goldfish" is, we calculate its similarity with the positive

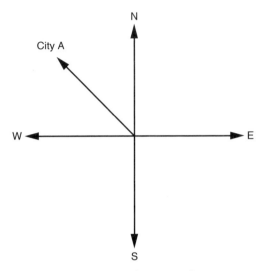

FIGURE 3.1   A two-dimensional vector.

paradigm words and produce from this measure the similarity of "goldfish" with the negative paradigm words.

Likewise, we calculated the abstractness of a given word by the sum of its similarity with twenty abstract paradigm words minus the sum of its similarity with twenty concrete paradigm words. We then used (for convenience) a normalization of the scale to map the calculated abstractness value to range from 0 to 1. The higher the score, the more abstract the word is. The details of this procedure are as follows.

We began with a corpus of 5×10^{10} words (280 gigabytes of plain text) gathered from university websites by a webcrawler. We selected our vocabulary from the terms (words and phrases) in the WordNet lexicon. We obtained the frequency of each WordNet term in our corpus and selected all terms in our corpus with a frequency of 100 or more. This resulted in a set of 114,501 terms.

Next we searched for up to 10,000 phrases per term, where a phrase consists of the given term plus four words to the left of the term and four words to the right of the term. These phrases were used to build a word-context frequency matrix **F** with 114,501 rows and 139,246 columns.

A row vector in **F** corresponds to a term in WordNet and the columns in **F** correspond to contexts (the words to the left and right of a given term in a given phrase) in which the term appeared.

The columns in **F** are unigrams (single words) in WordNet with a frequency of 100 or more in the corpus. A given unigram is represented by two columns, one marked *left* and one marked *right*. Suppose *r* is the term corresponding to the *i*-th row in **F** and *c* is the term corresponding to the *j*-th column in **F**. Let *c* be marked *left*. Let f_{ij} be the cell in the *i*-th row and *j*-th column of **F**.

The numerical value in the cell f_{ij} is the number of phrases found in which the center term is *r*, and *c* is the unigram closest to *r* on the left side of *r*. That is, f_{ij} is the frequency with which *r* is found in the context *c* in our corpus.

A new matrix **X**, with the same number of rows and columns as in **F**, was formed by calculating the positive pointwise mutual information (PPMI) of each cell in **F** (Turney and Pantel 2010). The function of PPMI is to emphasize cells in which the frequency f_{ij} is statistically surprising, and hence particularly informative.

This matrix was then smoothed with a truncated singular value decomposition, which decomposes **X** into the product of three matrices:$U_k \Sigma_k V_k^T$.

Finally, the terms were represented by the matrix $U_k \Sigma_k^p$, which has 114,501 rows (one for each term) and *k* columns (one for each latent contextual factor). The semantic similarity of two terms is given by the cosine of the two corresponding rows in $U_k \Sigma_k^p$. For more detail, see Turney and Pantel (2010).

There is a complex many-to-many mapping between words and meanings: a word may have many meanings, depending on context, and many words may have the same meaning. Unfortunately, we do not have direct access to meanings; we must infer meanings from word usage. As explained above, LSA uses statistical techniques to attempt to infer meaning from patterns of word usage in a large collection of texts (i.e., a corpus).

In this context, there are two parameters in $U_k \Sigma_k^p$ that need to be set. The parameter *k* controls the number of latent factors (hidden units of meaning) in the LSA model of a corpus. The parameter *p* determines the weight of each latent factor (the importance of each hidden unit of meaning in the model) by raising the corresponding singular values in Σ_k^p to the power *p*. The parameter *k* is well known in the literature on LSA, but *p* is less familiar. The use of *p* was suggested by Caron (2001). Based on our past experience, we set *k* to 1,000 and *p* to 0.5. We did not explore any alternative settings of these parameters for measuring abstractness.

USING SEMANTIC SIMILARITY TO MEASURE ABSTRACTNESS

Now that we had the relevant word matrix all we needed in order to measure abstractness were some paradigm words. Although Turney and Littman (2003) manually selected their fourteen paradigm words, here we used a "supervised learning algorithm" to choose our forty paradigm words of abstractness.

We used the MRC Psycholinguistic Database Machine Usable Dictionary (Coltheart 1981) to guide our search for paradigm words. This dictionary contains 4,295 words rated by human subjects with degrees of abstractness.

We used half of these words to train our supervised learning algorithm and the other half to validate the algorithm. On the testing set, the algorithm attained a correlation of 0.81 with the dictionary ratings. This result indicates that the algorithm agrees well with human judgments of the degrees of abstractness of words.

We split the 4,295 MRC words into 2,148 for training (searching for paradigm words) and 2,147 for testing (evaluation of the final set of paradigm words). We began with an empty set of paradigm words and added words from the 114,501 rows of $U_k \Sigma_k^p$, one word at a time, alternating between adding a word to the concrete paradigm words and adding a word to the abstract paradigm words. At each step, we added the paradigm word that resulted in the greatest correlation with the ratings of the training words. This is a form of greedy forward search without backtracking. We stopped the search after forty paradigm words were found in order to prevent overfitting of the training data.

Table 3.1 shows the forty paradigm words and the order in which they were selected. At each step, the correlation increases on the training set, but eventually it must decrease on the testing set. After forty steps, the training set correlation was 0.86. At this point, we stopped the search for paradigm words and calculated the testing set correlation, which was 0.8064. This shows a small amount of overfitting of the training data.

For another perspective on the performance of the algorithm, we measured its accuracy on the testing set by creating a binary classification task from the testing data. We calculated the median of the ratings of the 2,147 words in the test set. Every word with an abstractness above the median was assigned to class 1 and every word with an abstractness below the median was assigned to class 0.

We then used the algorithm to guess the rating of each word in the test set, calculated the median guess, and likewise assigned the guesses to classes 1 and 0. The guesses were 84.65% accurate. This procedure validated the abstraction rate.

After generating the paradigm words with the training set and evaluating them with the testing set, we used them to assign abstractness ratings to every term in the matrix. The result of this was that we now had a set of

TABLE 3.1. *The forty paradigm words and their correlation, in the training set.*

Concrete paradigm words			Abstract paradigm words		
Order	Word	Correlation	Order	Word	Correlation
1	donut	0.4447	2	sense	0.6165
3	antlers	0.6582	4	indulgent	0.6973
5	aquarium	0.7150	6	bedevil	0.7383
7	nursemaid	0.7476	8	improbable	0.7590
9	pyrethrum	0.7658	10	purvey	0.7762
11	swallowwort	0.7815	12	pigheadedness	0.7884
13	strongbox	0.7920	14	ranging	0.7973
15	sixth-former	0.8009	16	quietus	0.8067
17	restharrow	0.8089	18	regularization	0.8123
19	recorder	0.8148	20	creditably	0.8188
21	sawmill	0.8212	22	arcella	0.8248
23	vulval	0.8270	24	nonproductive	0.8299
25	tenrecidae	0.8316	26	couth	0.8340
27	hairpiece	0.8363	28	repulsion	0.8400
29	sturnus	0.8414	30	palsgrave	0.8438
31	gadiformes	0.8451	32	goof-proof	0.8469
33	cobbler	0.8481	34	meshuga	0.8503
35	bullet	0.8521	36	dillydally	0.8538
37	dioxin	0.8550	38	reliance	0.8570
39	USA	0.8585	40	lumbus	0.8600

114,501 terms (words and phrases) with abstractness ratings ranging from 0 to 1. Based on the testing set performance, we estimated these 114,501 ratings would have a correlation of 0.81 with human ratings and an accuracy of 85% on binary (abstract or concrete) classification.

From *sweet* to *sweetness*

Now that we had powerful tools, such as the ability to scale a word according to its level of abstractness, we could move to the next step. For testing our specific hypothesis, in the above list of words that were rated according to their level of abstraction we automatically identified 1,078 word pairs in the form X–Xness, for instance *sweet–sweetness*.

Let abs(X) be the abstractness level of word X. Following Peirce, our hypothesis is that abs(Xness) is significantly higher than abs(X). Let delta(X) = abs(Xness) – abs(X). Our hypothesis is that delta(X) is significantly higher than 0. To test this hypothesis we used a *t*-test for paired samples. The delta was found to be statistically significant (t = 4.914, p < 0.001). This result supports Peirce's idea of hypostatic abstraction.

Next, we calculated the difference between the abstraction level of Xness and X. If the difference was 0 or less we scored the word pair 0, and 1 otherwise.

Among the word pairs, 59% scored 1 and the rest 0. By using the sign test this result was found to be statistically significant (p < 0.001). Like the previous result, this result supports Peirce's idea.

We noted above that the sign of delta(X) was positive in 59% of the 1,078 pairs. This is statistically significant, but it raises the question of whether there is an explanation for why delta(X) is negative in some cases. We hypothesize that delta(X) is more likely to be positive when X is a high-frequency word, because *the more a word is used, the more opportunities there are for the word to become an abstract object*, through associations, connotations, and metaphors.

To test this hypothesis, we split our data into word pairs in which the difference between Xness and X was ≥ 0.10 (one standard deviation of the abstraction list) and word pairs in which the difference was 0 or less. We titled the first set "high abstraction" and the second "low abstraction." If our hypothesis was correct, then the average frequency of X in the high-abstraction set should have been significantly greater than the average frequency of X in the low-abstraction set. On the other hand, there should have been *no difference* between the groups with regard to the frequency of Xness.

To test this hypothesis, we used a one-way ANOVA and found a statistically significant difference between the groups (F (1, 1065) = 66.681, p < 0.001). The average frequency of X in the high-abstraction set was statistically higher than the frequency of X in the low-abstraction set (mean = 22,011 with 95% confidence interval of ± 645 versus mean = 15,380 with 95% confidence interval of ± 503, respectively). In line with our hypothesis, no statistically significant difference was found between the groups in the average frequency of Xness.

These results suggest that, as hypothesized by Peirce, the transformation of a word from a predicate into an object, from a monadic embodied quality into a dyadic object-in-relation, is associated with an increase in the level of abstraction.

Furthermore, it seems that this process is motivated by *language use*, which is probably the driving force behind the reification of the predicates. Predicates used more by the sign community may contribute to the emergence of more abstract objects. To better understand this dynamic, we move to the next phase of our study, which involves the in-depth analysis of two case studies. As I have argued, there is no substitute for a close and in-depth inquiry, and, despite the aforementioned results supporting Peirce's idea, delving more deeply into specific instances is a must.

THE LEXICAL CONTEXT OF THE WORDS

In order to better understand the "bag of words" associated with each sign in our X–Xness list, we used the word-context frequency matrix $\mathbf{F}$.

For each predicate in our word pairs (e.g., *dark*), we identified fifty words that tend to co-occur with the given predicate by examining the predicate's corresponding row vector in $\mathbf{F}$. The fifty largest values in this row vector select fifty columns in $\mathbf{F}$. The corresponding words for these fifty columns are the fifty words that co-occur most frequently with the given predicate. These are words that are "primed" by the given predicate: when we hear the predicate, these other words come to mind.

By reversing this process, we can also find the fifty words that prime the given predicate: when we hear one of these words, the given predicate comes to mind. We call these hundred words the "context" for the given predicate and use them for further analysis.

The unique bag of words produced by this procedure for each primed word was defined as its "context" and was used for further analysis.

For each of the 1,078 X–Xness pairs, we identified the context of X, the context of Xness, and the context of their intersection (e.g., words shared by *sweet* and *sweetness*). Moreover, we identified the complement context of X (i.e., words that exist in X but not in the intersection with Xness) and the complement of Xness (i.e., words that exist in the context of Xness but not in the intersection with X).

HOME, SWEET HOME: ANALYZING THE TRANSFORMATION OF *SWEET* TO *SWEETNESS*

In order to dig deeply into the dynamics of hypostatic abstraction, we used two case studies. The first case is the word pair *sweet–sweetness* and the second is the word pair *dark–darkness*. We chose to focus our analysis on the pair *sweet–sweetness* as it was used by Peirce to illustrate his idea of hypostatic abstraction. The pair *dark–darkness* was chosen because of the negative associations of dark color in many cultures, specifically the negative associations of darker skin color in some cultures, even in cultures in which people are characterized as having dark skin.

TABLE 3.2 *LIWC analysis of the context of* sweet *and* sweetness.[a]

Category	Sweet_Com	Sweet	Inter	Sweetness	Sweetness_Com
Social	2.47	2.93	16.67	5.45	2.38
Affect	12.9	12.7	8.33	34.55	42.86
Positive emotion	9.07	9.04	8.33	34.55	35.71
Negative emotion	3.57	3.46	0	5.45	7.14
Bio	7.14	8.24	41.67	14.55	7.14
Ingest	3.57	4.26	25	9	4.76
Friend	0.27	0	8.33	0	0

[a] Results are in percentages. Sweet_Com: complement of *sweet*; Inter: intersection of the contexts.

In order to understand the transformation and the abstraction of *sweet*, we first applied the Linguistic Inquiry and Word Count software (www.liwc.net) to study the word categories characterizing the context of *sweet*, *sweetness*, and their intersection. This software is a very simple text-analysis program that calculates the degree to which people use various categories of words. The software includes a dictionary of words sorted by human judges into different categories. The software works by simply segmenting the text and categorizing its words into the predefined categories. It is a powerful text-analysis program that has been validated and intensively used in psychological research (Pennebaker and Francis 2001; Tausczik and Pennebaker 2010). The results of the LIWC analysis appear in Table 3.2.

We may consider the intersecting context as a bridge between *sweet* and *sweetness*. Several interesting findings pop up from a first glance at the table. The first finding concerns emotions. The affect associated with *sweetness* is greater than that associated with *sweet*. This is mainly due to the difference in positive emotion associated with *sweetness*. Interestingly, this increase in positive emotions is mediated at the intersection by words in the category of social interaction (*social* and *friend*) and by words in the categories of biology and ingestion.

This categorization does not tell us exactly how *sweet* is transformed into *sweetness*. To better understand this process, we identified the most concrete and frequent words associated with *sweet*. Some of these words are: *bread, girl, cherry, tea, recipe, corn,* and *honey*.

Not surprisingly, *sweet* is mainly associated with sweet food. Eating and tasting sweet food is the denotational and most basic source of *sweet*. However, the most abstract and frequent words associated with *sweet* were *love, life, success, taste,* and *surprise*. When examining the most abstract and frequent words at the intersection of *sweet* and *sweetness* we found *love* and *life*.

This finding points to the link between the basic experience of sweet food and the psychological emotional attachment to the nurturing mother or father in terms of love. *Love is basically associated with those who gave us food and therefore life.*

Platonic love, a term usually used to denote nonsexual and immaterial love, is an ungrounded concept. One should recall that for Plato and Socrates "Platonic" love probably had quite a different meaning due to their great fondness for young men.

In this context, one may hardly deny the sexual aspect of "love." I argue that love is embedded and embodied in basic attachment patterns. Those who gave us food secured our life and hence gave us love. This common-sense knowledge, forcefully forgotten by hundreds of years of Western Christianity, has never been lost from the semiotician's point of view.

As will be further discussed, food is a symbolically loaded object with deep historical, cultural, and psychological layers of meaning, and several chapters of the book will elaborate on it.

We may ask what are the most abstract and frequent words associated as complementary of *sweetness* – the words that appear in the context of *sweetness* but do *not* exist at the intersection of *sweet* and *sweetness*. Among these words we find in descending order *good*, *give*, and *hope*.

This finding allows us to trace the emergence of *sweetness* from the basic embodied experience of *sweet*. As we are nurtured by our mother or father, the basic interaction is associated on the abstract level of analysis with *love* and *life*. These abstract concepts are carried and propagated to *sweetness* through the platform of biological and ingestion words, mainly associated with food, and through the field of personal interaction signaled by the friendship and social category. This trajectory clearly illustrates the way emotion is deeply associated with sense making through semiotic mediation.

One should remember though that, as argued by Adorno (in a letter to Walter Benjamin), "all reification is a forgetting." We can see that the words associated with our concrete embodied experience appear to a significantly lesser degree in the context of *sweetness*. In a sense, they are "forgotten" in favor of abstract connotations.

To prove this hypothesis, we measured the average level of abstraction of words at the intersection of the word pair. The average abstraction levels of words in the context of sweet, sweetness, and their interaction were 0.47, 0.58, and 0.54, respectively. These results support the above interpretation.

The associations of sweet are "grafted" to the "semiotic field" (Neuman and Nave 2009b) of *sweetness* and load this object with a high level of positive emotion and with words that extend its denotational source, such as *good* and *hope*. Indeed, the abstract notion of *hope* is deeply rooted in our basic attachment to significant others and the expectation that love and life will be materialized through the interaction of nurturing us.

To recall, the ancient Greeks metaphorically described hope as the "exiles' bread." Unconsciously, they made the association between expecting food and expecting a better future – hope.

The above interpretation, powerfully supported by our computational psychological cultural analysis, also explains why *sweet* and specifically sweet food is deeply associated with love. The fact that chocolate is one of the favorite gifts on Valentine's Day is just another indication of this deep-rooted dynamic. I will elaborate *love* and *sweet* in the forthcoming chapters of this book, deepening our understanding of the carnal and semiotic mediation of our mind. Now let us move from *sweet* and its positive associations to a concept with a clear negative sense.

ANALYZING THE TRANSFORMATION OF *DARK* TO *DARKNESS*

The context of *dark* is quite simple to understand if we examine its affective context (see Table 3.3).

We can see that the shift from *dark* to *darkness* involves an increase in negative emotions, specifically anxiety, and in social words. This transformation is mediated at the intersection through *sadness*. While affect is reduced at the shared context of *dark* and *darkness*, this is mainly due to the disappearance of positive emotions and the increase of negative emotions. This is a trivial finding, but the way it is created is less trivial.

The most concrete and frequent words associated with *dark* are *hair*, *skin*, and *eyes*. At the intersection of *dark* and *darkness*, we find two key words: *deep* and *despair*. The dark color associated with body parts and closed and deep places is associated with the horror of the abyss and death, as evidenced by *morbid* – the most abstract word in the context of *dark* – and in the intersection of *dark* and *darkness*.

Darkness is associated through the lack of light with death and morbidity: *trembles*, *battle*, *weeping*, *evil*, and *sin* are some of the words that appear as complementary of *darkness*. The basic horror of being in a place with no light (i.e., *deep*, *room*, *abyss*) is propagated to *darkness* and associated with *evil*.

TABLE 3.3 *LIWC analysis of* dark *and* darkness.[a]

Category	Dark	Dark_Com	Inter	Darkness	Darkness_Com
Social	0.39	0.42	0	2.4	3.23
Affect	7.28	7.31	6.45	8.8	9.68
Positive emotion	2.56	2.71	0	1.6	2.15
Negative emotion	4.53	4.38	6.45	7.2	7.53
Anxiety	0.98	1.04	0	1.63	2.15
Anger	0.98	1.04	0	1.63	2.15
Sad	1.77	1.46	6.45	2.44	1.08

[a] Results are in percentages. Dark_Com: complement of *dark*; Inter: intersection of the contexts.

This propagation is evident in the increase of negative emotions and may be traced to a positive feedback loop involved in the grafting procedure that starts from our basic embodied experience (Neuman 2009a).

Bad things are dark things associated with fear and propagated to the abstract realm of evil. In this context, the unfortunate negative associations of dark skin, hair, and eyes can easily be traced to our fear of dark places and the hypostatic abstraction that transforms this concrete fear into abstract concepts such as *evil* and *sin* and back into their concrete origin – the dark skin, eyes, and hair.

Interestingly, the dynamics described above may help us to trace the movement from "denotation" to "connotation" and "metaphor." While *dark* may be used as a denotation to point at the color of certain objects, it is also used as a connotation in the context of "dark thoughts," for instance. This transformation is comprehensible if we identify the abstract terms associated with the complement of *darkness*. "Dark thoughts" mean thoughts of *evil* and *sin*, as identified by our analysis, and these connotative senses result from grafting our basic fears from the denotations toward *darkness* as an object that stands in certain relations with other objects. In the case of *darkness* it is possible to identify these relations by using corpus analysis.

To gain more insight into the relations in which *darkness* is embedded we again used COCA. Through COCA, we identified the verb form collocated in a window plus four words to the right of *darkness*. The results were sorted according to frequency and minimum MI equal to 3. We found that *darkness* was associated with *descends, envelops, engulfs, enfolded, gropes, abides, gorged, extinguishing, cloaking, dwelled,* and *shrouds*. What does this mean?

In metaphorical terms, *darkness* is like the mythical predator or the abyss that might engulf us in death. Portraying darkness in this way is possible through the grafting procedure described above.

In sum, the abstraction of *dark* starts from simple association with the lack of light and the horror associated with this experience. This horror is the source of the metaphorical/abstract sense of *darkness* as an engulfing substance. *Darkness* is therefore loaded with our fear of being swallowed by a primordial form, a fear that echoes in our myths, psychological theories, and stereotypes.

For instance, an ancient myth that appears in the *Veda* tells us that Prajapati, the androgynous being and the primordial lord of creatures, felt an enormous emptiness when he gave birth to the world. This horrible emptiness caused Prajapati to reunite with his offspring by swallowing the newborn. When the newborn saw the empty mouth of his father he shouted in horror. This horror illustrates the fear of being swallowed into the darkness of death, of losing one's individuality and autonomy. This idea is clearly echoed in the writings of the psychoanalyst Melanie Klein, where the infant's aggressive fantasies of consuming from the mother's breast may symmetrically turn on him as the object consumed by the mother.

DISCUSSION

Due to the lack of appropriate computational tools, the complex relation between language and thought has been too easily dismissed and mis-represented in the psychological literature. By using state-of-the-art tools in natural language processing, we can delve deeply into this complex phenomenon.

The semiotic perspective presented in this chapter resonates with the notion of "embodied cognitive science" (Clark 2006) in which the mind is in a constant flux that is coordinated by the use of words. This approach, which defies "any simple logic of inner versus outer, or of tool versus user" (Clark 2006, 374), allows us to see the continuity of the conceptual system across species (Barsalou 2005) and to understand the way human beings may transcend their grounding in the perceptual realm through sign-medi-ated interactions with others.

According to this perspective, our sign system, which is social by nature (Saussure 1972), starts with referential denotational signs to the concrete reality/experience, whether external or internal reality (Danesi 2003). This reference to the embodied experience should be clarified in order to sharpen the difference between human and nonhuman cognition.

In contrast with animal communication, human language "deals mainly with entities" (Vauclair 2003, 12) rather than with holistic situations (e.g., the presence of a predator). Therefore, our language is a language of "reification" (Neuman 2003), as it allows us to "crystallize" the dynamic flux of sensorimotor experience into objects of reflection and contemplation (i.e., signs). Through experimentation with the sign system and mechanisms such as hypostatic abstraction, some of the signs may detach from their concrete embodiment. The fact that signs are primarily social tools of interaction explains the abstraction of the mind as a process of internalization (Lawrence and Valsiner 1993).

This point is very important for those interested in education. Cultivating the minds of young people (as well as those of adults) necessarily involves the internalization of models of interaction. The mind of a young child who is exposed to respectful and critical argumentative dialogues of significant others is totally different from the mind of a young child whose models disrespectfully force their will on their subordinates.

In human beings, words and gestures function not primarily to obtain a result in the physical world but rather "to direct another individual's attention (its mental state) to an object or event as an end in itself" (Vauclair 2003, 14). This object-oriented behavior develops differently in human beings from how it does in primates:

> A typical form of communication between the infant and a competent adult (e.g., the mother) arises in humans during object manipulation. This form is characterized by the mutual exchange between mother and infant regarding a large variety of discrete, movable objects … By contrast, the nonhuman primate mother does not appear to intervene directly in the infant's object manipulations.
>
> (Vauclair 2003, 20)

In other words, we think through the internalization of symbolic interactions with others as we relate with them to objects in the world.

These designated objects and the social-semiotic interaction through which they are enacted are internalized and used for autonomously reflecting on our sign system as an object in itself. Our thoughts become more abstract as the signs we use to reflect on the external and internal reality turn far from their embodied origin. This thesis may explain why the brain as a physical system needs language in order to become self-conscious (Neuman and Nave 2009a), as well as other quandaries left unanswered by the cognitive-mentalistic approach.

In sum, adopting a semiotic perspective and state-of-the-art computational tools, we have shown that Peirce's idea is empirically grounded.

Moreover, through case studies, we have portrayed a process that explains the trajectory of abstraction. This explanation is in line with our evolutionary context, modern conceptions of "embodied cognitive science," and the variance that exists at the cultural level of analysis. In this sense, it is fully in line with Luria and Vygotsky's (1930) vision that the human being should be studied as the synergetic product of three trajectories: the evolutionary, the developmental-individual, and the cultural.

Moreover, the methodology we introduced and used in this study – computational cultural psychology – is clearly in line with Valsiner's vision of the appropriate methodology cultural psychology should adopt (2007, 367).

First, we use signs as our unit of analysis. This choice naturally derives from the semiotic perspective we adopt in this book. Our signs are forms of mediation rather than simple causes in mechanistic causal models.

Second, our study is not a simple technical procedure for supporting a theory. As argued by Valsiner (2007, 367), "An empirical proof of a hypothesis is productive only if it leads to a new idea, rather than if it confirms an existing one." Our analysis opens new ways for inquiring into cultural mediation, as is evident from our case studies.

It is for future studies to identify the exact patterns through which an embodied experience is translated into a reified object. Moreover, our methodology actually consists of studying "multilevel causal systems" and "downward causation," because signs as forms of cultural mediations that emerge from collective and historically grounded interactions clearly influence the mind of individuals who contribute to this collective activity. In sum, there are many points of intersection between the methodological vision presented by Valsiner and our study.

Let me close this chapter with a reference to a cultural artifact, more specifically a movie. *Planet of the Apes* is one of the most successful and appreciated movies produced by Hollywood in the late 1960s. The plot is simple but the idea is tricky. A group of astronauts lands on an unknown planet. To their surprise they find a horrific reversal of the order known to them: the real rollers of the planet are apes, and human beings are subordinate to them. This role reversal echoes our innermost fears, and the movie – like another expression of role reversal, the carnival, insightfully analyzed by Bakhtin – is one strategy for managing our fears.

One of the figures in the movie is Dr. Cornelius, who is a young chimpanzee. In a religious kind of speech, he says:

> Beware the beast man, for he is the devil's pawn. Alone among God's primates, he kills for sport, or lust or greed. Yes, he will murder his brother

to possess his brother's land. Let him not breed in great numbers, for he will make a desert of his home and yours. Shun him. Drive him back into his jungle lair: For he is the harbinger of death.

The human mind's ability to abstract and reverse is responsible for a variety of impressive artistic creations like *Planet of the Apes*. Is there a real reason to reject the idea of apes having a mind like our own with abstract ideas such as God?

I titled this chapter in a provocative way to trigger a discussion about the human mind and its unique and semiotically mediated nature. The conclusion of this chapter is that our ability to signify objects in arbitrary mode and to subject this signification to increasing levels of complexity draws a watershed between us and other nonhuman organisms. Probably there is a good reason why apes don't have God, and the reason concerns their limited ability to manipulate their sign system.

This conclusion has nothing to do with the validity of Dr. Cornelius's critical speech. Our ability to detach ourselves from concreteness has definitely been used as an alibi for the worse. For generations human beings have murdered, enslaved, and exploited their fellow humans and other nonhuman organisms by blinding themselves to those others' sorrow and pain. Finding the similarities between human beings and animals, a rhetorical strategy known as *animalism*, has consistently been used to displace other human beings from the sacred position of the human and to subject them to exploitation. At the same time it is our ability to transcend the concrete that allows us to bring good to the world by seeing the suffering of others, by imagining possible and sometimes better worlds, and by pursuing these ideals.

One of my most illuminating encounters happened when I was a young student. I was talking with a graduate student in biology who immigrated from France and lived in an Israeli kibbutz. He was an "anarchist" with a highly sophisticated worldview, and I enjoyed our intellectual conversation. At a certain point and under the influence of my psychology professors I used the term "human nature" to support one of my arguments about the limited morality of human beings. He looked at me amused and said, "Well done. I'm a researcher in biology and have no idea what you mean by using the word 'nature' in the context of 'human nature.' It is rather surprising that psychologists can give biologists the answer."

His point was clear. Human beings are defined by their "potential" rather than by their "nature." The same human animal can potentially risk his or her life for the sake of an unknown human being or even for the sake of a nonhuman organism. On the other hand, he or she can potentially destroy his or her own habitat and even viciously murder, exploit, and torture those who are closest to him or her. Dr. Cornelius was right at least in his demand for morality. As argued by Bakhtin, "there is no alibi in existence." One cannot hide from one's deeds and our semiotic "nature" explains why.

4

Lost in translation: how to use automatic translation machines for understanding "otherness"

Abraham Wald (1902–1960) was an Austro-Hungarian-born Jew. As a Jew raised in a religious family he couldn't attend school on Saturday and therefore was homeschooled by his parents. This homeschooling was extremely successful as Wald graduated from the University of Vienna with a Ph.D. in mathematics. Wald was forced to flee to the USA when the Nazis came into power and developed his academic career in that welcoming country.

In retrospect, the Nazis' "thesis" of the Aryan race's superiority over the Jews was powerfully refuted when Jewish scientists, such as those who led the Manhattan Project, became the cutting edge of the war efforts. We could not imagine the war efforts of the USA without Robert Oppenheimer, Edward Teller, John von Neumann, and many others.

During the Second World War, Wald made his own personal contribution to the war efforts (Mangel and Samaniego 1984). The context of his contribution is extremely interesting. The American airplanes that returned from the front were, naturally, damaged by antiaircraft artillery. As a solution the army sought to add armor to the planes. However, covering the whole airplane's belly and wings with armor would necessarily result in a weight increase that would have fatal consequences. Therefore, as a commonsensical solution, the army considered adding armor only to areas that statistically showed the most damage.

A reasonable way to address this challenge is to identify the statistical patterns of bullet holes. To identify these patterns and map the weak spots of the planes the army asked for statistical advice from Wald.

Wald, however, was far from the typical statistical advisor. His brilliant and seemingly paradoxical insight was to "carefully determine where returning planes had been shot and put extra armor *everyplace else!*" (Wainer 1990, 343, my emphasis).

This is counterintuitive advice. However, Wald concluded that "since planes had probably been hit more-or-less uniformly those aircraft hit in the unmarked places had been unable to return and so those were the areas that required more armor" (Wainer 1990, 343).

I would like to discuss Wald's brilliant insight in general conceptual terms, in terms of translation or more accurately in terms of *what is lost in translation*. Wald's brilliance was to see that what is "lost in translation," metaphorically speaking, is of no less importance than what is translated, and that sometimes *absence* is no less important than presence in our understanding of reality, in the same way as silence is no less important than talk for understanding a conversation. In this sense, despite his different academic orientation, Wald is close to the poet Robert Frost, who suggested that poetry is what is lost in translation; to Lacan, who in a similar vein pointed to the nontranslatable part of the *real* as our source of enjoyment and anxiety; and to the linguistic anthropologist Alton Becker, who argues that culture is precisely that which is lost in translation.

Our interest is in cultural psychology, and therefore the question is whether we can find that which is lost in translation and, by using it, better understand culture and psychology. Therefore, I first discuss the idea that culture is what is lost in translation, and second propose a paradoxical way through which we may use the "stupidity" of automatic machine translation (MT) in order to get a better grasp of culture and psychology. In this sense, my attempt to understand culture through computational tools is a tribute to Wald's paradoxical logic. Let me start with another great mind, the Spanish philosopher José Ortega y Gasset (1883–1955).

In his insightful paper "The difficulty of reading," Ortega y Gasset (1959) points to the fact, that despite all utopian efforts, in reading a text there always remains an "illegible" residue. By reading a text we may identify things that the author has not meant to say and at the same time more than she or he plans. In this sense, "to read is to interpret and not anything else" (Ortega y Gasset 1959, 3). Ortega summarizes this observation under what he describes as the "Axioms for a New Philology" (2):

1 Every utterance is deficient – it says less than it wishes to say.
2 Every utterance is exuberant – it conveys more than it plans.

Alton Becker cites Ortega y Gasset's two "axioms" of "interpretative linguistics" and suggests that the role of the "interpretative linguist," and probably that of the cultural psychologist too, is in *correcting* our deficiencies and exuberances in understanding others. Think about this modest and impressive ambition: just correcting deficiencies and exuberances. Do you remember the nonunderstanding husbands I mentioned in Chapter 2? Those who divorce less than the understanding others? The nonunderstanding husbands are those involved in corrections. They are like the interpretative linguist discussed by Ortega y Gasset. In both cases, the focus is primarily on correcting our deficiencies and exuberances in understanding others.

In the ego-centered academia in which we live, it is probably impossible to "market" a research approach that aims at corrections only. However, I feel enormous respect for this modest approach. Life is about corrections, and our ability to correct is an essential part of it. As Darwin has wisely taught us, mistakes are the source of variation and therefore of life itself. Nevertheless, correcting "mistakes" at the micro level of interactions is what keeps us alive.

The rigor here is not the rigor of a theory but "the rigor that comes from the *particularity of text-in-context*" (Becker 2000, 73, my emphasis). By proposing this approach Becker is close in mind to the "pragmatic" approach as presented by Bakhtin, because the focus of our activity is on understanding the particularity of the situation through a contextual analysis. But what do we actually mean when we use the magic word "context"? This is a question repeatedly asked in this book. Do you remember Bateson and the metasignals? Volosinov and his description of context?

Shifting the burden of proof to context seems in many cases an excuse to avoid encountering the complexity of the situation. The fact that life is complex is not an excuse for not trying to understand it. Unfortunately, I have attended too many interpretative sessions in which the speaker's avoidance of saying something determinate or significant was covered with a big smile and the irrefutable argument: "It depends on the context."

Ortega defines context as "a dynamic whole on which each part exercises influence, modifies the others, and, vice versa, receives pressure from the others" (Ortega y Gasset 1959, 14) In other words, the rigor of interpretative linguistics is in interpreting or making sense out of a linguistic unit, whether a word or a sentence, by carefully examining the way it is both "influenced" by the wider "context" and recursively influences it. This idea does not locate the task of meaning making in a Newtonian universe of simple cause and effect. The meaning of an utterance is not determined by a single factor. Meaning is the way through which the whole, the context, dynamically supports the comprehension of lower-level units and vice versa.

In fact, there is nothing new in this idea, which has already b⁻⁻ described as the "hermeneutic circle." However, it is quite difficult eve metaphorically describe it, and one needs visual metaphors, such as the topology of a Klein bottle, where the whole is dynamically constituted through a smooth flow of outside into the inside.

Ortega and Becker urge us to read the text through a dynamic, multi-level process and to pay close attention to the "holes" through which the text is constituted. This idea, despite its complexity and difficult demands, is of great value for the psychologist who is seeking to understand a different culture. Let me elaborate this point through a simple example.

Let's assume that it is the late 1970s and you are a Chomskyan linguist hired by the Israeli Intelligence Service to try to understand, through the analysis of given texts, whether the Egyptian prime minister Sa'adat is serious in his intentions to establish peace with Israel. This is a kind of psychological "profiling" common in the various intelligence agencies, but with limited predictive success one should add. In fact it is a kind of forensic linguistics task that has become more popular today.

As a linguist interested in the theory and abstract mathematical structure of language – its grammar – you may have little if anything to say about the subject. However, if you are an interpretative linguist with sensitivity to the particularity of the Arab language in context then you may be interested, for instance, in the exact word the Egyptian prime minister used to describe peace. Is it سلام, meaning "real" peace, or الصلحة (sulha), a ritual that is considered a ceasefire for an unlimited time?

Indeed, I have heard that the exact terminology used by Sa'adat was of great interest to the Israeli intelligence community. According to the story I have heard, Sa'adat was insulted when asked whether he tended toward peace or *sulha*. *Sulha* is a term used by the Bedouin nomadic tribes, and Sa'adat, as a proud farmer from the banks of the Nile, did not like the idea that he was mistaken for a Bedouin nomad. This anecdote points at the importance of understanding another cultural mind through a careful analysis of its language and thought.

What is the methodology we should use in order to understand a different culture? The most intuitive approach is to translate the other culture into our own conceptual system. In contrast, Becker suggests the methodology of "back-translation": "starting from a translation and then seeking out the exuberances – those things presented in the translation but not in the original – and the deficiencies – those things in the original but not in the translation" (Becker 2000, 73).

Becker's idea is an interesting approach to understanding the particularity of language, with its deficiencies and exuberances. The interesting question is whether modern computational tools can help us in addressing this challenge. What I would like to suggest is that a paradoxical use of MT may be to identify the cultural particularities of a culture, those particularities that might be lost in translation. This use has materialized into a paper co-authored with my student Danny Livshitz and my colleague Howard Newton, and presented at a security informatics conference (Livshits *et al.* 2012).

In order to introduce this thesis let us first understand the general logic behind MT and the exact loss we experience in translation. The reason for using MT is twofold. First, there is no better way to understand the loss accompanying translation than by examining the most structured and formal attempt of translation known today. Second, instead of pointing at the problems and errors of MT, I suggest using it in order to better understand cultural particularities and discrepancies. The second suggestion is somehow counterintuitive as we positively think of eliminating errors and solving problems. Sometimes, however, errors can be used for the better, as will hopefully be illustrated later. This logic is the logic underlying advances in levels of martial arts: use your opponent's energy and errors for your own benefit.

I have no aim of providing a comprehensive introduction to the subject of MT, and the interested reader is referred to introductory texts in natural language processing and computational linguistics, or to books that provide a more detailed presentation of MT (Koehn 2010). However, let me present the idea of MT in a nutshell.

In summary, MT involves the automatic translation of a text from a source language to a target language. As the algorithms underlying the best MT engines, such as Google Translate, are not public (Kit and Wong 2008; NIST 2008), we may only intelligently evaluate their logic and the logic combining statistical machine translation (SMT) with rule-based methods.

Words are considered our basic units of meaning and therefore the first step in translating a text is tokenization and the breaking of the text into words. The words are categorized according to their role. This phase involves identifying the parts of speech. A word can be identified as a noun, adjective, verb, adverb, preposition (e.g., in), and so on.

When we have words available for further processing we should resolve issues of polysemy and homonymy. Polysemy concerns the fact that the same word may have different senses. For instance, the word "cat" may be used to denote the feline creature or as slang for a jazz player. On the other hand, homonyms are words that have different senses despite being spelled the same. For instance, the word "interest" can be used in the sense of curiosity as well as in the sense of a fee paid for a loan.

These issues must be resolved when an MT deals with the alignment of words from the source text with words from the target text. How do we find the appropriate word or phrase from the target language that matches the meaning of the word or phrase in the source language? Here we get into the first problem, which involves the correct lexical choice.

To solve this problem, SMT uses "parallel corpora" in which the same texts exist in the source language and as experts' translations in the target language. In this case, we have a corpora annotated by human experts who translated the text from the source to the target. This is an important point. When presenting a new methodology for understanding cultural otherness through MT, I actually draw on statistical machine extrapolations of texts annotated by human experts. Therefore, MT – and more specifically SMT – is not the ultimate example of "artificial intelligence" but an instance of "augmented intelligence."

One should notice that the meaning of words is dependent on the domain in which they "live." The use of parallel corpora for translation is constrained by this fact, and therefore successful MTs are usually those developed for a limited and well-defined textual domain such as newspapers. However, trying to automatically translate poetry by relying on a corpus of translated news may end in bitter disappointment. Given these constraints, the use of a parallel corpus is a highly successful strategy of translation. By using such corpora we may find, for instance, that a certain word X is usually translated to a target word Y, and we may use this statistical pattern in our translation.

As one quickly realizes, this procedure may apply the best learning algorithm for identifying the target word, but *context* is an inevitable source of information and difficulty. This fact is clearly stated by the developers of Google Translate, who say: "We're constantly working to improve the quality of our translations. Even today's most sophisticated software, however, doesn't approach the fluency of a native speaker or possess the skill of a professional translator. Automatic translation is very difficult, as the meaning of words depends on the context in which they're used" (http://translate.google.com/support).

This is a wonderful statement, as it perfectly serves the methodology that I have developed. If context is at the core of translation, then a failure in context understanding may give us some indications about the culture from which this context has been drawn!

Let me emphasize again the difficulty of translation, a difficulty resulting from contextual constraints. For example, a colleague of mine who is a French psychiatrist and psychoanalyst was impressed by a paper I published in a psychoanalytic journal and asked for my permission to translate it from English to French. This paper is going to appear in a francophone psycho-analytic journal.

One of the keywords in my paper was "loophole," but how do you trans-late "loophole" into French? In this case, we don't have a simple problem of disambiguating a word by examining its local linguistic context. This is not a case in which we have to decide whether "bass" is used to signify a fish or a musical instrument, or whether a "tank" is used in the sense of a container or a war machine. Here we have a more difficult case in which a word is "loaded" with meaning that is not trivially matched by a word in the target language.

Loophole is a word that involves a semantic composition of "loop" and "hole." The emerging meaning of this composition cannot be identified by reduction to the composing components. It is a hole through which you may enter yourself through a kind of a "topological" loop.

In my paper, I used the term "loophole" to describe the paradoxical way one may reflect on oneself, but translating this sense to French was a very difficult and probably an impossible task, and we finally settled for *point de flee*, a phrase that grasps only a certain and limited portion of the original sense.

In the case where you have two parallel corpora regarding a specific form of discourse, such as parliamentary debates, the problem may be of minor importance. However, when you come into other forms of discourse, such as poetry, the idea of using a word for a word in order to translate the meaning of the text is known as "literal translation," and its naiveté was rec-ognized long ago.

It is Peirce again who can explain the reason for the shortcoming of this naive approach, and the reason is that meaning can never be reduced to a simple dyadic correspondence between words or between a word and a concept. The meaning of a word, a phrase, a sentence, and so on always involves an intricate *network* of associated signs through which the target word is loaded with associations, connotations, emotions, and the informa-tion used to entail the meaning of other words as well.

The connotations of a word are of great importance to the cultural psy-chologist. The metaphor "my lawyer is a shark" (Kintsch 2000), which will be discussed several times in this paper, may be read by an American as a positive metaphor in which the lawyer is described as "target oriented," for instance. However, in Farsi the word "shark" (كوسه ماهى) has the connota-tion of baldness, nonmasculinity, and therefore even implied homosexuality (I thank S. Moussaiey for informing me of this cultural meaning). Therefore, a Farsi metaphor "my lawyer is a shark" may have a totally different sense than the one it has in the USA.

In contrast with some past conceptions, metaphors and connotation are not anomalies of language use but are rather probably at the heart of language use, specifically in ancient cultures, such as the Farsi culture, in which layers on layers of meaning have been built through generations. In contrast with signaling systems evident in nonhuman organisms, our language is usually characterized by deep and constantly changing layers of nonliteral use that make it far from trivial to grasp using MT.

The task of MT does not end with finding the appropriate corresponding words. Words are organized in a syntactical structure, and the fact that "languages differ in their syntactic structure causes some of the hardest problems for machine translation" (Koehn 2010, 56).

As a text is multilayered, the problem does not even end at the sentence level of analysis but exists at the discourse level of analysis – for instance, anaphora resolution. Text is not translated word by word but sentence by sentence. Therefore, we not only have to match the appropriate source to target words but also align the sentences themselves. In fact, Koehn (2010) argues that the best-performing MT systems are not those that translate isolated words but those that translate phrases: small word sequences.

By focusing on multiword sequences, MT may better address the ambiguities associated with the translation of isolated words. In fact, the surroundings of a given word are actually its context, and context even at the minimal level of word sequences is crucial for understanding the meaning of a word.

The translation process does not even end at this point; it involves multiple phases that include "decoding," or the finding of the best translation among the potential alternatives, and then the smoothing of the text.

The lesson we have learned so far is that the failures of MT in grasping the deep nonliteral level of a text may be used in order to approximate a certain portion of that which is lost in translation, and through this loss we may better understand the culture that is our target.

To gain insight into this lost residue we may use back-translation but our focus should be on lost meaning that exists, to recall Ortega, neither at the micro level of the target word nor on the macro level of the context, but in between or at the "mesoscopic" level of analysis.

In sum, my proposal is that, by using the deficiencies of MT, we may better understand our own deficiencies in trying to grasp the otherness of culture. Before introducing the detailed methodology through which this challenge may be addressed, we may ask whether this paradoxical use of MT may have any practical benefits.

HOW IMPORTANT IS IT TO UNDERSTAND OTHERS?

The importance of identifying cultural discrepancies may be of great interest to ethnographic intelligence (ETHINT) or cultural intelligence (CULINT) (Coles 2005; Delp 2008; Renzi 2006), where the collective mind of a given society is elucidated for intelligence aims.

The importance of cultural awareness for intelligence analysis was recognized a long time ago, although there are ups and downs. As argued by Johnson and Berrett (2011, 1), "Cultural inertia is easily underrated, and American decision makers have shown a need for help in isolating and understanding the complexity, weight and relevance of culture as they consider foreign policy initiatives."

Kipp *et al.* (2006) even argue that conducting military operations in a low-intensity conflict without ethnographic and cultural intelligence is wasteful and clumsy. They further criticize the US military for neglecting the cultural aspect, and they introduce the Human Terrain System, which aims to address shortcomings in cultural awareness at the operational and tactical levels. If you recall my story of the American troops in Iraq and the ability to know the smell of a different culture and its sense of humor, the above criticism makes a lot of sense.

As language is recognized by the above authors as an indispensable source of cultural information, they propose to study texts ranging from political rhetoric to texts taught in school as a part of "cultural topography" – a new research tool for intelligence analysis. There is nothing new about this proposal and it resonates with leading approaches in cultural psychology (Valsiner 2007) that consider culture in terms of dynamic sign systems that frame people's minds and direct their behavior. In fact, successful intelligence agencies have always paid close attention to the study of strategic competitors' texts. In this chapter, I present a novel automatic textual analysis methodology that is able to identify "shortcomings" and inadequacies in cultural understanding or awareness. I'm not familiar with the technologies secretly developed by intelligence agencies. However, from what is known to me, the methodology I have developed is novel and illustrates the benefits of computational cultural psychology. Let me present the methodology in detail.

LOST IN TRANSLATION

As I have argued before, the most common approach to understanding a different culture is to translate it into our own terms. This is precisely the role of a talented CULINT analyst who is familiar with the languages and conceptual spheres of both cultures.

The idea of back-translation as a method of increasing cultural awareness is very important but its implementation in practice is far from trivial for two main reasons.

The first concerns our cognitive limitations. A text – written, for instance – comprises words and their relations. These relations produce a dense network of nodes (signs) and edges (relations), which the human mind may have extreme difficulty processing for the identification of structural properties.

The second challenge, closely related to the first, is that intelligence agencies handle a massive amount of data. Although an expert analyst with sufficient knowledge of anthropology and discourse analysis may probably increase our cultural awareness through a close, in-depth examination of a few texts, this ill-structured and energy-consuming process does not provide a scalable solution to a massive amount of data.

CULINT THROUGH BACK-TRANSLATION OF NETWORK MOTIFS

To the best of my knowledge, there is no systematic computer-based methodology for identifying shortcomings in cultural awareness. Our methodology first assumes that the meaning of the text under analysis is encapsulated, as proposed by Becker and others, in a *set of relations*.

The operationalization of this idea was proposed in a paper I wrote with Dan Assaf and Yochai Cohen (2012). The paper, which will be described in detail later, suggests that these relations may be conceptualized as "motifs" – sub-graphs – of a semantic network.

Our idea is simple. I will present it first in a nutshell and later return to it to develop and elaborate it further. A text may be represented as a graph of objects/nouns. This graph is built by first automatically representing the sentences as a set of binary relations between words. By applying a set of rules this representation is converted into a graph with nodes/words and their relations. The graph as a whole is of no interest to us, only its motifs.

Motifs are sub-graphs that appear with a significantly greater frequency than that which could have been expected by chance (Milo *et al.* 2002).

Through algorithms and software developed specifically for the identification of motifs, these sub-graphs are identified and processed further. For instance, Figure 4.1 presents three different types of three-node motifs. Each motif has a unique identification number that represents a unique connection between the signs (words) that occupy its three edges. In some

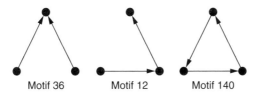

Motif 36   Motif 12   Motif 140

FIGURE 4.1 Three-node motifs.

of the motifs all signs are related in a single direction while in others there are bidirectional relations, reflecting co-dependence between the signs.

While examining the meaning of words comprising the nodes in a certain motif has not been of interest in motif analysis, we have suggested that, by identifying the words comprising the nodes of significant motifs, we actually identify "themes" in the text: patterns of significant semantic relations.

It must be emphasized that common motif analysis is purely *structural* and focuses on the identification of statistically significant patterns of subgraphs. In contrast, traditional textual analysis is usually *interpretative* and focuses on the "meaning" of signs or texts without taking into account statistical structural regularities.

What is unique in the methodology we have developed is that it merges *form* (i.e., structural motifs) and *content* (i.e., semantics of nodes) in order to identify meaningful patterns of relations in the text. After we understand this basic idea we can move forward.

To increase our cultural awareness of given textual data, we aim to identify what is lost in translation in terms of the above motifs/themes. This process is automatic and paradoxically relies on the deficiencies rather than on the success of automatic MT.

Our methodology uses the facts that automatic MT is far from perfect and that there are many sources hindering the quality of the translation at different scales of analysis (Koehn 2010). However, in our case we are not bothered by the deficiency of automatic MT but turn this deficiency into an advantage for identifying lost cultural themes.

The rationale underlying the methodology is easy to grasp. If we would like to increase our cultural awareness by identifying gaps in our understanding of certain cultural texts then we first have to identify the motifs comprising them.

Second, if we automatically translate the texts into different target languages assuming that the translation is insensitive to cultural nuances, the meaning will be lost in translation. The use of many target languages may solve the difficulties associated with the use of a single and particular target language.

After the texts have been translated, we translate them *back* from the target languages into the source language/culture and again identify the themes in the back-translation. If our logic is valid then discrepancies between the themes in the source culture/language and the themes returned in the back-translation should be indicative of cultural differences and therefore increase our awareness of the shortcomings in understanding the source culture. The following analysis provides the first empirical support for the validity of our methodology.

METHODOLOGY

To test our methodology, we analyzed thirty speeches that were downloaded from an internet site that includes the most important speeches in American culture, as rated by experts (www.americanrhetoric.com).

Each speech was automatically translated by Google Translate into three languages representing different families: Arabic (representing Afro-Asiatic languages), Chinese (representing Sino-Tibetan languages), and German (representing Indo-European languages).

Before it was translated, each speech was automatically parsed through the Stanford Parser to produce a "dependency representation" of the text (de Marneffe and Manning 2008). This parsing creates binary relations between pairs of words. For instance, the phrase "she looks beautiful" presents a binary relation of adjectival complement between "looks" and "beautiful."

Following this phase, we applied a set of rules to the dependency representation to create a network of nouns from the text. These rules are not perfect, and therefore the network also includes a fraction of words that are not nouns.

We represented each speech as a network of words and automatically extracted three-node motifs by using FANMOD software (Wernicke and Rasche 2006). The choice of three-node motifs, the most basic motif structure, is supported by theoretical justification (Neuman 2011) as well as by the need for saving computational load and gaining parsimony in interpreting the results.

For each speech, we identified the significant motifs in its original English language, translated the speech into each of the three other languages, translated it back to English, and repeated the same procedure of motif identification. In sum, we compared the themes that characterized each original speech with the themes that characterized its back-translations.

While most of the motifs (89%) that were found in the source language returned in one or more of the back-translations, it was found that
most of the words that populate these motifs in English did not return
in the back-translations; only 17% in Arabic, 7% in Chinese, and 25% in
German.

For each speech, we identified the returned motif with the highest frequency in the speech. The words comprising the nodes of these motifs were
translated back and forth, and by using Google's search engine we compared the chance of finding them together in a document compared to finding them separately.

In other words, we measured the conditional probability of finding Word
1 *and* Word 2 *and* Word 3 given the probability of findingWord 1 *or* Word 2
or Word 3. The measure produced by this calculation is an indirect measure of the motif's cultural significance. If a triadic combination of words
characterizes a certain culture, we should find it in a statistically significant
higher proportion in the source culture than in language corpora of other
cultures to which it has been translated.

We compared the above probability with the one produced by using the
translation of the three words into each of the three languages and conducted the search in the target languages: Arabic, Chinese, and German. As
a representative linguistic corpus we used Google's search engine.

RESULTS

Across speeches it was found that, on average, the prevalence of our cultural themes was higher in English (2.05%) than in German (1.62%), Arabic
(0.65%), or Chinese (0.53%), a difference that by using a t-test for paired
samples was found to be statistically significant for English and Arabic
($t = 2.42$, $p = 0.02$) and English and Chinese ($t = 3.08$, $p = 0.005$), but not
for English and German, two cultures that are relatively close and belong to
the same language family.

These results provide preliminary and minimal empirical support that
our methodology exposes some kind of cultural differences and may be
used for increasing cultural awareness. The meaning of these cultural differences is illustrated by analyzing emotions associated with the themes.

AFFECT IN THE MOTIFS

We identified the most frequently returned motifs in each language and
analyzed the words that were the most frequent nodes in each motif. For

TABLE 4.1 *Words categorized by LIWC as emotionally positive and negative emotions associated with the returned motifs.*

	Positive Emotion (%)	Negative Emotion (%)
English (original)	3.66	1.97
German	7.41	0.74
Chinese	6.02	5.09
Arabic	10.08	8.53

better understanding the meaning of these nodes we used the LIWC software. I introduced LIWC in Chapter 3 when analyzing some of my data.

When using the LIWC software interesting differences were found. While in the English source the percentage of affect words characterizing the motifs was 5.63%, for the German back-translation it was 8.15%, for the Chinese it was 11.11%, and for the Arabic it was 18.61%. In other words, on average, the words that returned with the motifs were actually more emotionally loaded than they had been in the source language/culture!

This result is supported by analysis of the percentage in which words categorized by LIWC as emotionally positive and negative emotions were associated with the returned motifs (see Table 4.1).

What is the meaning of these findings? We don't have the baseline to decide whether the speeches are high or low emotionally in comparison to some baseline of American culture. We can say, however, that if culture is what is lost in translation then American culture is reflected as *more positive and at the same time (to exclude the German case) more negative than it actually is.*

The bottom line is that this procedure reflects our discrepancy in understanding the affective aspect loaded with cultural texts. This is in itself not news, as the cultural psychology of emotion (for a review see Mesquita and Leu 2007) reveals clear differences in the ways different cultures process their and others' emotions. In fact, the idea of language as context (Feldman-Barrett *et al.* 2007) – which has been shown to be highly important even in identifying the emotion of facial expression – is highly relevant to our methodology. The idea is that different cultures support their members with different linguistic-conceptual schemes that may constrain the processing of emotions. The methodology hereby presented suggests a practical way to understand cultural discrepancy in emotions.

For instance, if an Arab CULINT expert analyzes American speeches using our methodology, he can infer that American–English culture will be conceived by his cultural milieu to be more emotionally loaded than it actually is.

This is a very important conclusion with clear practical implications, as it may raise cultural awareness of the fact that, in an Arab–American cultural encounter, the American side might be mistakenly conceived as more emotional than it is. In fact, this should not be manifested as a conclusion but rather as a hypothesis that is worth further consideration. To better illustrate our methodology we include a case study analyzing a classical political speech.

NIXON'S STRENGTH – A CASE STUDY

Let us take as an example Nixon's famous speech "The Great Silent Majority" (November 1969). As a researcher who invested efforts in understanding the psychology of political rhetoric through interpretative tools (Neuman *et al.* 2001; Neuman *et al.* 2002; Neuman and Levi 2003), I found it interesting to combine my old methods with the power of the computational methodology we developed.

In a very famous television address concerning the American policy in Vietnam, Richard Nixon responded to the public protest against the war and justified the American presence in Vietnam.

Figure 4.2 is a visual representation of the speech as produced by Wordle (www.wordle.net/create); the representation is limited to the eighty most frequent words.

We can easily see that the most salient words in the speech were words such as "Vietnam," "war," and "peace." This is a rather trivial finding. However, in this book I am obliged to say much more.

By analyzing this speech through our methodology, we identified the significant motifs in the speech and the words that were most frequently associated with the nodes in the motifs.

For instance, the most frequent words that populated Motif 36 were "think," "strength," and "war." "Think" is not a noun and was included in the results as a result of a failure of the Stanford Parser. Errors are inevitable when one uses statistical computational tools for natural language processing.

To gain a more complex representation of the speech we created a map in which nodes/words shared by two motifs glued together several motifs. This procedure produced the representation shown in Figure 4.3.

This representation includes some of the most common words and also words that were marginal in terms of frequency, such as "nightmare" and "strength." The first theme that associates "Vietnam" and "strength" is of

FIGURE 4.2 Visual representation of Nixon's speech as produced by Wordle.

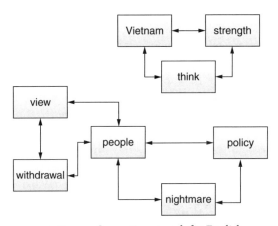

FIGURE 4.3 Semantic network for English.

specific interest, as "strength" is a marginal, almost unnoticed word in the speech. The word "strength" appears only four times in the speech:

1 The South Vietnamese have continued to gain in *strength*.
2 This withdrawal will be made from *strength* and not from weakness.

3 Well, one of the *strengths* of our free society is that any American has a right to reach that conclusion and to advocate that point of view.

4 I pledge to you tonight that I shall meet this responsibility with all of the *strength* and wisdom I can command, in accordance with your hopes, mindful of your concerns, sustained by your prayers.

(my emphasis)

"Strength" first appears at the beginning of the speech, where the South Vietnamese gained strength and as a result caused casualties among the American forces. From a psycholinguistic point of view, and following Hoey (1991), the first appearance of "strength" in the context of Vietnam is very important, as this is a lexical unit that frames the meaning of "strength" and provides the first link to establishing a coherent understanding of the concept.

The second use of "strength" suggests that the withdrawal from Vietnam will be made from "strength." The third use concerns the "strength" of the American society, which enables it to tolerate the antiwar protest, and the fourth use of "strength" concerns the strength of the president to pursue his policy.

The word "think" appears twice in the same paragraph:

But I had a greater obligation than to *think* only of the years of my Administration, and of the next election. I had to *think* of the effect of my decision on the next generation, and on the future of peace and freedom in America, and in the world.

(my emphasis)

Based on these data we can now interpret our findings. The first motif and its associated words expose a possible theme of the speech that focuses on the issue of "strength." Let me explain.

While the speech argues in favor of the "great silent majority" and against the protest, it is actually about "strength": the "strength" of the Vietnamese to "take over combat responsibilities from our American troops," withdrawing from a position of "strength" equivalent at least to the "strength" of the Vietnamese opponent and not to express weakness.

The "strength" of the society in the face of its opponents is a Janus face. It is the "strength" to face the enemy and at the same time the "strength" to face the internal protest that may be conceived as an internal enemy.

The final sense of strength is that of the leader, Nixon himself, who in the same way as the nation strives to courageously and with "strength" face his external Vietnamese as well as his internal opponents, which seem to be threatening to the same extent.

The following paragraph appears as a context for the first appearance of "nightmare" in the speech:

> We saw a prelude of what would happen in South Vietnam when the Communists entered the city of Hue last year. During their brief rule there, there was a bloody reign of terror in which 3,000 civilians were clubbed, shot to death, and buried in mass graves.

And the word itself appears in the following context:

> With the sudden collapse of our support, these atrocities at Hue would become the *nightmare* of the entire nation and particularly for the million-and-a-half Catholic refugees who fled to South Vietnam when the Communists took over in the North.
>
> (my emphasis)

This is the only place in the speech where "nightmare" appears. "View" appears three times in the speech; first "in view of these circumstances" where "the war was causing deep division at home and criticism from many of our friends, as well as our enemies, abroad." Second, in the sense of "point of view," specifically regarding the "minority who hold that point of view" of protesting against the war. The use of "that" to describe "point of view" is a clear case of "empathetic deixis," in which an emotional distance between the speaker and his critics is created through linguistic means.

The story portrayed by the above themes and their links is a story of *fear*, of a *nightmare*, of a "bloody reign of terror" that threatens the nation (the American nation?) and Christians in particular (Vietnamese but probably good American Christians too).

It is a story about a vicious and strong opponent that should be responded to by the strength of the nation and by the strength of the leader, who struggles to prevent the evolving nightmare but also has the strength to face his domestic opponents.

The American people – who are "do-it-yourself people," "impatient people" – are probably located in the map shown in Figure 4.3 between the nightmare expected as a result of a harsh withdrawal and the strength needed to support Nixon's policy (which contrasts with the "view" of the protesters).

This interpretation of the themes and the way they mutually nurture each other is lost when we translate the speech into Chinese and identify the themes in the back-translation (see Figure 4.4).

"Collapse" appears in the text three times: once in the context of "the sudden [American] collapse of our support" and the expected nightmare;

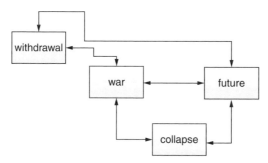

FIGURE 4.4 Semantic network for Chinese (back-translation).

once as the "collapse of confidence in American leadership not only in Asia but throughout the world" as a result of the "first defeat in our nation's history"; and once in the context of the danger that withdrawal "would mean a collapse not only of South Vietnam but Southeast Asia."

The major theme of "strength" evident in the English source and its deep association with "nightmare" facing those who oppose Nixon's policy has disappeared in favor of another picture portraying a rather shallow image of danger facing the withdrawal from Vietnam.

The central theme of "strength" in the face of evolving nightmare and internal (communist?) opponents is a theme deeply related to the cultural zeitgeist of the USA in the 1960s, and specifically the conservative political leadership that was immersed in the fears of the Cold War. For a Chinese, these cultural delicacies would have been lost in translation. However, they are clearly exposed through this methodology and its accompanying interpretation.

An intelligence analyst reading Nixon's speech through my unique methodology would have grasped the deep, layered meaning of Nixon's speech. The speech's theme of "strength" is actually what Freud would have called "reaction formation," a sign of weakness rather than of strength. In talking about "strength" Nixon is actually a weak president who signals in the speech the end of his regime and the end of the American involvement in Vietnam. Whether such an approaching tipping point could have been anticipated in real time is a difficult question to answer.

Life is built along the logic of the "forking paths" described in one of Borges's stories rather than along the lines of a simple linear universe. In this context, our ability to predict is severely limited, a fact that doesn't dismiss our deep motivation to understand and forecast the future. An amusing anecdote will be used to conclude this chapter.

As a young student I worked at the Office of the Chief Scientist at the Israeli Ministry of Education. I was a "senior research coordinator" who was given the wonderful opportunity to critically analyze studies, and share my analysis and recommendations with my boss. One day we got an invitation from the Chief Scientist of the Police proposing to establish a task force of chief scientists, whose role was to forecast social and economic changes that might have significant implications for crime and the work of the police. In those days, more than twenty years ago, the social sciences were not very familiar with the idea of chaos. In my report to the Chief Scientist, I explained that no one had predicted the collapse of the Soviet Union, Gorbachov's perestroika, the fall of the Berlin Wall, the massive wave of Russian immigrants to Israel, or the fact that the prostitution "industry" in Israel had suddenly changed to be governed by ladies from the former Soviet Union, a fact that had suddenly and desperately increased the demand for Russian-speaking policemen.

Forecasting in a chaotic environment is a risky task and, like other organisms that have developed remarkable tools for living in a chaotic environment, we too should better plan our steps despite our arrogant theories.

CONCLUSION

My colleague Mark Last directed me to an interesting article published in a hardcore fundamentalist Farsi newspaper, *Kayhan*. In its November 2012 issue one can find the following text:

رهبر انقلاب در اجتماع پرنشاط جوانان خراسان شمالي:
پيشرفت حقيقي و تمدن ريشه دار در انتخاب مكتب توحيد است

Google translates this text as: "Young *gay community* leader in North Khorasan [is saying]: 'Real progress and civilization is rooted in monotheism school choice'" (my emphasis).

This title may shock the naive reader. A fundamentalist Islamic newspaper in Iran quotes a "young gay community leader"? After all, under the regime of the fundamentalists, gays are viciously persecuted and sometimes executed. Is the above title a sign of a changing society? Misinterpreted, this translation may give great pleasure to some analysts from the American Department of State. Surely, if an Iranian newspaper is citing the young leader of a homosexual community in North Khorasan, the Arab Spring has fully blossomed and a real change is evident in Iran.

Unfortunately, the Department of State people may be wrong again. The correct translation is: "The revolutionary leader at the joyful assembly of the youth of North Khorasan …"

In other words, no gay liberation in Iran and no spring in Tehran. Like a Swiss cheese, translation is full of holes, in the same way as our understanding. In this context, it is better to identify the holes, as wisely proposed by Becker.

In this chapter, I have introduced a novel methodology for identifying shortcomings in cultural awareness. The methodology is built on the identification of themes in textual graphs and on the paradoxical use of automatic MT for identifying themes lost in translation. I don't have any pretentions of presenting a complete methodology for understanding a different culture, and I am well aware of the current shortcomings and technical difficulties associated with what I have presented. However, my aim is to provide (1) a methodology worth examining and developing, and (2) proof of concept that the methodology may indeed expose cultural discrepancies.

The strength of the methodology is in examining both structural and semantic aspects of the data as two complementary aspects, and in providing an automated method that may be used for analyzing a large quantity of data in a short time.

As there is no magic or fully automated solution to the challenge of CULINT, I must stress the fact that the methodology presented in this chapter cannot be a substitute for the intelligence analyst but only a tool that may help him or her to better address the challenge of CULINT. As in other cases mentioned in this book, there is no substitute for the winning combination of a scientific structural analysis accompanied by an in-depth and sensitive interpretation. Therefore, this chapter concludes by pointing to the great potential of the methodology but at the same time urges researchers to develop it further. As I said at the beginning of the chapter, my aim is to use this example of computational cultural psychology for corrections only and for raising our awareness of the deficiencies and exuberances in understanding a different culture.

5

Spies and metaphors: automatic identification of metaphors for strategic intelligence

In May 2011, *Wired* magazine published a paper under the provocative title "Spies, meet Shakespeare: intel geeks build metaphor motherlode." This title generates curiosity, as spies and Shakespeare belong to two different "semantic fields." Although some notable writers, particularly British writers such as W. Somerset Maugham and Graham Greene, belonged to the intelligence community, Shakespeare was probably not one of them.

The author of the article, Lena Groeger (2011), introduces the Intelligence Advanced Research Projects Activity (IARPA) – "the mad science unit of the intelligence community" – and its metaphor project, which aims to "exploit the use of metaphors by different cultures to gain insight into their cultural norms."

In fact this project has drawn wide attention; *The Economist* joined the celebration by publishing the article "Metaphors we do everything by?" (R.L.G. 2011), and other newspapers have published similar stories.

IARPA is a relatively new American agency that was established to develop "the next generation of spycraft technologies" (Bhattacharjee 2009).

In the context of "spycraft," metaphor identification isn't the most salient tool. Our images of the spy world are nurtured by Hollywood rather than by the real world. We can imagine agent 007 – James Bond – driving a car that turns into a war machine. We can imagine the tech geeks who operate the most sophisticated technology to locate the place where Jason Bourne, the hero of *The Bourne Identity*, is calling from. However, we would hardly imagine a spy movie in which a secret agent bursts into the technology geeks' office shouting, "Urgent! I need the metaphors used by the Iranians to describe the United States."

Surprisingly, in 2011 IARPA launched an open solicitation call for the "Metaphor Program." If IARPA were not a spy agency, then the Metaphor

Program could have passed the wider audience by. So why is an agency seeking to understand the metaphors used by people?

The general context is the context of "strategic intelligence," which involves a country seeking to understand the general picture emerging from a variety of information sources produced with regard to a strategic opponent. Understanding your opponent is not an easy task. Intelligence agencies gather a huge amount of information from open sources. Such information from newspapers is known as OSINT; that from human informants is known as HUMINT; and that from tracking down messages and other digital signals is known as SIGINT.

The information gathered must somehow be integrated into a meaningful picture. Without a meaningful pattern the huge amount of information has no value. Is a certain strategic opponent "really" planning to increase its scope of influence by dominating the politics of neutral countries? Is the leader of a dictatorship heading toward armed conflict? Answering questions concerning strategic intelligence is a difficult task because it involves understanding the behavioral processes of human beings in vivo, outside the comfortable lab of the psychologists. In this context, we may better understand why understanding metaphors is relevant for intelligence agencies.

Understanding the meaning of a target concept, such as the concept used by the enemy to describe us, is naturally performed by human beings through mapping of deep structural relations from a source concept to the target concept. This is what metaphor is all about. For instance, when someone says "my surgeon is a butcher" he doesn't mean that his surgeon is working extra hours at a butcher shop slicing pieces of beef.

Metaphor is a psycholinguistic device for describing one concept in terms of another one. For instance, when one says "my surgeon is a butcher," one may mean that, despite his intensive education and expertise, the surgeon is no more than a "meat cutter." This metaphor is therefore loaded with negative connotations.

According to the metaphorical view, human thinking is deeply rooted in conceptual metaphors that underlie processes of knowing, learning, and experiencing. That is, our thoughts are mediated through language, and conceptual metaphors are one of the main tools that guide this mediation. We may conclude that understanding people is possible by understanding the metaphors they use.

While metaphors have been studied since antiquity, the importance of *conceptual metaphors* for understanding human thinking has been propagated by Lakoff and his colleagues (Lakoff 1999, 2002; Lakoff and Johnson 1980, 1999) and developed by others who have studied among other things

the universal embodied aspect of metaphors as well as their cultural particularities (e.g., Bowdle and Gentner 2005; Gibbs *et al.* 2004; Kovecses
2002, 2007).

Understanding metaphors can be supported by computers, which may
be used to analyze a massive amount of data. For instance, we may want
to understand the way in which the Muslim population in the USA is represented in the minds of conservatives. As newspapers represent a certain
collective consciousness, we may analyze the articles of the *Wall Street
Journal* in order to identify metaphors associated with Muslims. However,
we first have to "teach" the computer to differentiate between metaphorical
and literal language use.

Computational models of metaphors and algorithms for differentiating
nonfigurative from figurative language have been explored in the natural
language processing and cognitive sciences literature (e.g., Barnden 2008;
Birke and Sarkar 2006; Gedigian *et al.* 2006; Kintsch 2000; Krishnakumaran
and Zhu 2007; Shutova 2010; Utsumi 2006; Veale and Hao 2008). However,
as quite recently and critically reflected by Veale (2011, 278, my emphasis):
"While computationally interesting, none has yet achieved the scalabil-
ity or robustness needed to make a *significant practical impact outside the
laboratory*." This is of course a challenge that I and my team successfully
addressed, as will be described below.

The reason for the failure described by Veale is probably that, despite
some efforts to develop a methodology for metaphor identification (e.g.,
Pragglejaz Group 2007; Steen *et al.* 2010), "There is virtually no set of reli-
able, replicable methods that can be employed to identify words as metaphorical, or for relating systemic patterns of entire expressions to underlying
conceptual metaphors" (Gibbs 2007, 7).

In other words, two challenges still facing the field of natural language
processing are to automatically (1) identify metaphors and (2) extract their
underlying conceptual structure. If you think about these abilities, you can
understand why we may be interested in automatic analysis of metaphors
for strategic intelligence.

For example, let's assume that we would like to understand what the new
Islamic government in Egypt is thinking about the West. We can automatically analyze a huge amount of text produced by the government and identify the metaphors it uses to describe the West. By using these metaphors we
can somehow portray a general picture of the Egyptian worldview.

Automatically identifying metaphors associated with a target term that
we would like to understand is not a simple task. Here I would like to introduce this task and examine several solutions.

At this point I should stress the fact that my group was one of the winners in the IARPA Metaphor Program and that, together with Dan, my research assistant, and Yochai, my programmer, I was responsible for developing the core algorithms for the identification of metaphors (e.g., Assaf *et al.* 2013; Neuman *et al.* 2013a).

As an aside, let me just say that it is one of the wonderful vicissitudes of life that a guy like me, with no formal background in computer science, was able to win this huge project and to develop novel algorithms that have outperformed the state-of-the-art algorithms. I'm serious about it because the new technological era has enabled science to be more democratic and pluralistic than ever. Science is not about the degrees you have, the disciplines you have mastered, or the sophisticated rhetoric you have learned. Science is about the free and creative spirit of the human mind and its ability to solve problems and to invent new ones. Let the best man or woman win! Unfortunately, after a year of research and development and after winning the project's second year, my group was "backstabbed" in a way that taught me an important lesson about the so-called "free market" and the way national interests and taxpayers' money are sacrificed for greed and ego interests. Nevertheless, this is another story …

In the context of the information technology era our ability to think "conceptually" may be a great advantage. To think at the "ideas" level of analysis is to "bootstrap" the problem from its basic embodiment and captivity in the lower-order material realm. Many problems are like the Hydra, a mythical monster that Hercules exterminated by detaching it from the ground. We must detach the problem and examine it on a conceptual level. Then of course we should return to reality, as mere abstract thought is nonproductive. If you accept this logic then you understand the importance of interdisciplinary and conceptually oriented teams. You don't have to be an MIT graduate in computer engineering to design sophisticated algorithms. Indeed, Dan Assaf, who designed the algorithms with me, is a medical student with a background in psychology, and Yochai Cohen, who programmed the algorithms, got his bachelor's degree in mathematics from the Hebrew University and learned programming independently of his academic qualification.

The idea that automatic processing of conceptual metaphors may be used for identifying the meaning(s) of a target concept appeared in a paper I published in *Information Sciences* with Ophir Nave, who was then a graduate student in applied mathematics (Neuman and Nave 2009b). This idea has been partially developed (under a one-year contract with the Israel Ministry of Defense) and implemented in a rather naive system – "Pedesis" – that, given a target concept, harvests the Web for metaphors associated with the target by using a simple lexical pattern (X is like Y) and identifies the relevant source concepts (Neuman *et al.* 2010). Pedesis is limited to a simple lexical pattern and therefore cannot differentiate between figurative and nonfigurative language. Nevertheless, it has been successfully applied to the automatic screening of depression in free text (Neuman *et al.* 2012), and the pattern we used, whether "simile" or "real" metaphor, was found to be extremely informative.

Later, and together with Peter Turney, we developed a state-of-the-art algorithm for differentiating between figurative/metaphorical and nonfigurative/literal language (Turney *et al.* 2011). This algorithm and its use in the metaphor project are detailed below.

At this point let's turn from the biography of our project back to the issue. A conceptual metaphor involves mapping from a source concept to a target concept. As the target concept is the *explanandum* – the object that needs to be explained – we hypothesized that the source concept will be more concrete and familiar than the target. This simple idea underlies the preliminary approach we developed with Peter Turney. The unique approach we developed is grounded in another algorithm developed by Turney for determining the "abstractness" level of a word (Neuman *et al.* 2012). This algorithm, which is detailed in Chapter 3, achieves 85% success in binary classification of data annotated by subjects. It means that in 85% of the words where the algorithm was "asked" to decide whether a word was abstract or not, it achieved agreement with the decision made by human beings. To recall, the algorithm resulted in a set of 114,501 terms (words and phrases) with abstractness ratings ranging from 0 to 1, and we have further used it for several interesting applications.

In Turney *et al.* (2011) we used the abstraction level of words in order to determine whether the use of a word in a word pair or sentence was figurative (literal) or not (i.e., metaphorical). For instance, we analyzed word pairs comprising an adjective and a noun such as "dark chocolate" and "dark thoughts." In the first case, the adjective "dark" is used in a literal nonmetaphorical way, as "dark" is used to describe the color of the chocolate. In the second case, "dark" is used in a nonliteral, metaphorical way, as it does not describe the color of the thoughts. Thoughts have no color. In this case, "dark" is used as a synonym of "vicious."

The algorithm simply looks at the abstraction level of the noun. If the abstraction level is high, such as in the case of "thoughts," then the decision is that the adjective is used metaphorically. If the abstraction level of the noun is low, such as in the case of "chocolate," then the decision is that this is a case of literal use. Simple but … no one thought about it before.

Our algorithm, titled "Concrete–Abstract," produced very nice results but, as will be shown later, failed in cases where the adjective did not have an embodied base. Let me now return to IARPA's call and the way we addressed it.

Our original algorithm for identifying metaphorical language uses the average noun's level of abstraction as the predictor of whether that target concept – whether a noun, a verb, or an adjective – is used metaphorically or not. This algorithm can be extended to other forms of metaphors. For instance, the metaphor "my lawyer is a shark" (Kintsch 2000) can be represented through a verb phrase (i.e., "is like") associating the target ("lawyer") with the source ("shark"). The abstraction level of "lawyer" is 0.41 and the abstraction level of "shark" is 0.22. As the source concept is used in order to explain the target concept, the abstraction level of the source is lower when the source is metaphorical and higher if it is literal. If one says "my lawyer is stupid," then "stupid," which is rated higher than "lawyer" on the abstraction scale (0.69), is used literally.

Another instance is the sentence: "His life took a left turn." By using a grammatical representation of the sentence, we can easily identify "turn" as the relevant argument and "took" as the metaphorical verb. The abstraction level of "life" is 0.63, that of "took" is 0.61, and that of "turn" is 0.54. The algorithm identifies "turn" as metaphorical and therefore the argument "turn" and the predicate "took" were both selected for further analysis.

This simple heuristic is powerful enough to determine whether the source that is grammatically associated with the target is used metaphorically or not. We originally suggested extending the same logic with variations to more complex sentences ("my lawyer is a vicious shark") or to the analysis of verbs, as has been shown in Turney *et al.* (2011).

The bottom line is that Concrete–Abstract achieves 79% accuracy in predicting classification of human-annotated adjective–noun pairs (e.g., "dark mood," "dark chocolate") and 73% accuracy on 25 verbs that appear in 1,965 sentences from Birke and Sarkar's (2006) results.

Identifying metaphors is not enough, and IARPA also asked us to generate a "semantic frame" and to identify "conceptual metaphors." Generating a semantic frame and identifying a conceptual metaphor is far from a trivial task. For instance, let's analyze the sentence: "His life took a left turn." To understand the meaning of this metaphor we may use FrameNet (https://framenet.icsi.berkeley.edu/fndrupal), which is a resource of "semantic frames." If we search FrameNet for "turn" we get the semantic frame of "change_directions." Using this semantic frame we can understand the above sentence as a metaphor involving a change of direction. That is, the semantic frame involves the mapping of our metaphors into general lexical patterns involving our encyclopedic knowledge.

Mapping the above metaphor into a "change of direction frame" is a relatively easy task. However, what about the metaphor used by Forrest Gump's mother: "Life is like a box of chocolates"? Identifying the conceptual metaphor underlying this expression is not an easy task. According to Gump's mother, life is like a box of chocolates because "you never know what you're going to get." In other words, life involves an element of uncertainty and surprise with positive affective orientation. What about Shakespeare's metaphor "All the world's a stage"? This metaphor too is far from trivial, as one would hardly reason out from "stage" to the theatrical notion of life as a play written by the almighty playwright for the PLAYERS=HUMAN_BEINGS. In sum, identifying the semantic frame(s) (i.e., mapping) and the underlying conceptual metaphor(s) of a given target concept is far from trivial, and currently there is no algorithm for addressing this challenge.

The problem is even more acute in other languages and cultures. For example, the metaphor "my lawyer is a shark" cannot be trivially interpreted to Iranian Farsi. In Farsi "he is a shark" (کوسه ماهی) has a different sense than in English because, and as I have mentioned before, the word کوسه is associated through deep levels and historically layered connotations with a man who can't grow facial hair and as such is impotent or even homosexual.

To address the challenge of identifying the semantic frame and the conceptual metaphors for a given target, we first proposed to reduce the problem to one of representing a metaphor in terms of "analogical relations." The focus on analogical relations is firmly grounded, as relational knowledge is fundamental for higher cognition (Halford *et al.* 2010), specifically in the context of analogical reasoning and metaphor comprehension (Turney 2008). Unfortunately, we haven't fully exhausted this proposal; nevertheless, it may be interesting to investigate it here. Let me explain it by first focusing on three simple metaphorical structures.

In addressing real-world problems sometimes a useful strategy is to identify several simple structures underlying the complexity of the real process. Among social scientists there is sometimes antagonism against this strategy and for good reason, as they are familiar with the simplistic and hardheaded reductionist ventures that populate the field. Nevertheless, the model that should inspire social scientists, cultural psychologists included, is the one that looks for relatively simple motifs or building blocks underlying the complex structures under inquiry. For instance, although mathematics is a field miles apart from the social sciences, mathematicians have joined forces in an amazing scientific venture that resulted in the classification of "finite simple groups."

Despite the fact that metaphorical language use can be instantiated in an enormous variety of linguistic expressions, we thought that it might be helpful to identify basic metaphorical structures. Following this logic and Krishnakumaran and Zhu's (2007) metaphor classification, we can differentiate between type I, type II, and type III metaphors. As you can see, triadicity is evident in this case too …

Type I metaphors involve a verb of the "be" form where two objects/nouns are associated (e.g., "he is a lion"). Type II metaphors involve a verb acting on a noun (e.g., "he planted good ideas in their minds"). And type III metaphors involve an adjective acting on a noun (e.g., "she has a sweet smile").

Now, to identify whether a certain linguistic expression is metaphorical or literal we can identify type I, II, and III structures in the linguistic expression; represent them as analogical relations; and operate a procedure to determine whether these analogical relations are metaphorical, and what the conceptual metaphors underlying them are.

For example, Adolf Hitler, one of the most murderous and vicious dictators known in history (and the competition is extremely strong), used to excite the German mob through his passionate rhetoric. His rhetoric was full of metaphors, many of them used to portray the Jewish people in a monstrous sense.

Among Hitler's metaphors (Musolff 2008) we find the metaphor JEWS-ARE-PARASITES (Rash 2005). When we first encounter this expression we can easily identify it as an "A is B" structure. If we have a procedure that may help us to identify this expression as a metaphor, then representing it in analogical terms may help us to elucidate its meaning. For instance, this metaphor can be represented as JEWS:B::PARASITES:D. That is, "Jews are parasites" because the parasites stand in some functional relation with an object D in the same way as the Jews stand in a functional relation with B.

One possible interpretation of this anti-Semitic metaphor is that, just as parasites invade the body, the Jews invaded the German nation. In this context, identifying the semantic frame and the conceptual metaphor involves the identification of the relevant *relations* and *arguments* holding between the constituents of the analogical representation.

The same logic holds for the type II metaphors. With regard to type II metaphors, we have the analogical pattern T:S::Q:G, where T signifies the target and S the source. For instance, the metaphor "the land gave birth to

Bolivar" (Aponte Moreno 2008), used by Hugo Chávez (the former president of Venezuela), can be represented as Land:Bolivar::Q:G. In this case, for Q and G we should seek for arguments sharing the same relation(s) as those holding between "land" and "Bolivar" (i.e., gave_birth). For instance, the land gave birth to Bolivar in the same way as a mother gives birth to a child. Identifying the semantic frame through analogical analysis may therefore support us with a powerful tool for understanding the metaphors and those who use them.

For instance, if we analyze the target "land" and find the metaphor "the land gave birth to Bolivar," then we are seeking other arguments that "give birth" (e.g., mothers) to others (e.g., babies).

The arguments/phrases of a given relation may be further analyzed to determine the "selectional preferences" of the vertices (Light and Greiff 2002; Resnik 1996); that is, the objects most likely to function as arguments for the relation.

Let's examine the metaphor used by Chávez in 2006 (Aponte Moreno 2008, 43):

> Miren, uno siempre busca el auxilio de los sabios, de los sabios, porque yo solo sé que no sé nada como dijo un filósofo, uno siempre anda buscando el auxilio de Dios, el conocimiento de los sabios, y Bolívar, uno de los más grandes sabios que parió esta tierra, que ha parido esta tierra.

This excerpt has been translated by my colleague Zvi Bekerman as follows:

> See ... We always look for the help of the sages, of the sages, for I only know I know nothing as the philosopher said, one is always looking for the help of God, the knowledge of the sage, and Bolivar is one of the greatest sages in this land, one that the earth has *given birth to*.
>
> (my emphasis)

By applying critical metaphor analysis (Charteris-Black 2004), Aponte Moreno (2008) argues that in the above excerpt "land" is metaphorically portrayed by Chávez as a mother giving birth to Bolivar. This insight based on manual analysis along the lines of critical metaphor analysis can be automatically implemented as follows. First, we identify through the algorithm the source (e.g., Bolivar), the target (e.g., land), and their metaphorical relation (e.g., gave birth), which is the focus of our analysis. Next, we search a relevant linguistic corpus for instances of the 3-tuple pattern $<*, R, *>$, where R stands for the metaphorical relation and $*$ stands for a wild card, which is an object noun co-occurring with R in a window of 1–4 words and functions as its argument.

For instance, we searched COCA for the nouns collocated with "give birth" at a window of −4. We found the following nouns in descending order of frequency: (1) woman, (2) mother, and (3) female. The same search within a window of +4 produced the nouns (1) child, (2) baby, and (3) twins.

With respect to the metaphorical relation "give_birth," this analysis exposes well-defined clusters characterizing the source and the target. For tagging them, we may choose the most abstract objects or the lowest shared node in the semantic hierarchy. The resulting conceptual metaphor for the metaphorical expression associating "land" with "Bolivar" is FEMALE-GIVE_BIRTH-CHILD. In other words, the land gave birth to Bolivar in the same way as a female gives birth to a child.

Another example is the metaphor we discussed before – "Jews are parasites," from Hitler's *Mein Kampf*:

> Er war deshalb auch nie Nomade, sondern immer nur *Parasit* im Körper anderer Völker.
> For that reason he [the Jew] was never a nomad, but only and always a *parasite* in the body of other peoples.
> (cited in Musolff 2008, my emphasis)

Using COCA, we conducted a corpus analysis of "parasites" in the context of "Jews." This analysis revealed that the highest-scored verbs "base" (a form of verbs in COCA) collocated in a window of +4 with "parasites" are "infect," "invade," and "crawl."

Interestingly, if we use the pattern "Jews infect" in Google's search engine, the first search result is "Jews infect food with cancer and send it to Muslim countries." If we use the same pattern with "crawl," we find as the first entry a statement by Abu Al-Subh (Hamas former Minister of Culture) saying that "Jews are the most contemptible nation to crawl upon the face of the earth." It seems that, regardless of European efforts to acknowledge the genuine representation of the Palestinian people, these genuine representatives who have been elected in free democratic elections are precisely those who in their rhetoric reflect the shadows of the fascist Europe.

Both of these anti-Semitic uses of the "parasite" metaphor appear in an Islamic fundamentalist site and indicate the way metaphors are used for "cultural transmission." If as cultural psychologists we ask, "Where have Hitler's metaphors gone?" the answer we get is that these metaphors have been transmitted for the use of Semitic Muslims, those who Hitler despised as inherently inferior.

In the next phase of our analysis, we identified the preferentially selected arguments for each of the source concept's preferentially selected predicates.

Following our "parasites" example, we found arguments that have, according to WordNet, a clear classification in one group, which is ANIMAL (e.g., worms, viruses, snakes, and rats). As ambiguity is a source of concern, we should emphasize that the tagging of the source/target domains can be conducted by an automatic voting procedure that takes into account the majority of source domains belonging to a given hypernym.

For example, although "rat" has the connotation of an "informer" or "betrayer," in the context of the metaphor JEWS-ARE-RATS only its first sense optimally converges with the other animals used to describe the Jews: snakes and worms. Therefore, the metaphor "Jews are parasites" can be semantically represented as JEWS-ARE-ANIMALS. Moreover, by applying the methodology, we may find that the mapping from the source concept "parasites" involves "invade" and "infect," and reconstruct analogical relations such that parasites infect an organism in the same way that Jews infect the German nation.

Thus far I have introduced the importance of identifying metaphors in texts and analyzing them. I have also introduced the original algorithm my colleagues and I designed with Peter Turney and some ideas on how to identify the semantic frame and conceptual metaphor underlying a given expression. In the next sections I delve deeply into the solutions we actually found and the way computational tools can be used for metaphor identification and understanding.

IDENTIFYING METAPHORS

There have been various approaches to the identification of metaphors, ranging from the use of "word sense disambiguation" (Birke and Sarkar 2007) to WordNet (Krishnakumaran and Zhu 2007). Our starting point is the Concrete–Abstract algorithm of Turney *et al.* (2011), which gives state-of-the-art accuracy for this task. To recall, the rationale of this algorithm is as follows. Type III metaphors, comprising adjective–noun phrases (as in "dark thoughts"), generally involve the use of a concrete concept ("dark") to describe a more abstract concept ("thought"). Therefore, for the task of distinguishing between metaphorical and literal phrases, Turney *et al.* (2011) used only one element: the abstraction rating of the noun in the phrase.

The idea is that the fact that the noun is abstract indicates that the adjective is likely used in a concrete sense to explain the meaning of the noun, and therefore the phrase functions as a metaphor.

The abstractness of different words was estimated based on their distributional similarity and dissimilarity with prototypical abstract and concrete words. As this procedure relies on a vector space representation of word meaning, it is prone to inherent problems with such methods (Turney and Pantel 2010), such as contextual influences on the abstractness score of a given word. For instance, although "cat" and "American eagle" are both concrete objects belonging to the same category (animal), "cat" scores 0.29 on the abstraction scale while "American eagle" scores 0.47. This is probably because the American eagle is also often used as a symbol, and so is contextually associated with more abstract concepts in texts.

Moreover, Concrete–Abstract assumes that the abstraction level of the noun is indicative of metaphorical relations. However, the noun may be relatively concrete and still constitute a metaphorical phrase. For instance, the metaphor "broken heart" includes a relatively concrete concept ("heart") that scores 0.37 on Turney's abstraction scale.

As the words rated by the abstraction scale have not been disambiguated, the concrete "heart" is used in the sense of the body organ, while the "heart" in "broken heart" is used in the sense of emotion, kindness, and spirit. In the following section I present a new algorithm for metaphor identification designed to remedy the problems associated with the Concrete–Abstract algorithm.

METHODOLOGY

I assume, as do Turney *et al.* (2011), that a metaphor usually involves mapping from a relatively concrete domain to a relatively abstract domain. However, it is important to consider what those specific conceptual domains are.

Literal use of a concrete adjective will tend to be more salient with regard to certain semantic categories of concrete objects and not others. For instance, in its literal use, the word "dark" may be associated with certain word categories such as physical objects (e.g., "table") or body parts (e.g., "hair"). This notion leads directly to the Concrete Category Overlap (CCO) algorithm I developed with my team (Assaf *et al.* 2013). The algorithm assumes that, if the target noun of an adjective belongs to one of the concrete categories associated with the literal use of the adjective, it is probably literal; otherwise, it is probably metaphorical.

In a sense, this new method combines the notion of measuring concreteness with that of using selectional preference, as has been well explored in previous work on metaphor identification (Wilks 1975). This hybrid approach, however, overcomes the well-known issues of the pure selectional preferences approach (Fass 1997; Shutova 2010), in particular its tendency to over-generate metaphor hypotheses and be misled by common conventionalized metaphors.

For readers who have some inclination toward scientific formality, the pseudocode of the CCO algorithm is as follows:

Input: an adjective–noun pair $<A,N>$.

1 Let $N(A)$ be the θ_{num} nouns most frequently modified by A, with mutual information of at least θ_{MI}.
2 Let N^C be the κ most concrete nouns in $N(A)$.
3 Let $Cat(A)$ be the set of all semantic noun categories containing at least θ_{cat} nouns in N^C.
4 If N belongs to one of the categories in $Cat(A)$, then return LITERAL, else return METAPHORICAL.

As you can see, this short pseudocode is grounded in deep logic, metaphorically speaking … The basic idea is that an adjective is assigned to a set of semantic categories based on the most frequent and concrete nouns that it modifies. In practice, we require these pairs to have a minimum of MI as well, in order to ensure that the nouns are significantly associated with the adjective.

In our experiments, we identified these nouns by simple collocation in COCA, setting θ_{num} to 1,000 and θ_{MI} to 3. The most concrete nouns are identified based on the abstraction scale developed by Turney *et al.* (2011); we have found a κ of 100 to work well, though (as we show below) the results are not very sensitive to the exact value.

To classify noun semantics, we used the WordStat noun categorization based on WordNet, which classifies 69,817 nouns into 25 categories, of which 13 are concrete categories (e.g., "artifact"). As we selected the most concrete nouns, we expected them to be categorized only in these 13 categories. Based on statistics calculated from the most frequent 10,000 nouns in COCA, we found that on average each noun is assigned to two categories. Therefore, if we randomly assign 100 concrete nouns to the 13 concrete categories we would expect, on average, 15.4 words in each category.

We thus set $Cat(A)$ to be all categories containing at least $\theta_{cat} = 16$ nouns from N^C. This helps to avoid choosing categories that do not really represent literal use of the adjective A. To test the algorithm we used several data sets as described below.

DATA SETS

Data set 1

Our first data set was an extended version of the 100-phrase corpus used by Turney *et al.* (2011). Five hundred adjective–noun phrases were drawn from COCA according to the same procedure used by Turney *et al.* (2011). The set included 38 different adjectives (and 321 nouns) with a clear embodied base (e.g., "warm," "soft," "deep," "big," "sour"). Idioms were removed (based on Wiktionary: www.wiktionary.org), leaving 433 adjective–noun pairs. Ground-truth labels (metaphorical/literal) were based on the judgment of two experts in metaphor analysis, who used the Wiktionary definitions as a point of reference to determine whether the adjective was used in its most salient embodied/concrete sense or in a secondary, extended metaphorical sense.

For instance, in the case of "bitter lemon," the first embodied definition of the adjective "bitter" is "having an acrid taste (usually from a basic substance)." When asked to judge whether the phrase "bitter relations" is literal or metaphorical, the judges used the basic denotation of "bitter" to make a decision; as "relations" cannot have an acrid taste, the phrase was judged to be metaphorical. Disagreements between the judges were resolved through reconciliation. Inter-annotator agreement was 96%. In the final version of this data set, 215 phrases were judged as literal and 218 as metaphorical.

Data set 2

Since Turney *et al.*'s Concrete–Abstract algorithm works by examining the abstraction scores of nouns, we would expect it to be considerably less effective for metaphors with less abstract nouns, such as the metaphor "broken heart."

In data set 1, nouns in metaphorical phrases scored significantly higher on abstractness than nouns in literal phrases ($\mu = 0.55$, $\sigma = 0.13$ vs. $\mu = 0.32$, $\sigma = 0.09$, respectively). A t-test for independent samples showed a statistically significant difference between the metaphorical and literal conditions ($t(257) = 15.87$, $p = 0.00$). As the fraction of metaphors in the overall type III population with highly abstract nouns is unknown, Concrete–Abstract may have a serious blind spot.

To deal with this issue, we also constructed a corpus in which there was no significant difference in the abstractness of the nouns comprising the phrases in the metaphorical and literal conditions.

This second data set was constructed starting from the sentences and phrases in the Berkeley master metaphor list (Lakoff 1994). We used the processed corpus prepared by Krishnakumaran and Zhu (2007) and parsed each sentence using the Stanford Parser (de Marneffe and Manning 2008).

Adjective–noun pairs related by the syntactic amod relation were extracted, and manual expert analysis identified literal and nonliteral adjective–noun phrases using the methodology described above. We then extended the set by retrieving adjective–noun phrases from COCA associated with several target nouns from the first set. The final data set included 182 phrases, out of which 95 were literal and 87 metaphorical.

In this corpus there was no statistically significant difference between the abstraction level of the nouns comprising the metaphorical and literal conditions; hence we expected the Concrete–Abstract algorithm to not perform well with it.

RESULTS

We reproduced the Concrete–Abstract algorithm by binary logistic regression for literal/metaphorical classification based on the noun abstraction score, evaluated by tenfold cross-validation. This sounds impressive, but to the nonexpert it should be clarified that it is a simple scientific procedure. The regression is actually a statistical analysis in which we try to examine how good our independent variable is in predicting the dependent binary variable. The tenfold cross-validation is actually a technique that aims to assess the validity of our prediction by partitioning our data set in training and test sets, measuring our prediction, and moving on to another round of partition-prediction. The results of our algorithm are averaged across the folds, in our case ten folds.

The CCO algorithm requires no training; we also evaluated a hybrid algorithm, using logistic regression including noun abstractness with the output of CCO. The results for data set 1 are given in Table 5.1. "Accuracy" is a measure of the algorithm's success. It is calculated by taking the number of cases in which the algorithm correctly identified metaphors and non-metaphors and dividing this sum by the total number of cases. "Precision" is another measure that calculates the proportion of "true positives," cases in which the algorithm correctly decided a phrase was a metaphor out of the total number of cases the algorithm decided a phrase was a metaphor. "Recall" is the proportion of true positives out of the total number of true metaphors in the corpus.

TABLE 5.1 *CCO algorithm results for data set 1.*

Method	Accuracy (%)	Precision (%)	Recall (%)
Concrete–Abstract	85.0	87.6	88.4
CCO	82.5	88.6	**90.2**
Combined	**88.7**	**90.4**	86.7

TABLE 5.2 *CCO algorithm results for data set 2.*

Method	Accuracy (%)	Precision (%)	Recall (%)
Concrete–Abstract	48.6	44.2	26.7
CCO	**73.6**	**76.0**	**65.5**
Combined	73.2	75.6	65.1

TABLE 5.3 *CCO algorithm results for data sets 1 and 2 together.*

Method	Accuracy (%)	Precision (%)	Recall (%)
Concrete–Abstract	74.6	74.9	73.4
CCO	**79.8**	**84.9**	72.1
Combined	78.4	79.5	**75.8**

These results replicate the findings of Turney *et al.* (2011) and also show that CCO, in combination with Concrete–Abstract, noticeably improves metaphor identification. The results for data set 2 are given in Table 5.2. In this case, remember that we tested the ability of the Concrete–Abstract algorithm to differentiate metaphorical and literal language use when the adjectives/attributes don't have an embodied base.

As hypothesized, Concrete–Abstract failed to provide any significant prediction of whether a phrase was a metaphor or not. This is an important finding as it exposes a blind spot in the state-of-the-art algorithm. In contrast, CCO provided a significant improvement over the baseline.

Finally, let me present the results for a combined data set, including all 615 phrases from data sets 1 and 2. The results are given in Table 5.3.

CONCLUSIONS

I opened this chapter by introducing IARPA's Metaphor Program. This project represents a deep understanding that comprehending other minds is, as suggested by Ortega y Gasset, projecting ourselves into their language. Understanding the language use of a given group or person through the analysis of massive amounts of text is a difficult task. IARPA understood that using computers may be of great help as long as the computers can identify metaphorical language, which is common among human beings. The aim of this chapter was to present my thoughts about this project and a new algorithm for identifying one type of metaphor. This algorithm, CCO, has been shown to work well, even in cases where the Concrete–Abstract algorithm fails utterly.

As it is still unclear what fraction of naturally occurring metaphorical expressions fall into the "easy" and "hard" cases for any particular approach, we first considered the CCO algorithm as just the first of an ensemble of methods to be developed for identifying various sorts of metaphorical expressions. Indeed, in Neuman *et al.* 2013b my colleagues and I present the extension of the algorithm to other types of metaphors. However, quite recently and regardless of the IARPA project, I have developed a simple and elegant algorithm that is grounded in Opposition Theory (Assaf *et al.* 2013). This algorithm was tested on the original test set used by Turney *et al.* and resulted in 89% accuracy in predicting whether a phrase is metaphorical or not. I mention this algorithm as it is a wonderful expression of how old structuralism can provide us with inspiration for developing intelligent tools.

Despite the success of our algorithms, we should acknowledge the fact that languages evolve based on unique cultural and historical factors, and it is highly unlikely that the complexity of metaphors can be fully captured by algorithms adhering to a universal form of reasoning.

Indeed, some metaphors have a cultural-historical logic that cannot be fully captured by our algorithms (Trim 2007), and improving the identification of metaphors across language/cultural contexts will ultimately need to take into account various irreducible processes that turn literal into metaphorical use.

What is the lesson cultural psychology may learn from the IARPA Metaphor Progam? The grand lesson is clear. Cultural psychologists who are trying to understand the sign-mediated nature of the human mind have been enriched with powerful new tools for their toolkit. Instead of qualitatively analyzing a limited number of metaphors, these psychologists can now analyze a large quantity of textual data to gain a more comprehensive view of their research subject. Given our increasing textual resources, we can learn how the metaphors associated with God, for instance, have been changed through the documented textual history of the Christian West, to understand the similarities, differences, similarities of differences, and differences of similarities in the metaphorical use of vicious dictators, and to gain awareness of the way metaphors of both female and male bodies change and transform our self-representation.

Computational cultural psychology urges us to enrich our toolkit, and automatic metaphor analysis is just one instance of a tool, one of many to come in the future.

6

Scent of a woman: the mediation of smell and automatic analysis of extended senses

It is five years since my last return to England: During the first years I could not endure my wife or children in my presence, the *very smell of them was intolerable.*

(Jonathan Swift, *Gulliver's Travels*, my emphasis)

FROM THE MOUSE'S NOSE TO BORGES'S SCULPTURE

The above quotation from *Gulliver's Travels* is funny as it shockingly violates our cultural norms. Swift, known for his wicked sense of humor, has touched on a sensitive point. How can the smell of a beloved one be so intolerable?

For the cultural psychologist there is no greater pleasure than in showing how "natural" biological psychological processes are mediated despite their nonmediated and "natural" appearance. In this context, smell is of specific interest as it is a common belief that we have a poor sense of smell, attributed mostly to our evolutionary heritage, and that smell is such a basic perception that the role of mediation is minimal if any.

There is probably a universal aspect of smell, at least with regard to the dimension of "pleasantness." The smell of roasted meat is probably attractive to most of us, excluding a minority of vegetarians, and even in this case I doubt whether the smell is unpleasant. A famous supporter of vegetarianism likes to present to his audience the following argument. Let's put in front on an infant an apple and a bunny. The infant will probably play with the bunny and eat the apple. Hence, we are born vegetarians. Not exactly. Let's assume the child grows up. We place in front of him a roasted bunny and an apple. The smell would probably change his mind. Now this person will prefer to play with the apple. It must be emphasized that I don't present an argument against vegetarianism but just an argument in favor of our animalistic brain.

In fact, the Bible teaches us that originally human beings were vegetarians and that permission to consume meat was given to them by God after the great flood and God's recognition that human nature is quite different from what he (or she) expected at first. This is an important lesson, as consuming meat is presented as morally wrong but psychologically justified as a compromise only. In fact, thousands of years ago and from its early days, Judaism has paid close attention to animal rights and at the same time realized the danger in ideological vegetarianism. Those who deny their animalistic part and are not ready to compromise with it and live with it under strict constraints are too arrogant and therefore fail to recognize the danger encapsulated in their animalistic nature. But let us now return to smell.

In contrast with the appealing smell of roasted meat, the smell of rotten organic matter may be categorized as unpleasant or disgusting. This is probably why modern houses are equipped with various fragrances that aim to cover the smell of excrement in toilets.

These two examples should be qualified of course by contextual factors, in the same way as any argument in favor of psychological universalism. The either (universal)/or (particular-contextual) approach is firmly rejected in this book. The complexity of human psychology is such that complex human behavior emerges as a synergetic product of lower-level processes. The complexity cannot be reduced to simpler/universal strata, but the existence of these strata cannot be denied or dismissed in the same way as the unique contextual factors.

Regarding the above examples, the smell of roasted meat may be highly attractive to human beings but how about the smell of human flesh? Is there a difference between the smells of the roasted flesh of human and non-human organisms?

In one of my courses on psychoanalysis, I raised this question. One of my students, who was a military paramedic, shared with me a traumatic experience from his military service as a result of which the smell of burning human flesh had been "burned" into his mind. The smell, as he told me, was extremely similar to the smell of a barbeque, although the emotions attached to this experience were painfully negative.

The same is true with regard to the smell of human excrement. In his famous and provocative book *The Lady of the Flowers*, the French novelist Jean Genet describes the autoerotic feeling of smelling his own excrement. Whether Genet's preference is pathologic or not is an open question, but it is clear that our disgust at the smell of our own excrement is significantly less than our disgust at the excrement of others.

This contextual sensitivity is evolutionarily grounded, as we are disgusted with excrement, which might threaten our health. The transformation and contextualization of this disgust is common in our culture. For instance, the psychological conflicts around excrement have been of great interest to psychoanalysis and a source of artistic amusement, from Philip Roth's *Portnoy's Complaint* to a variety of "bowl satires."

To recall, our psychology is grounded in our carnal body. From a biological perspective, the sense of smell starts with a sniff of molecules that enrich the olfactory epithelium. The repertoire of the mammalian olfactory receptor is estimated to include 1,000 different receptor types (Buck and Axel 1991). Human beings, however, functionally express approximately 350 of these receptors and "recent genetic studies show a decline in the number of functional olfactory receptor genes through primate evolution to humans" (Shepherd 2004). In other words, as we have become human, we have lost some of the rich potential and rich repertoire of receptors that we previously shared with other mammals.

The loss of some genes targeted toward smell does not simply entail the deterioration of our sniffing abilities. This would have been the case if the sense of smell could have been reduced to genes, receptors, and a simplistic key-and-lock model of smelling, where smell is produced through the binding of certain molecules to certain receptors. According to this popular metaphor, biological recognition, of smell for instance, involves the simple correspondence between a key (i.e., a molecule) and a lock (i.e., a receptor), and *voilà*! Here you have a smell! The lock-and-key metaphor cannot explain smell in the same way as it cannot explain other forms of biological recognition such as antigen recognition by the immune system (Cohen 2000; Neuman 2008).

Let us start with the key. "Though we now know almost everything there is to know about the molecules, we don't know how our nose reads them" (Turin 2006, 6). So maybe the answer is with the lock? The receptors? The answer is negative. The number of genes coding the olfactory receptors does not simply correlate with the sense of smell, at least with regard to the complex recognition of scents. Indeed, a shark can sense the smell of blood from a distance but the repertoire of smells identified by a shark is not necessarily richer than that of a human being. If there were a simple mapping between the number of olfactory receptor genes and the human sense of smell, then the rich repertoire of the French fragrance industry would probably not have existed.

Or let's talk about French cheese. There are around 400 different types of French cheese, which I doubt any reasonable mouse, with its rich repertoire of genes, would find reasonable to discriminate. These cheeses are described as dry, dust, sweet, fruity, alcoholic, green, plastic, and even … bad (Curioni and Bosset 2002). A mammal consuming food it describes using the adjective "bad" is necessarily a highly contextualist and semiotic creature. The reason is that complex culture transcends our most basic inclinations.

Think about the way food that smells "bad" and that should have resulted in immediate rejection has turned into gourmet food. Another example is poisonous food. Think about the fugu – the Japanese poisonous puffer fish – prepared only by highly qualified chefs and according to strict rules of Japanese law. Why should a normal human being take the risk of eating such a dangerous food? Although the chef is responsible for the dangerous part, there is always a chance of a mistake, as happens from time to time.

Human pleasure, as Freud teaches us, is built around tension reduction. The cheese whose smell evolutionarily signals "danger" is a tension-evoking food in the same way as the fugu. Eating these smelly cheeses or the fugu is a tension-reduction activity: I'm alive despite the awful smell and the fish poison! This conclusion suggests that the contextuality of taste and smell is a contextuality grounded in our psycho-logic and cannot be dismissed as irrational cultural particularities.

Human beings are "astonishingly good at odor detection and discrimination" (Yeshurun and Sobel 2010, 223) and, believe it or not, people have been shown to be able to distinguish their own T-shirt from a hundred identical T-shirts worn by others for twenty-four hours (Lord and Kasprzak 1989).

In contrast with smell detection and discrimination, people are "astonishingly bad" (Yeshurun and Sobel 2010, 226) at identification and naming. Sobel (Yeshurun and Sobel 2010) describes an amusing anecdote in which he asked a family member to close her eyes and let her smell a jar of peanut butter, which he asked her to name. This subject used to eat peanut butter everyday but she was unable to name it! This is an interesting anecdote, and maybe we have some kind of "smell aphasia" in which our brain finds it difficult to relate its olfactory patterns to language.

We may conclude so far that the size of our genetic or receptor arsenal is not the most important factor in smell. As sexologists like to remind men, size (of the penis) is not the most important thing.

If smell does not exist in the molecules or in the genes that code the receptors, then a simple correspondence between the sign and the signified does not exist. This conclusion may depress men who buy expensive fragrances just to hit the right button of potential females. The idea that just using the appropriate "sign" of smell will turn any man into a female attractor is a fantasy nurtured by the advertisement industry, but like other fantasies it is empirically groundless. As poignantly suggested, it is not that "fragrance works for the opposite sex the way shit works for flies" (Turin 2006, 15). While the sense of smell cannot be exhausted through simple models, its complexity is fully comprehensible from a semiotic perspective; a sign does not have a simple correspondence with the signified, probably even for a fly.

In this context an inevitable question is how we can reconcile a relatively high sensitivity to smell with a relatively low number of olfactory receptors in the nose (Shepherd 2004, 573). The trivial answer is that the complexity of smell cannot be simply reduced to the genetic level. A less trivial answer concerns the way in which high-level brain functions that involve *language* and *memory* are involved in constructing the complexity of smell.

While memory is a factor shared by other nonhuman organisms, the role of language is less trivial; but, as argued by Shepherd (2004, 574), "language is necessary for human smell." How is language associated with smell specifically, given the poor human ability to name smells?

To address this question let's turn to Borges's "Two metaphysical beings," a two-page essay that appears in his book on imaginary beings (Borges 1974). Through his poetic imagination, Borges illustrates the way in which the simple sense of smell may give birth to the complexity of the mind. In fact he attributes this description to Condillac, who describes a marble statue inhabited by a soul that had never perceived or thought. This statue has one sense, which is smell.

As Borges describes it, "a whiff of jasmine is the start of the statue's biography" (1974, 144). "In the statue's consciousness once there is a single odor we have attention." Once the odor lasts after the stimulus has faded there is memory. The ability to differentiate past and present is the ability to compare, and if there is likeness and unlikeness involved then we have judgment. When judgment recurs we have reflection and so Borges continues by describing the emergence of mental faculties from a single sense "the least complex of all" – that of smell. The peak of this process is the emergence of the "I." What a beautiful epistemic and aesthetic move by Borges! Think about it, the *self*, this sacred and cherished thing invented by European Christianity and modern psychology, is turned into a function that evolved from … the nose!

While Borges describes the bottom-up process through which the complexity of the person evolves from the sense of smell, it is clear that the complexity of smell is embedded in the complexity of the individual through a top-down process as well. Indeed, the meaning we attribute to a smell is weaved through multiple threads of memory, comparison, language, and judgment, all of them deeply rooted in our cultural schemes and practices.

Now, arguing that language is somehow involved with the "mediation" of smell is nice, but what do we actually mean? To explain the role of mediation, I would like to draw on a thesis I have developed elsewhere, and to do so I will start with the concept of "dimension."

DIMENSIONS OF EXPERIENCE

Informally, the dimension of a space is the minimum number of "coordinates" we need in order to specify a point within it. It is helpful to explain this idea through a simple example. I used this example to explain the idea of dimensionality to my son when he was a little child. At the current phase of writing this book he is seventeen years old and a talented young man with excellent grades in physics, which means that my dimensionality explanation has somehow shaped his mind …

Here is the example. Let's assume that we would like to build a moving laser cannon that will target an annoying fly. The idea popped into my mind during one of the hot Israeli summers in which a drop of sugar would always attract a fly. To hit the fly we must specify its position. Now if the fly is traveling along a straight line then we need only one coordinate to target it. If the fly is walking on a two-dimensional paper then we need two coordinates to specify its point. If the fly is flying in a three-dimensional room we need three coordinates or dimensions: height, width, and depth. Even if we specify the coordinates, we still have to take into account the fact that the fly is a moving target and therefore anticipate its future location, which means that time is added as another dimension. This form of anticipation convinced the engineers of the Second World War that anticipation and intention are not empty mentalist concepts and that even a murderous device such as a cannon needs them to be able to hit its target. However, this is another story.

It is important to realize that the idea of specifying a point through coordinates is not limited to concrete spaces or objects and may be extended to the mental realm as well. For instance, let us take the first-person experience of wine tasting. One may describe the taste of a certain wine by using one dimension – likeness – ranging from 0 (disgusting: I want to spit it out!) to 10 (heavenly taste). This simple dimension represents our most binary and basic approach to food, tasty/in and disgusting/out, as extended to a continuum.

This point is interesting as the idea of binarism is the hallmark of structuralism. In a postmodern era, structuralism has been under heavy attack and has been mocked for its simplicity. However, there is a deep truth in structuralism, and binarism cannot be simply dismissed, although it should definitely be qualified and used as a starting point only for evolving complexity. Nevertheless, it is clear that beyond cultural variations the "in" and "out" differentiation is the one standing at the basis of our smell experience.

The use of a single dimension might be overly simplistic and we may want to describe the taste of a certain wine by adding a second dimension such as "aroma" or a third dimension such as "softness." Describing the taste of a certain wine through these independent (i.e., orthogonal) dimensions is done by specifying a point residing in the space that is constructed by the three dimensions. The space is the abstract concept constituted by the dimensions.

We feel extremely comfortable in working with low-dimensional spaces such as the in–out likeness dimension. This preference is evolutionarily clear. Our ancestors were not interested in the rich repertoire of Italian wines, the fascinating tastes of French cheese, or the delicate variety of chocolate.

The evolutionary imperative was simpler. First, sensitivity to potentially harmful food ingredients, and second a preference for nutrition with evolutionary advantage.

As argued by Yeshurun and Sobel (2010), "pleasantness" is the primary dimension of smell. Pleasantness may vary of course between individuals, cultures, and contexts, as well as across time. However, at the most basic level the pleasantness of a smell has a clear evolutionary function: "The primary function of olfactory can be viewed as to signal approach or withdraw" (Yeshurun and Sobel 2010, 230). When we approach a poisonous food it is better to withdraw, and when we sniff the smell of a barbeque our nostrils lead the way to this rich source of protein.

Interestingly, and surprisingly as it may seem, there is a deep relation between our sense of smell and the psychological concept Freud described as the "superego." There is a quite convincing argument in psychoanalysis and attachment theory that our superego has evolved primarily as an *observing* and *regulating* mental function that aims to keep us away from trouble (Holmes 2011), and let me add even culinary trouble.

Therefore, it is possible to speculate that a part of the origins of our delicate and abstract form of the superego and moral consciousness has evolved from our need to distinguish proper and nonproper food. As you can see,

Borges was extremely insightful when he located the origins of the self in the sense of smell.

Let me add from my psychoanalytic interest another speculation, which is the possibility of diagnosing a person's superego through his metaphors of smell. A suspicious personality, one whose exploratory function is minor in comparison with the security function, will be sensitive to the otherness of smells.

A rigid superego will use the smelly metaphor of "stinks" to describe anything that falls behind its boundaries and threatens its sense of security. According to these materialistic albeit semiotic speculations, the education toward multicultural sensitivity passes through the stomach and nose rather than through our rational brains. The English who were first exposed to Indian cuisine were making a step toward a more accepting superego and therefore a more liberal society. History could have been totally different if Britain had colonized cultures with less attractive and rich kitchens.

The materialistic proposal that I presented before, with its reductionist flavor toward the dimension of pleasure, has its limits. As amusingly suggested by Merleau-Ponty (1996, xii), "It is true, as Marx says, that history does not walk on its head, but it is also true that it does not think with its feet."

Low (2005) reminds us of the way in which smell contributes to bipolarities, such as those of good and evil, and to the way these bipolarities are used for constituting boundaries between people (us and them). However, he reminds us that the complexity of smell cannot be reduced to dichotomies. Although our natural history originated from simple preferences, such as the preference toward pleasantness, it has evolved into a complex behavior.

In this context we are in deep trouble because, when we encounter an experience characterized by high-dimensionality, our ability to visualize or imagine it is extremely limited. I must emphasize at this point that the high-dimensionality of sensation has two directions: natural-biological and cultural.

As explained by Yeshurun and Sobel (2010), olfaction is considered a multidimensional sense, as around 1,000 different receptor types contribute to the percept. This is the bottom-up source of multidimensionality. The second source involves factors such as the use of learned and cultural linguistic tags that may add to this dimensionality in a top-down manner. Let me illustrate this point through a concrete example. Once, when writing a paper involving the concept of dimensionality, I became aware of a bottle of wine that was located in front of me. If the curious reader is wondering, the answer is negative and I'm not a drinker ... A sticker on the bottle poetically described the unique character of the wine in an attempt to tempt potential buyers. Here is an illustrative excerpt of this description:

> This wine is mostly composed of Merlot so that its character is governed by the *roundness, devotion,* and *seductive softness* of the Merlot but also enjoys the *compressed, wild,* and *youthful* character of ...
>
> (my emphasis)

This excerpt includes six dimensions of taste marked by italics, and the whole poetic description of the wine includes twelve different dimensions. Now think about it. We cannot even imagine how to specifically visualize the taste of this wine as a point in a twelve-dimensional space, as these dimensions are probably grounded in continuous physical dimensions. So what does it mean to experience in twelve dimensions?

The limitations in verbally describing a complex phenomenon such as wine tasting is probably the reason why wine tasting is considered by some people as a snobbish and empty pretension that is not grounded in our basic experience. Indeed, it is quite difficult to point to the "interestingness" of the wine by a superficial examination of its physical sensory characteristics. Is wine tasting an empty snobbish ritual as some people think? Is the king really naked? My answer is somehow complex, and in order to present it I would like to draw on another mathematical metaphor.

The abstract "phenomenological space" of wine may be metaphorically comprehended through the mathematical concept of the "manifold" (Novikov and Fomenko 1990). In mathematics, a point on the manifold *cannot be directly accessed* as it lacks a system of coordinates to specify its location. It must be emphasized that what we lack in the manifold is a general system of coordinates that may help us in specifying a point on the manifold. It is as if we are lost in the sea with no available coordinates to guide our navigation.

However, a point on the manifold is always accompanied by other points that constitute its "local neighborhood." This local neighborhood may serve as a "limited space" through which we may represent the point (Novikov and Fomenko 1990). Let me explain this idea by using a simple example (Novikov and Fomenko 1990, 127).

If we want to draw a map of the earth's surface, then we can represent points that exist on the three-dimensional spherical surface of the globe on the two-dimensional plane. Practically, it is impossible to achieve one-to-one mapping of a sphere to a plane, as reduction of dimensionality inevitably results in loss of information: some points that were separated on the three-dimensional sphere may be condensed into the *same point* on the two-dimensional plane.

A pragmatic solution used by cartographers to represent a sphere on a plane is to cut the sphere into small pieces each of which is projected *separately* onto part of a plane. The original sphere is therefore represented by gluing together these patches onto a single map of the globe.

Is it possible that when we encounter a complex high-phenomenological experience we operate along the same lines and "glue" the whole from simple "patches"?

Let us see the way in which the same process is evident in wine tasting. The experience of tasting wine cannot be directly represented, in the same way as the point cannot be specified on the manifold. In itself, the complex experience of wine tasting is beyond words, similarly to the experience of being in love or standing amazed in front of nature's beauty.

However, we can describe the taste of wine by using its "local neighborhood" through signs such as "softness," "aroma," and "interestingness." As we can see, natural language as the ultimate form of symbolic representation and mediation plays a crucial role in providing us with the "coordinates" or dimensions for representing the high-dimensional experience: projecting it to lower dimensionality and reconstructing it through an "atlas of signs."

Although the primordial experience of wine tasting or fragrance smelling is beyond words, it is approximated by the "symbolic patches" weaved through natural language. The smell of a baby is beyond words but language allows us to approximate it.

A trivial question is whether the rich primordial experience does not really exist without naming it. The nontrivial answer that I would like to provide is that indeed the experience exists but in a very primordial form, in a simple and behavioral form. It exists as a primordial experience but not as a *mental object* that can be manipulated and "complexicated." We experience it but we cannot manipulate or reflect on it. Let me illustrate this point.

The smell of a rose involves at the basic level a primordial multidimensional experience that cannot be easily identified or named. If you have experienced certain forms of Zen Buddhist meditation then you should understand the way trivial objects lose their meaning when turned into objects of contemplation. The reason is obvious. The complexity of the object and its mysteriousness are enacted whenever it becomes the focus of attention. Being attentive to objects, from the rose to your cat, "nullifies" their meaning as it exposes their "true" nature. Language helps us to make things simpler and much more complex at the same time. Only when the smell of the rose is described through words such as "pleasant" may the rose turn, at certain historical points of Western society, into the ultimate sign of beauty or the symbol of "virgin."

A nonhuman organism has its nonsymbolic preferences. The smell of roasted meat probably signifies "good" to my cats in the same way as it does for me. However, as my cats cannot symbolically articulate the smell of roasted meat through abstract metaphorical language, it is doubtful whether a community of cats will ever symbolize other forms of "good" objects by using meat as a sign. My cats cannot say, for instance, "When you scratch my back I feel a 'meaty' form of pleasure."

In sum, the role of symbolic mediation is in providing us with discrete lower-dimensional tools for representing high-dimensional and continuous experience. These symbolic representations recursively turn into objects of reflection, and through a complex evolving network of associations, connotations, metaphors, metonyms, and other devices turn into complex objects in themselves.

These signs are used to make sense out of the primordial smell, and as they load it with meaning it is reinvented as a cultural product. In contrast with the naive realist who believes in a world simply evident just before his eyes (e.g., the smell is in the molecules/receptors) or the naive postmodernist who believes in a world devoid of order (e.g., the smell is a personal narrative), the picture that I portray in this book is much more complex. Symbolic mediation does not invent a world *ex nihilo* nor represent a world simply given in advance. It is a complex process through which we reflect and refract our experience in dialogue with reality.

The above theorization raises a question regarding the high/low dimensionality of cognition. On one hand, the olfactory system involves the perception and representation of smell in high-dimensionality. On the other hand, it seems to be grounded and motivated by one dimension, which is pleasantness. The question is: why bother with high-dimensionality when the final behavior is motivated by a single dimension only?

The answer that I would like to provide originated from my observation that intelligent adaptive systems such as the immune system or natural language involve a delicate dialectics between high- and low-dimensionality. Let me use the immune system as an example. For the nonexpert the immune system is portrayed as a simple mechanical system that identifies threats, such as viruses and bacteria, and strives to eliminate them. However, this simple representation is far from the complexity of the immune system.

One of the major agents of the immune system is the B cell, which plays a crucial role in recognizing potential threats – antigens. The recognition of antigens involves the binding of a molecular structure of the B cell known as the antibody to the antigen. The structure of the antibody is fascinating. This receptor has a variable region that is not genetically determined. In other words, the structure of the "lock" that involves recognition of the "key" – the antigen – is not genetically determined but "epigenetically" manufactured from genetic raw material (Cohen 2000, 144).

The potential diversity of this structure is therefore enormous. The variability of the antibodies is explained by the need of mammals to cope with the extremely fast mutation rate of antibodies' enemies – viruses, for instance.

Think about a situation in which you have to cope with a vicious enemy that tries to invade your body. This is not a horror film but the daily reality of complex organisms. Now in order to target your opponent you first have to recognize it. The problem is that your enemy changes its shape and the trap you use may not recognize and catch it anymore.

The solution provided by the immune system is in line with the principle of "requisite variety" brilliantly formulated by Ross Ashby (1958). To address the variety of your opponents you have to introduce the same amount of variety!

This is precisely the principle guiding the behavior of the B cells. In terms of dimensionality, it means that, to survive a hostile and changing environment that produces an enormous number of combinations, one has to introduce a corresponding combinatorial system that implies high-dimensionality/complexity/variety.

This principle holds for both the immune system and the olfactory system. The smell receptors, such as the receptors of the B cell, represent this evolutionary answer to the need to survive in a changing and challenging environment. However, the "curse of dimensionality" directs any intelligent system seeking a simple behavioral response to project the high-dimensionality forced by the evolutionary game into a low-dimensional space, such as the dimension of pleasantness.

In sum, the high-dimensionality is forced by evolutionary need and the curse of combinatorial complexity, and dimensionality is compensated by projection into low-dimensionality.

Culture introduces complexity to this story by providing another source of variety that is not biological-evolutionary. The result is a fascinating dialectics between high- and low-dimensionality, complexity, and simplicity that is an incredible source of variability and creativity.

THE SWEET SMELL OF LOVE

In order to understand a complex process we may use computational resources, and here computational cultural psychology comes into the picture. How can computational cultural psychology contribute to our understanding of smell beyond the micro level or cross-cultural studies?

The case that I would like to present illustrates the way smell is mediated through language, and I start with a simple mapping of adjectives describing smell. To identify these adjectives I used COCA and searched for the adjectives identified one position to the right of "smell." I got a very long list of attributes used to describe the experience of smell: "sweet," "faint," "bad," "musty," "strong," "acrid," "sour," and so on. The most frequent adjective was "sweet." Next I searched for the smell adjectives describing "woman" and again found "sweet" to be the dominant one. My aim was to use the scent of a woman as a case study for understanding the mediation of smell.

Assuming that we are not cannibals and that describing the scent of a woman as "sweet" does not point to her sugary taste, the interesting question is how the connotation of "sweet" as pleasant, friendly, and so on emerged from its sugary taste.

We addressed this before where we tried to understand how language enables abstract cognition. However, in this chapter I would like to present a computational model and experiment that delves deeply into the way connotations emerge from denotations. This model is the first step in explaining how the complexities of sign-mediated experience emerge from our more basic embodied experience, and to the best of my knowledge the model described by Neuman *et al.* (forthcoming) is the first to simply explain the emergence of connotations from denotations.

Let me start presenting my thesis by elaborating the difference between denotation and connotation, two concepts that have repeatedly been mentioned in this book.

We all know that the adjective "dark" in the word pair "dark hair" functions in its literal sense, while in the word pair "dark humor" it functions in a connotative sense meaning "wicked humor." The same is true for "sweet cake" versus "sweet woman." These examples illustrate the difference between *denotation*, the literal sense of a word, and *connotation*, its extended meaning.

It is argued that the denotation of a word, or at least of simple words, is embodied in our basic sensorimotor interactions with the world (Lakoff and Johnson 1999). This point has also repeatedly been mentioned in this book. In fact, even the meaning of abstract concepts can be traced to embodied origins. For instance, the abstract concept "explanation" has its origins in *ex* (out) + *planus* (flat plane). In other words, explanation can be visually imagined as an invisible object taken out and put on the plane, visible for all.

While the idea of embodiment has deep historical roots, in recent years neuroscience has provided its own support for this thesis. More specifically, the embodied aspect of word sense has gained support from recent neuro-cognitive studies (e.g., Just *et al.* 2010) pointing to the embodied representation of word meaning.

In fact, support for the embodied notion of word sense has also been gained from systematic psychological research into language and conceptual development (for a recent review see Arunachalam and Waxman 2011). This research has shown that infants begin learning nouns by first identifying nouns and mapping them to object categories – for instance, understanding that Kitty is a cat. That is, categorization that is grounded in perceptual similarity has been recognized as a preliminary and crucial process in learning word sense.

Despite the apparent differences between several possible senses of a word, the way in which the human mind differentiates between them has not been resolved in either psychology or linguistics. This is not a surprise because, as argued by Harnad (2005), cognition is mostly about categorization.

It has been argued by my colleague Marcel Danesi (2003) that connotation results from "grafting" basic associations from the original context of the denotation to the new context in which it is applied. For instance, to follow his example, the word "snake" has a clear denotation. However, in the statement "the professor is a snake," certain associations such as "slyness," "danger," and "slipperiness" are grafted from the conceptual domain "snake" to the conceptual co-domain "professor." In other words, connotation extends the denotation through "association-by-inference" (Danesi 2003).

Nevertheless, the vast network of associations linked to a target word and the high density of our semantic network make it difficult to understand the way a connotation is grafted from its denotative origin without losing its origins in the vast forest of associations. This point is far from trivial. In my attempts to trace the connotations of words, I have analyzed corpora of associations gathered from human subjects. Trying to trace these associations has led nowhere, as in a few steps everything is associated with everything, as trivially deduced from the small-world topology of linguistic networks.

Connotations do not pop up from denotations through brute force and simple associations. As proposed by Danesi, connotations involve associations-by-inference, and identifying this mechanism of inference is a must in order to bring some order to the emergence of connotations.

While the literature in linguistic pragmatics, in psychology, and in semiotics emphasizes the importance of "encyclopedic knowledge," "context" (Allan 2007), "co-occurrence" (Corrigan 2004), and "grafting" (Danesi 2003) in establishing the connotation of a word, it is far from clear (1) how this process actually takes place, and (2) how to build intelligent systems that model and simulate this intelligent ability.

The current chapter presents a computational model explaining how a connotation of an adjective emerges from its denotative sense. Based on this model, I present an algorithm that identifies the correct sense of the connotation of the word and test it on a multiple-choice test. I must emphasize that in designing this algorithm my aim was *not* to directly test its psychological reality by comparing it to human performance or to test it on a human-like task. Indirectly one may use my results to infer the logic of the human mind and even the unique cultural habitats through which different connotations are shaped specifically, for example how the scent of a woman has become "sweet."

THE MODEL

First I present a cognitively inspired model of the way connotations emerge from denotations. The model is limited to attributes/adjectives only, and future developments will extend it to other forms of connotations.

As argued by Waxman and Lidz (2006, 320): "The process of mapping adjectives to their associated meanings is surprisingly elusive." However, my starting point is the vast psychological knowledge indicating that word-sense learning is grounded in categorization that is embodied, though not limited to our sensory motor experience.

To understand the denotation of an attribute such as "sweet" we first identify the "prototypical concrete objects" modified by the adjective. That is the first phase in identifying the prototypical concrete and embodied objects modified by our adjective. This phase follows the realization that "the precise meaning of a given adjective is influenced by the noun it modifies" (Waxman and Lidz 2006, 317). An infant may learn that a cake is sweet but that so are ice cream, potato, and chocolate. The infant doesn't have to be familiar with all of the sweet objects in the world. Memory limits may drive us to keep in mind just several prototypical objects, those mostly associated with the category and naturally best representing it.

In another culture an infant may use a similar word to describe totally different objects or to describe different objects by using totally different attributes. In this sense the model that I present is adequate for describing the way cultural variations emerge in different cultures.

The common denominator of the objects described by our adjective "sweet" is their sugary taste, which is the most basic embodied denotation of "sweet." The big question is how the different connotations of "sweet" emerge from this basic sense.

Again, following the extensive literature in psychology and the work of Waxman (e.g., Waxman and Klibanoff 2000), *comparison* and novel word learning may play a crucial role. For example, the child may hear his mother addressing him by asking "Who is a sweet child?" or his father pointing at his "sweet smile" and then wishing him "sweet dreams." Comparison of the prototypical concrete and abstract objects modified by the adjective is such that the child may learn that the new category of objects modified by the adjective is different from the first embodied category and has greater similarity to other words appearing in the same context of language use, such as "friendly" and "pleasant." As argued by Harnad (1990) in his famous "symbol grounding" paper, it is clear that categories stand at the heart of cognition and our signs are somehow grounded in categorization. However, the complementarity of categories and language systems is necessary to explain the way senses are extended from their original sense.

This basic model is materialized in the ConoSense algorithm described in the next section. As will be seen, this algorithm can be used with high success to identify the connotation of an adjective appearing in an adjective–noun phrase.

CONOSENSE – A CONNOTATION-IDENTIFICATION ALGORITHM

ConoSense implements the above cognitive model but its success aims to empirically support that model. Following the distributional semantics hypothesis (Harris 1954) and the importance of prototypes for category learning (Rosch 1973), the algorithm first identifies the prototypical concrete and abstract objects modified by the adjective under inquiry.

In practice, my colleagues and I used COCA as the best available corpus of American English and searched for the most frequent 1,000 nouns collocated one place to the right of an adjective. That is, we first identified in a large corpus the objects for which our adjective functions as an attribute.

The second phase involves ranking the nouns according to their level of abstractness/concreteness and choosing the fifty most concrete and the fifty most abstract nouns. To perform this task we used the algorithm developed by Turney *et al.* (2011) and their list of over 100,000 words and phrases scaled according to their level of abstraction.

The aim of the third phase is to identify the prototypical concrete and abstract objects modified by the adjective. We analyzed the concrete/abstract nouns separately and called the two sets of words the "master list." For each of the fifty nouns in the master list, we searched COCA again in a window of plus/minus three lexical units and identified the fifty most concrete (in the case of concrete) or abstract nouns collocated with each noun. If a noun that was found in this search also appeared in the master list, then a directed edge was sent from the search word that appeared in the master list to the noun that was found in its context. By using this procedure rigorously and formally (as described in Neuman *et al.* 2013a), the output is a directed graph of concrete/abstract nouns (self edges removed).

Phase four involves the identification of the nine most prototypical objects in each category. They are simply selected by using the normalized number of connected edges for each word. That is, we selected the ten objects with the largest number of connected edges.

For example, the prototypical concrete objects of "sweet" were: "potatoes," "butter," "rice," "syrup," "fruit," "cream," "bread," "honey," "peas," and "corn." The prototypical abstract objects associated with sweet were: "nostalgia," "intimacy," "solace," "sadness," "affection," "longing," "pleasures," "honesty," and "regret."

To evaluate the relevance of the prototypical concrete/abstract nouns for the identification of connotations we conducted experiment 1.

EXPERIMENT 1

We used the prototypical concrete/abstract objects in the metaphor-identification task developed by Turney *et al.* (2011). The task comprised five adjectives ("dark," "warm," "sweet," "hard," and "deep"). For each of the five adjectives there were twenty word pairs in which the first word was an adjective and the second was a noun. Overall there were a hundred word pairs. In some of the pairs the adjective was used in its literal sense (e.g., "dark hair") and in others it was used in its extended metaphorical sense (e.g., "dark thoughts").

Turney *et al.* (2011), who developed the state-of-the-art algorithm for metaphor identification, used the abstractness level of the noun as the only relevant variable to predict whether the phrase was literal or metaphorical. They tested the algorithm against the judgment of human experts as a criterion and obtained 79.4% accuracy. For testing the relevance of the prototypical concrete/abstract nouns we measured the similarity of the target noun in the word pair to the concrete/abstract nouns.

For measuring the similarity we used a vector space model of semantics (Turney and Pantel 2010) by specifically using the "term-to-context" matrix developed by Turney *et al.* (2011). We summed the vectors of the concrete or abstract nouns and measured the sum's distance from the vector of the target noun. If the similarity of the noun in the word pair was higher with the abstract nouns, we decided it was metaphorical; if not, it was literal.

A binary logistic regression with ConoSense prediction as the independent variable and the human judgment criterion used by Turney *et al.* (2011) resulted in 81% accuracy ($\chi^2 = 49.54$, $p < 0.001$). While the recall rates gained by ConoSense were lower than those gained by Turney *et al.*'s (2011) algorithm (71.4% vs. 76.4%, respectively), the precision gained by ConSense was much higher (93% vs. 85.71%, respectively).

Using a backward conditional binary logistic regression analysis with Turney's independent variable, our prediction showed that the abstractness level of the noun did not contribute to the prediction of ConoSense, and it was finally removed from the analysis. The results of experiment 1 supported the relevance of the prototypical objects for the identification of connotations.

Now that we had the ten most prototypical objects for the concrete and abstract objects modified by our adjectives, we could move on to the next phase and try to identify the *synonyms* of the adjective, which represent its connotative sense. We used COCA and selected the first ten synonyms of the adjective. For instance, for "sweet" we identified the following synonyms: "kind," "fresh," "musical," "pure," "friendly," "attractive," "gentle," "pleasant," "caring," and "cute."

Phase six involved the measurement of similarity between each of these synonyms and the concrete and abstract nouns in order to select the synonyms that have abstract connotative meaning.

By using the similarity-measurement procedure described in experiment 1, we measured the similarity between each of the synonyms and the concrete/abstract objects. As an arbitrary cutoff point, only values equal to or greater than 0.10 were considered in the analysis. Synonyms that gained similarity measures equal to or greater than 0.10 relative to the abstract context and did not have significant similarity with the concrete context were selected as potentially representing the connotations of the adjective.

After completing the implementation of our cognitive model *in silico* we could turn to the final phase, which was implementing it in a connotations-identification task.

Materials

Following the proposal to test artificial intelligence similarly to human subjects (Bringsjord and Schimanski 2003), we designed a multiple-choice test. Again, we chose the five adjectives that were used by Turney *et al.* (2011) for their metaphor-identification algorithm. The adjectives were: "sweet," "dark," "hard," "warm," and "deep." For each adjective we searched WordNet to identify the adjective's different senses, relevant examples of two-word phrases illustrating its connotations (e.g., "dark thoughts"), and the synset of the adjective for identifying adjectives that are synonyms of the word's connotations.

For instance, the fourth sense of "dark" is a connotation that means "stemming from evil characteristics or forces," and "sinister" is a synonym of this sense. Based on this sense we selected the word pair "dark deeds."

Our experiment included twelve word pairs for each adjective followed by four possible senses in which one of them indicated the correct connotation of the adjective. In the case of "dark deeds" the correct sense is "sinister." Overall, ConoSense was tested on sixty multiple-choice questions.

Each word pair in our experiment was followed by the four possible answers. The correct answer and the competing answers were selected mainly from WordNet, Oxford Online Dictionary, and COCA, where we looked for frequent adjectives associated with the target noun and with a minimum pointwise MI of 3. Therefore, in many of the cases the competing answers were adjectives significantly associated with the noun, an association that seriously challenged the discriminative performance of the algorithm.

Procedure

To decide which of the four possible answers is the most appropriate, our algorithm performs a simple procedure and measures the similarity between (1) the synonyms selected in phase X as representing the connotation of the adjective + the target noun and (2) each of the possible answers. For instance, given the phrase "hard look," the algorithm has to choose between the following answers that indicate the adjective's true sense: (1) "dispassionate," (2) "brief," (3) "close," and (4) "firm." The relevant connotations identified for "hard" at phase X were "difficult," "powerful," "violent," "intense," and "challenging."

Therefore the first vector includes the sum of all of these words' vectors *plus* the vector of the target word "look." Then ConoSense measures the similarity between this vector and the vector of each of the possible adjectives: "dispassionate," "brief," "close," and "firm." In cases where the same similarity score was calculated for two answers or more, a decision was made based on decimal number.

Results

Across the sixty questions our algorithm gained 90% success, which is significantly higher than what could have been expected by random guess. However, this is not enough. One may ask whether a simple similarity measure between the phrase (e.g., "dark look") and each of the potential answers may give similar or better results. To test this hypothesis, we compared the performance of our algorithm to that of a document-to-term similarity procedure implemented by Boulder's LSA engine (http://lsa.colorado.edu) and to the similarity score between the phrase and each possible answer as calculated through Turney's term-to-context matrix (TTC).

Our algorithm identified the correct answers in 90% of the cases, compared with 63% for TTC and 37% for LSA. Using a *t*-test for proportions, our algorithm outperformed TTC ($Z = 3.65$, $p < 0.001$). These results indicate not only that ConoSense performed better than random guess but also that it outperformed a simpler procedure implemented through LSA and TTC.

DISCUSSION

In *Scent of a Woman*, Al Pacino plays the role of Lt. Colonel Frank Slade, a tough and rude army veteran who has lost his sight. The plot involves a student by the name of Charlie Simms whose job is to take care of Frank during the Thanksgiving weekend, and the unfolding of their relationship with each other, with others, and with themselves. In one of the scenes Lt. Colonel Frank Slade says:

> Ooh, but I still smell her. [*inhales deeply through nose*]
> Women! What can you say? Who made 'em? God must have been a fuckin' genius. The hair … They say the hair is everything, you know.

*Have you ever buried your nose in a mountain of curls ... just wanted
to go to sleep forever? Or lips ... and when they touched, yours were
like ... that first swallow of wine ... after you just crossed the desert.
Tits. Hoo-ah! Big ones, little ones, nipples staring right out at ya, like
secret searchlights. Mmm. Legs. I don't care if they're Greek columns
... or secondhand Steinways. What's between 'em ... passport to heaven.
I need a drink. Yes, Mr. Simms, there's only two syllables in this whole
wide world worth hearing: pussy. Hah! Are you listenin' to me, son? I'm
givin' ya pearls here.*

(my emphasis)

In his cynical and alcohol-driven monologues Lt. Colonel Slade gives
"pearls" of wisdom to the young Charlie Simms. However, his cynical
"pearls" are indicative of his depression and his innermost wishes for true
love. Although the "only two syllables" worth hearing allegedly represent
his chauvinist attitude, it is the hair (of a woman) one can bury oneself in
that is God's true genius.

The metaphorical use of "bury" is important for understanding the scene.
The hair is metaphorically portrayed like the ground, which is a place where
one can rest in peace forever. As written in Genesis (King James version
3:19): "In the sweat of thy face shalt thou eat bread, till thou return unto the
ground." The "ground" is the archetypal mother, warmly accepting human
beings to rest in peace, like a real good mother (and father).

When imagining himself "buried" in a woman's hair, Slade exposes not
only his suicidal wishes but also his wish to be held and contained by a good
mother/woman. Why does the movie's title point to the *Scent of a Woman*
(or in the Italian origin *Profumo di donna*)? I believe that the association
with Slade's blindness and the idea of compensating for the loss of sight
through smell is not a good explanation as it is ungrounded in the movie's
plot. However, as I showed above, the most important smell associated with
a woman is "sweet." In answer to the question of what the scent of a woman
is, we can definitely answer: sweet! However, it is the meaning of this smell
that both reflects and constitutes its deep association with the concept of
"woman."

The sweet scent of a woman is the pleasure associated with the woman,
first and foremost the woman who nurtured us. This pleasure is relocated to
other women and motherly figures as well.

In this chapter, I have pointed to the culturally laden meaning of smell.
While originating in our carnal bodies, the meaning of smell extends its
basic embodiment. It is the logic of this extension that I have described in
this chapter. The simple model I have proposed suggests that basic attributes

are originally associated with the prototypical concrete objects and object categories we encounter in our daily experience. The complexity of our sign system, and cognitive processes such as comparison, allow us to go beyond this limited context to the rich realm of connotations and metaphors. It is the social interaction between infant and significant others through which the infant may develop his mind, understanding that "sweet" may be used in the sense of "pleasurable," for instance.

In fact, "pleasurable" may be considered as a sign signifying the abstract Janus facet of "sweet." Indeed, sweet is pleasurable and if I had a pleasurable dream then *ipso facto* it is a sweet dream … The importance of understanding this logic has far-reaching consequences for education, for instance. The fact that our biological containers/bodies are forced to be schooled according to a physically constrained manner that has been shaped through the industrial revolution is diagrammatically opposed to what we know about bodies and "souls" alike.

Our mind is developed through physical interactions and its extension through social-semiotic and attachment-based forms of interactions. This is quite remote from what public education is all about.

Lt. Colonel Frank Slade was giving us "pearls," but in a different way from how he cynically meant. He shows us that even tough colonels have been helpless infants that longed for a holding mother. The cradles of our mind are the basic attachment patterns with significant others. Extending our mind toward distant territories is therefore an extension built on our trust in significant others and the way through which they settle the ladder of signs for emotional, mental, and personal growth.

7

Dolly Parton's love lexicon: detection of motifs in cultural texts

Dolly Parton is one of the most famous singers in the USA and is known as the queen of country music. She is well known not only because of her songs but also through her unique physical appearance: her feminine aspects are grotesquely overemphasized, the most salient of them being her huge (artificial) breasts and lips.

One of Parton's albums, released in 1974, is titled *Love Is Like a Butterfly* after one of the album's songs. The first lines of the song, written by Parton herself, go like this:

> Love is like a butterfly
> As soft and gentle as a sigh
> The multicolored moods of love are like its satin wings

If we carefully analyze the song, we may identify words and phrases describing or associated with the experience of love: soft, gentle, sigh, multicolored, satin, wings, heart, feel, strange, inside, flutters, flight, rare, with me, kiss me, touch, warm, tender, with you, laughter, bring me, sunshine, spring, happy, by my side, precious, share, sweet, together, belong, daffodils, butterfly.

From this list I have chosen fifteen words as best representing this experience: soft, gentle, sigh, wings, inside, rare, touch, warm, tender, sunshine, spring, happy, precious, sweet, together. I call this list Dolly Parton's love lexicon.

One may ask why in a book dealing with cultural psychology we should care about this song that metaphorically portrays love as a butterfly. This question is specifically relevant in a book introducing the idea of computational cultural psychology. Now the question immediately proposed by our highbrow critic is why we should care about this lexicon of love clichés. It is after all a song that is the expression of kitsch and vulgar culture, and the way it represents love is not worth anything. Why shouldn't we read, one may ask, Shakespeare's love sonnets? However, there is a good answer to the critique.

With all respect to Shakespeare (I even wrote a paper on masturbation in his first sonnet!), there are probably more people in the USA who have listened to Dolly Parton's love songs than who have read Shakespeare's sonnets. If one is interested in the way love is represented in popular American culture, Parton's song may be of great interest.

Moreover, high culture is a term used to describe the cultural artifacts most praised by the elite. Classical music, including opera, is considered by many to represent high culture. It is a symptom of the vicissitudes of history that opera is considered to be high culture, given its origins and the fact that the first opera performances looked like carnivals, with food sold during the show and prostitutes offering their services to the distinguished guests. When trying to understand a given culture one should not be biased by the artifacts admired by the elite; one should instead pay close attention to the "low" culture consumed by the nonelite.

I believe that today no serious researcher in cultural psychology would deny this methodological imperative. Trying to understand British culture through Shakespeare is only of minor relevance and does not take into account less admired and more popular artifacts consumed by the common people such as pub songs and comic newspapers. The idea that one should take into account "low" culture in order to understand the multiple facets of a given culture is not new, and I fully adopt it. In this context, analyzing Parton's song as an attempt to understand something about the American cultural representation of "love" and about love as a psychocultural construct may be an interesting intellectual exercise. What can we learn about love from Parton's song?

The challenging question that I would like to address through computational cultural psychology is how to move beyond the clichés of the song toward a deep understanding of culture. To address this challenge, I first used Google Book Search (http://googlebooks.byu.edu).

This corpus, which was released in May 2011, includes 155 billion words and ranges over a period stretching from 1800 to 2009. I used "love" as a target word and searched for whether words from our love lexicon appeared within a window of plus or minus four words. In addition, I used a limit of minimum MI of three. Let's take for example the word "soft." Table 7.1 presents the results of the search. The numbers in the table's cells indicate frequency of occurrence. For instance, the expression "the soft breath of love" first appeared in 1800 and appears just once. It was found that the most frequent appearance of the words in the lexicon was in the nineteenth century.

TABLE 7.1 *Google Book Search for "soft."*

	Words																					
	Total 1810–2009	1800s	1810s	1820s	1830s	1840s	1850s	1860s	1870s	1880s	1890s	1900s	1910s	1920s	1930s	1940s	1950s	1960s	1970s	1980s	1990s	2000s
and soft dreams of love	110				5		12	14	13	23	9	15	6	3	1	4	2	2	1			
with soft tales of love	69					4	4	7	14	13	20	3	2	1					1			
soft and full of love	59				5	5	2		1		6	6	4	2	1	3	1	5		5		13
the soft breath of love	50	1	2	5	6	9	2		2			6	3	6		4	2	1				
soft airs of promised love	46							1	2	18	13	8	2			1					1	
lute's soft tone do love	45								4	4	2	11	6	7	2	2	1	5				1
thousand soft recollections of love	43							1	1	6	11	9	5	1	2		4			2		1

This finding is of great interest as it shows that the real inspiration for Parton's modern love lexicon is a period described as "Romanticism," an aesthetic zeitgeist emphasizing emotion as the core of the aesthetic experience and nature as a major inspiration for metaphorical language.

To understand this Romantic representation of love, think about Lord Byron or the Brontë sisters. Interestingly, the associations of "inside," "rare," and "together" have their peaks much later. For instance the peak of "together" occurs around 1990 and 2000. This is an interesting finding because it may hint that, despite the fact that Parton's love representation may be traced to the nineteenth century, it was only later that love became deeply relational in our social representations of love. This point will be emphasized when analyzing one of the most successful romantic comedies of Hollywood: *When Harry Met Sally*.

Let's return to Parton. The fact that a modern American country music singer is so much identified with this song, which is considered as her "signature," tells us something interesting about the way love is represented and mediated through images, metaphors, and signs that reached their peak approximately a hundred years before this woman born to a poor family from Tennessee decided to form her meaning of love.

Attributing the cultural heritage of this song to Romanticism should be qualified, of course. Passionate images of love and naturalistic metaphors for describing it exist even in the Bible. Nevertheless, the fact that Parton's lexicon reached its peak in textual data of the nineteenth century is of certain significance. Yes, one may counter, but the corpus you analyzed is a corpus of textual data in a period when most people were illiterate. Aren't you analyzing high culture again?

Whether the high culture of written books influences the popular oral culture or whether the oral popular culture has been represented in high textual culture is a question we cannot and maybe should not answer due to the interweaving threads of culture.

The fact that through corpus linguistic analysis we have "discovered" Parton's source of inspiration may end as a linguistic anecdote, but we may ask several difficult questions such as to what extent this Romantic image of love still exists today and whether it differentiates between the way men and woman conceive love. We may also ask: what is the cultural evolutionary trajectory through which "soft," "sweet," and "tender," for instance, have become associated with love?

To better understand my subject, I used the Corpus of Historical American English (COHA) (http://corpus.byu.edu/coha). COHA is the largest structural corpus of American English, and it allows the search of

400 million words of text of American English from 1810 to 2009. First, I used the fifteen adjectives that appear in the lexicon and that were found to be associated with love. Next, I checked what kinds of objects they describe. For instance, I used "soft" and searched the corpus for nouns that appeared in a window of three words to the right. After identifying the objects described as "soft," I chose only objects that appeared in the 1810s or 1820s and that were literally described as "soft" (e.g., "soft hair") and excluded from the analysis metaphorical descriptions (e.g., "soft words"). What I found were the following objects: hair, touch, cheek, snow, lips, wood, fingers, velvet, soil, moss, sigh, pillow, wings, beds, palm, and cushion. I then used the association of a descriptor and noun (e.g., "soft hair") and searched its associated adjectives within a window of plus or minus four words.

The results were sorted by identifying adjectives that appeared in the song or that were semantically associated with the original list. The objects that shared more than one adjective with the song were: "beds" (warm, sweet), "hair" (tender, warm), "touch" (sweet, tender, warm), "cheek" (warm, happy, glad), and "lips" (delicate, warm, sweet).

These results point to the embodied nature of the softness of love. Describing love as soft is mostly associated with body parts – hair, cheeks, and lips – and with the activity of touch and the object "bed." Love is soft through the embodied experience of touching the cheeks, lips, and hair of our beloved one or being touched by those who love us.

As we can see, even when a sexual extrovert such as Dolly Parton is representing love she chooses to do it by echoing the most basic attachment patterns of interactions. She doesn't choose sexual images hinting, like some rap singers, toward intercourse (e.g., nipples or penises) but instead describes love through cheeks, hair, touch, and lips. Our romantic images of love therefore echo more basic attachment patterns that in themselves are not sexual.

When Parton is longing for love she is longing for the gentle-soft-man or more precisely for *gentle relationships/interactions*. This finding is very similar to the one discussed with regard to *Scent of a Woman* and Lt. Colonel Frank Slade in Chapter 6. However, the embodiment of love cannot exhaust the complexity of Dolly Parton's love lexicon nor Lt. Colonel Slade's love representations. To enrich our understanding we must delve deeper.

Now let us return to Romanticism and discuss Jane Austen, the author of *Pride and Prejudice*, which is one of the most popular images of romantic love, albeit in a different sense than the one mentioned before. Austen is considered to be a novelist not necessarily affiliated with the zeitgeist of Romanticism. The center of her novels is the country gentleman, who strives (and is defined) by a solid set of ideals, manners, values, and rituals.

In reading her novels, the postmodernist reader may find himself amazed by the rigid and nonreflective set of practices that guide the characters' lives. There are appropriate things that should be said or done with specific timing and in the right place. Any deviation from these rigid norms might be suspected as being bad manners, which are immediately associated with the vulgarity of the lower class. Here you can sense the social-political context in which the distinction between "low" and "high" culture emerged. This context is a clear material symbolic context. Bad manners are not necessarily those that are "inherently" bad but rather those characterizing the lower class.

For instance, the "gentleman" is not really "gentle" in the kind of sense mentioned in Parton's song, but rather is primarily a male who is wealthy enough that he doesn't have to work! An evolutionary psychologist would jump to his feet arguing that this is quite trivial. When Parton is longing for "gentle" love she is singing about the sublimation of the gentleman concept. He would argue that Parton is actually longing for a wealthy man who will take care of her. The more sophisticated metaphorical sense of "gentle" is only secondary to the most important motive, which is to find a wealthy husband. This is a trivial evolutionary explanation that I would like to refine.

This is a crucial point in an argument that I would like to develop later and that explains the deep relation between Parton and Austen. Parton, who is longing for a gentle and tender love, is longing for the man who has been "refined" by a *surplus of wealth and social manners*. The idea of "surplus" and its relevance to understanding culture will be developed in Chapter 10, dealing with dinner.

Let me further reflect on the idea of the gentleman to better explain the above argument. The gentleman, in contrast with the vulgar lower class, is a restrained person with an advanced sense of judgment, sensibility, and good manners. Bad manners are left to those who have to strive for a living and to struggle in the jungle of daily life. In this sense, good manners are not appreciated for their own sake but as an *indication of wealth and social class*. Those men with good manners are those who can allow themselves to *transcend nature*.

Along a similar line, the women in Austen's novel strive toward elegance, which again can be contrasted with the vulgar taste and manners of the lower class. Again "elegance," originating from the Latin sense of "tastefully refined," is a merit of those who transcend their basic needs and may refine their "taste," which is an embodied concept. After all, our taste is basically associated with food, not with expensive furniture.

I'm emphasizing this idea because we sometimes and naively confuse value and class. The "gentlemen" established "appropriate" social norms and values, but these values are no more than an indication of *class markers,* and one should not mistake them for ethical norms. It goes without saying that a critical reading of class and ethics would find no moral superiority in the gentleman.

The context of Austen's novels is clearly not a reflective context of the kind I mentioned above. No hungry children, no criticism of the lack of equal opportunities, and no critique of the social norms. It is also a context in which love and sexuality are subordinated, at least as an ideal, to the social norms.

In fact, the body in its material sensual form is almost totally absent from Austen's novels. No breasts, hair, cheeks, lips, clitoris, or penis. Is there a sharper contrast than the one that exists between Jane Austen, the spinster and asexual author of *Pride and Prejudice,* and Dolly Parton, with her overemphasized feminine sexuality?

Let me discuss the similarity between Parton and Austen in the context of Romanticism. "Romantic" is a term derived from the literary genre of romance and associated with ideas of chivalry, adventure, idealized love, and the supernatural. Lord Byron, whom I cited before, was a living instantiation of Romantic ideas.

In fact, the variety of artistic forms and writers has led to a critical examination of the term "Romanticism" and its replacement by the term "Romantic" to designate a particular period (Bainbridge 2008).

McGann (1983 cited in Bainbridge 2008, 13) suggests that we should adopt historical distance from a text in order to identify its ideology or false consciousness. The Romantic, he explains, celebrated the poet, the imagination, and the natural world at the cost of failing to deal with historical, social, and political problems.

Austen is not a typical representative of the imagination or the natural. Therefore, reading her as epitomizing Romanticism might be a mistake. However, she clearly represents what Mellor (1993) describes as "feminine romanticism" indicating a *relational self.* Austen may therefore be considered a romantic novelist in the modern sense of a novel focusing on romantic love, relations, and a happy ending.

However, Austen does not clearly fall into this rubric either. Reading her sophisticated novel *Emma,* one understands the deep relationship between

Austen and Parton, as *Emma* is primarily a novel about *relationships* and of a very typical kind.

In Chapter 9 I am going to describe the novel's plot in order to discuss it through culturally changing consciousness and to identify and elucidate the relationships within it through computational tools, allowing us to identify themes – units of meaning – in a text.

To delve into my computational approach to identifying themes in texts we first have to closely understand the meaning of a relational self. Chapter 8 is dedicated to this task. Then, Chapter 9 explains the new methodology I have developed and implements this methodology to better understand Parton and our modern concept of love as representing a high point of synergism between the embodied, ontogenetic, and cultural threads of love.

8

The relational matrix of the I

I concluded the previous chapter by suggesting that the modern representation of love is comprehensible only as synergetic threads. The gentle love described by Parton can be traced back to our most basic embodied patterns of attachment to significant others. However, locating the peak of those metaphors in Romanticism suggests that our concept of love has been somehow transformed by culture and at a specific point of our cultural history. I have suggested that love has become more *relational* and sublime. However, the meaning of this term "relational" should be explained. To explain the relational nature of modern love and its very specific sense, I first dedicate this "noncomputational" chapter to explaining the meaning of our relational self. In trying to explain the relational nature of the self and to introduce the methodology through which we expose relational patterns in text, I first explain an important aspect of our language and our "trust" in guiding us to deep layers of meaning.

From the perspective of semiotic cultural psychology, relations are exposed mainly by analyzing the language of those who establish relations. Understanding the relations of Harry and Sally in *When Harry Met Sally* is impossible without paying close attention to the things the characters say and of course avoid saying. Understanding family as a relational system is impossible without carefully analyzing the verbal communication patterns between members of a family. However, analyzing language in order to expose deep layers of meaning assumes basic trust in the way language can guide us, whether to expose the deep psychological layers of a person or of a given culture.

In this context, we first have to acknowledge the deficiency of language in providing us with a simple door into the soul of the individual.

As early as 1920, Bakhtin (1990) suggested that abstract thought and language convert the individuum (from the Latin sense of an atom) from a unique, dynamic, ontological singularity into a reified object of reference. To quote from his seminal treatise "Author and hero in aesthetic activity":

[Sign-mediated] thinking has no difficulty at all in placing *me* on one and the same plane with all *other* human beings, for in the act of thinking I first of all abstract myself from that unique place which I – as this unique human being – occupy in being.

(Bakhtin 1990, 31)

Bakhtin's observation is that on the most basic level, language, as a social abstract system of signs, fails to represent the individuality and singularity of a unique human being. This is of course an inherent property of language. Language constrains the flux of the Heraclitean river by providing us with nominal categories through which we may gain stability and understanding with the ultimate price of losing the singularity of the lived experience. This criticism echoes in the writings of several great thinkers from Dilthey to Bion.

Wilfred Bion (1962a), a famous and rather obscure psychoanalyst, considered "thought" to be the integration of a "preconception" with "frustration." For instance, the baby who anticipates his mother's nurturing breast may be frustrated by its nonappearance, which means that hunger is not satisfied. Bion argues that, if the infant has a normal capacity for frustration, the absent breast turns into a thought, *here interpreted as a category associated with the signified breast*, not mechanically and brutally through a dyadic relation, but triadically, with the mediation of the ego, indicating that which is not directly accessible.

In other words, if the infant can bear the frustration, the missing breast is converted into a category and a sign. This is a fascinating point, as what is converted into a sign is actually the absent.

The sign produced through this process is an abstraction, as Bakhtin noted. It is not a simple association between two elements, what Peirce described as "secondness," but a triadism that includes the sign, the signified (i.e., the missing breast), and the interpretant, which is the evolving ego machine linking the sign and the signified. This interpretation will be elaborated below through Peirce's semiotic theory.

Bakhtin's general suggestion is instantiated with regard to the unique status of the first-person pronoun "I." Bakhtin made the insightful observation that, unlike other linguistic signs, *the sign "I" has no clear reference*. The sign "flower" indicates the concept of a flower, the sign "number" corresponds to the object well defined by Bertrand Russell, but what object does the sign "I" indicate? To where does it point? It is an object that cannot be even trivially associated with perceptual experience.

The answer is that the sign "I" fulfills the mysterious function of associating the lived experience of the individual with a communicable and social form of expression. As beautifully explained by the Bakhtin scholar Michael Holquist (1990, 28), "Much as Peter Pan's shadow is sewn to his body, the 'I' is the needle that stitches the abstraction of language to the particularity of the lived experience."

From the above discussion it is clear that a tragic, built-in breach exists between the mature subject and herself, a breach created by the language and the way it distances the subject from the lived experience. The existence of this breach was realized by Bakhtin, who discussed it in the context of Dostoyevsky's novels:

> *Man is never coincident with himself.* The equation of identity A = A is inapplicable to him. In Dostoyevsky's artistic thought, the genuine life of the personality is played out in the point of his departure beyond the limits of all that he is in terms of the material being which can be spied out, defined and predetermined without his will, "at second hand."
> (Bakhtin 1973, 48, my emphasis)

In other words, the unique psychosemiotic status of the first-person-singular pronoun exposes a duality, a separation, between the inner "I" – here signified as "I_0" – and the social, communicable "I." This is a crucial point that was echoed later in Lacan's writing. As soon as our language reaches a certain level of complexity a breach is evident between the experiencing subject and his or her reflecting consciousness. It is a form of alienation resulting from the fact that language as a symbolic activity necessarily distances us from the experience as it is.

This duality between the symbolized represented "I" and its corresponding "genuine" being is illustrated in Borges's witty parable "Borges and I" (Borges 1964). In this parable the author (i.e., Borges) begins by differentiating between the speaking "I" and Borges: "The other one, the one called Borges, is the one things happen to" (Borges 1964, 246).

This statement refers to the breach noted by Bakhtin. However, the parable concludes with, "I do not know which of us [Borges or I] has written this page" (Borges 1964, 247), and therefore alludes to the paradox of the subject who is both differentiated and intermingled with himself at the same time.

In this context, the meaning of the first-person-singular pronoun is far from trivial, and the method for relating the use of it to the subject's lived experience is even less trivial, as is evident from Bion's revolutionary attempts to map the transformations from the inaccessible I_o to its communicable products (Bion 1965).

From a relational perspective, and a semiotic perspective à la Volosinov and Bakhtin is always relational, it is clear that the only way to understand the I_o is by carefully *weaving the matrix of objects and relations in which it is embedded*. One may even argue that what we describe as the I_o is no more than the sum of objects and relations in which the so-called individual is embedded. Do you remember the manifold analogy that I used to understand the experience of wine tasting? Do you remember the "atlas of signs" we use to reconstruct this complex experience? This is precisely the way the I is constructed.

In other words, approaching the *inner life* of a person does not involve archeological excavation of that which is *beneath* the surface, beneath the *persona* (i.e., from Latin "mask") but rather the weaving of a tapestry showing what is *in between* the singularity of the first-person perspective and the second- and third-person perspectives (Neuman 2004a).

This is a highly important point for cultural psychology, as it urges us to understand people not as isolated atoms but neither as marionettes of social forces. The individual is comprehensible only as the dynamics existing in between the singularity of the first-person perspective and the social perspectives where language, or more generally our semiotic systems, functions as the "glue."

Moreover, according to this "interactional" epistemology (Neuman 2003), which was developed by people such as Peirce, Bakhtin, Volosinov, and Bateson, language is neither a representation of reality nor an autonomous system of simulacra, as portrayed by Baudrillard (1981).

Language is the communicational medium we use to translate (and reconstruct) our inner experience into the "language of outward expressedness" (Bakhtin 1990, 31). Thus, our access to the inner world is always mediated. Our access to the representation of love is always mediated, and to better understand love, for instance, we must identify the relational patterns in which love is weaved.

The above suggestion does not lead to empty particularism in which saying something significant about the subject is impossible. *Regularity may be found in patterns of mediation*. In other words, instead of looking for the unknowable metaphysical and Platonic form of the "transcendental self," or desperately withdrawing to the interpretative position that our language is a game *in and for itself*, the interactionist perspective urges us to examine the logic of mediation as a constitutive logic of the mind (Neuman 2003).

In this sense, this chapter presents a specific perspective on issues of language, interpretation, validity, truth, and reality.

PEIRCE AND THE RELATIONAL MATRIX

Long before the concept of "thirdness" (Benjamin 2004) or "three-ness" (Ogden 1985) entered the psychoanalytic dictionary, Peirce, among other great minds such as Bakhtin, realized that a triad is the basic relational position of the subject and the interpretative activity. Let us further discuss Peirce's perspective. Our point of departure is Peirce's distinction between the sign, the signified, and the interpretant. To quote:

> We must distinguish between the Immediate Object, – i.e., the Object as represented in the sign, – and the Real (no, because perhaps the Object is altogether fictive, I must choose a different term; therefore:), say rather the Dynamical Object, which, from the nature of things, the Sign *cannot* express, which it can only *indicate* and leave the interpreter to find out by *collateral experience* [i.e., previous experience with others that makes novel situations comprehensible].
>
> (Peirce 1992, vol. II, 498)

In other words, the dynamical object, the signified, the "O," can never be directly indicated by the sign. It is a particular hypothetical object beyond our reach. We need the complementary third ring of the Borromean knot, which is the interpretant – the ego machine that associates the sign with the "dynamical object."

The interpretant comes into being when a link is established between the dynamical object and the sign. In our case, we may differentiate between the dynamical I – (I_o), the sign I, and the interpreting I ("I_R"). That is, our genuine I is a particular and dynamical object that cannot be directly and simply approached. However, when we are semiotically socialized we learn the use of the sign I. We refer to ourselves by using this sign, whose meaning can be understood only through a relational matrix.

According to this suggestion, and as Winnicott (1965a) realized, the use of the sign "I" is a watershed in child development, as it indicates a child's entrance into the social relational world where she becomes a member of a sign community able to reflect on herself.

Moreover, Peirce's suggestion that the dynamical object can only be "found out" through the interpreter's *collateral* experience with the other is consistent with Winnicott's "paradox" that an object must be created in order to be found (Winnicott 1965b).

In this context, an interesting question is how the I_R is found out and created through collateral experiences with significant others. To address this question, I would like to discuss several other aspects of Peirce's theory, aspects that have been presented before.

To recall, in Peirce's theory of relations there are three basic relational types that correspond to his three categories of being: firstness, secondness, and thirdness. I have introduced these categories before but would like to mention them again. Firstness is the "mode of being of that which is such as it is, positively and without reference to anything else" (Peirce 1931–1966, vol. VIII, 328). For example, the basic sense of being, the most basic sense of consciousness, falls under the rubric of firstness. It is the most basic feeling of being alive. Peirce's conception of firstness seems to be non-relational, a kind of monadic quality, indifferent to anything else. This is wrong. Peirce uses this type for analytical reasons only and recognizes the fact that even firstness is relational, as our mind is relational in nature. Like Kohler's hen, even the most basic experience of "dark" is a difference that makes a difference.

We enter the relational domain with the secondness/dyadism that "consists in one thing acting upon another" (Peirce 1931–1966, vol. VIII, 330). This is a pure binary relation. No third is involved.

Thirdness/triadicity is "mental or quasi-mental influence of one subject on another relative to a third" (Peirce 1931–1966, vol. V, 469). It is the "mode of being of that which is such as it is, in bringing a second and third into relation to each other" (Peirce 1931–1966, vol. VIII, 328).

A sign positioned in a triadic structure of a sign, signified, and interpretant is a form of thirdness. Winnicott's "potential space," having the form of the symbol, the symbolized, and the interpreting subject (Ogden 1985, 132) is also a form of thirdness. Culture as a potential space is a realm of thirdness. In fact, wherever you find meaning you find thirdness.

As Bion noted, albeit in the context of knowledge, a dyadic relation in which the I functions as the first object is an assertion of a relationship (Bion 1989). Indeed, switching from monadic language (in which the I is meaningful only insofar as it is associated with basic qualities of the individuum) to dyadic language (in which the I functions as a relational sign) to triadic language (in which the I is related to another through a third) is an important developmental phase in the transformation of the mind, and may be indicative of the subject's or the group's relational matrix, which reflects and refracts his/its identity.

The next issue concerns the transformation between different types of relations. Peirce stated that a genuine triadic relation is *irreducible* to lower-order relations and that the complexity of higher-order relations can be reduced to triads. In other words, any system of relations can be expressed (in principle) by the three "atoms" of monadic, dyadic, and triadic relations. This statement is very important for establishing a relational matrix for the I through which the dynamical object I_o is expressed in the activity of the I_R.

Another important suggestion made by Peirce concerns his idea of "hypostatic abstraction" (Peirce 1931–1966, vol. IV, 235, 227–323). The idea of hypostatic abstraction (intensively elaborated in Chapter 3, on the way language abstracts thought) is that there is a procedure that converts a quality expressed as an adjective or some part of a predicate into an additional object. For example, the expression "honey is sweet" may be converted into "honey possesses sweetness."

The transformation is actually a transformation from a monadic relation to a dyadic relation that results in a *reification* of the basic quality precisely as described by Bakhtin. This conversion takes place, for instance, when the basic quality of the first object turns into a second object "possessed" or "contained" by the first one. In a case where I functions as the object, basic feelings such as frustration or aggression may be converted through a collateral experience with a significant other into reified objects contained or possessed by the I. Here we should merely mention Bion's idea (1956) that the aggression experienced in the case of frustration with respect to the nonexistent signified (e.g., the bad breast) might result in a pathological reification and compartmentalization of ego-related particles. On the other hand, our ability to turn our emotions, for instance, into objects of contemplation is very important for emotional self-regulation. Think about anger, for instance. Anger may flood us and conquer our mind. Our ability to turn the anger from an overwhelming experience into an object of reflection is crucial for managing the anger and reducing its effect. Language is therefore crucial for gaining control with the inevitable price that this form of control alienates us from the primordial experience in its purity.

The lesson we can learn from Peirce is that the relational matrix in which the I is woven can be reconstructed if we pay close attention to the objects, relations, and transformations that constitute it. Specific attention should be given to hypostatic abstraction, which transforms qualities into dyadic relations, and to triadic relations, which form the core of the relational matrix.

The Glass Menagerie

To illustrate how the I_R functions, is created, and is found out in collateral (i.e., social) experience I use Tennessee Williams's famous play *The Glass*

Menagerie (Williams 1988). *The Glass Menagerie* is a psychologically ori-ented play and is therefore a wonderful text for illustrating the above theor-ization. Moreover, through this play we may speculate about more general cultural patterns, with the appropriate qualifications of course. The play will be qualitatively analyzed but in Chapter 9 I will show how to automatically extract themes out of it.

The characters in the play are the mother, Amanda Wingfield; her daugh-ter Laura; her son Tom; and Jim O'Connor, the "gentleman caller," who is described as "a nice, ordinary young man." If you remember our previous discussion on the concept of gentlemen then you can immediately establish a link in your mind between Jane Austen, Dolly Parton, and the major char-acter in the play –the family's mother, Amanda, a Southern lady. Amanda cherishes the ideals of the old American South, among them the concept of the gentleman, which is actually the British concept of the gentleman.

Amanda is a key figure in constituting the family's pathological relations. Her husband deserted her years ago, and she has "failed to established contact with reality" and "continues to live vitally in her illusions." Laura, the daughter, is disabled and lives cut off from reality to the point that she is like "a piece of her own glass collection, too exquisitely fragile to move from the shelf." Tom, who is also the narrator of the play, is a "poet" who works at a warehouse to support his mother and sister. He is the healthiest member of the family and constantly challenges his mother's fantasies by mirroring them to her.

To follow how Amanda patterns the relations surrounding her I_0 and to understand how she co-constructs her relationships with the others, I identified all the sentences in which Amanda uses the first-person-singular pronoun. Using an algorithm for identifying the predicate–argument struc-ture of a sentence (Lin and Smith 2006), I examined whether each I was an argument in a monadic, dyadic, or triadic relation. Only triadic relations were further analyzed.

This simple technique results in key sentences that, when interpreted in the appropriate context, may help us reconstruct the relational matrix of the "I"s. Let us illustrate this procedure with an example (Williams 1988, 25–6):

AMANDA: Girls that aren't cut out for business careers usually wind up married to some nice man. [Gets up with a spark of revival.] Sister, that's what you'll do!
[Laura utters a startled, doubtful laugh. She reaches quickly for a piece of glass.]
LAURA: But, Mother –
AMANDA: Yes? [Crossing to photograph.]
LAURA [in a tone of frightened apology]: I'm – crippled!

AMANDA: Nonsense! Laura, I've told you never, never to use that word.
Why, you're not crippled, you just have a little defect – hardly noticeable,
even!

Let us analyze a segment of the last sentence, where the I appears in
a triadic relation: "*I've* told *you* never, never to use that *word*." "I" is the
first object in the triad; "you" is the second object, and "[that] word" is
the third. The use of *emphatic deixis* "that" to point to "word" is interesting, since emphatic deixis is commonly used by speakers to distance themselves emotionally from a negatively charged object (Levinson 1983). In the
above scene, this object is the word "crippled," a basic property Laura uses
to describe herself in the *monadic* relation "I'm – crippled!"

While Laura uses a monadic relation to talk about herself, as opposed to
her mother's fantasies, her mother responds with a triadic relation in which
her pattern of denial is evident: "*I've* told *you* never, never to use that *word*."
She repeatedly denies this basic monadic relation ("you're not crippled")
and uses hypostatic abstraction to convert the quality (i.e., crippled) into an
object (i.e., defect) contained in Laura's I: "*you* just have a little *defect*."

This scene clearly illustrates how collateral experience, in our case an
interaction between a mother and daughter, transforms a painful acknow-
ledgment of reality ("I'm – crippled!") into a command to deny reality ("I've
told you never, never to use that word.").

This command indicates a relational pattern that results in the *reification*,
possession, and *transformation* of the basic, painful feeling. "That word,"
which is so threatening to Amanda that it cannot be said, has been safely
transformed into an allegedly harmless object (i.e., "little defect") contained
in Laura, although as a reified object it becomes a part of Laura and not a
basic cause of anxiety.

The reification of Laura's "little defect" is not a simple denial, since in
another context Amanda uses the same "word" that she firmly forbids her
daughter to use. The prohibited word appears in a quarrel between Amanda
and Tom.

The context of this quarrel is Amanda's desperate longing for a "gentleman
caller" who will save Laura and herself from their misery. The gentleman is
the woman's savior as he can provide her with wealth and the accompanying
social status. Amanda pushes Tom to invite one of his friends to dinner. In her
fantasy Amanda considers this young man, whom the family barely knows, to
be the ultimate "gentleman caller." To her disappointment she finds out at the
end of the evening that "Our gentleman caller was engaged to be married!"
(Williams 1988, 90). She blames Tom for this, and when Tom tries to avoid his
mother's fury by going to the movies, she tries to evoke guilty feelings: "Go to

the movies, go! Don't think about us, a mother deserted, an unmarried sister who's *crippled* and has no job" (Williams 1988, 91, my emphasis).

This context illustrates that the "sacred prohibition" on using the forbidden word is context- and relation-dependent. As part of a relational pattern of reifying her daughter's feelings, Amanda prevents Laura from using the word. Laura's I_o is converted from a dynamic nexus of qualities into a basket/container of objects and therefore an object in itself, which is defined, like a mathematical set, by its single member – the "little defect."

Instead of responding to Laura's feeling of frustration with recognition and empathy, Amanda imposes on her reification and denial. This interpretation is further established if we examine Amanda's triadic patterns of relations.

Triadic relations in the play in which the I functions as a first object are few, but they converge into an indicative pattern of relations. The following is a list of sentences in which Amanda's I functions as an argument in a triadic relation. Arguments in a triadic relation are italicized.

1   Context: Amanda finds out that Laura has dropped her typing lessons: "*I* thought that *you* [Laura] were an *adult*, it seems that I was mistaken" (Williams 1988, 21).

2   Context: Laura gets up to bring in the blancmange. Amanda stops her: "you be the lady this time and I'll be the darky ... *I* want *you* [Laura] to stay fresh and pretty for *gentleman callers*" (16).

3   Context: After supper, Amanda asks Tom to do her a "favor" and comb his hair: "There is only one respect in which *I* would like *you* [Tom] to emulate your *father*" (43).

4   Context: After speaking with his mother about Laura and saying that she is "crippled," Tom says he is going to the movies: "*I* don't believe *you* [Tom] always go to the *movies!*" (51).

5   Context: Tom forgets to pay the electric bill and the lights go off after the dinner with the "gentleman caller." Amanda turns to Jim (the gentleman caller) and says: "*I* might have known better than to trust *him* [Tom] with *it*" (68).

6   Context: Amanda realizes that Jim is engaged. She is angry at Tom for not knowing this: "*I* suspect that *you* [Tom] would never give it *a thought*" (49).

7   Context: Amanda finds out that Tom was reading a book by "Mr. Lawrence" (probably D. H. Lawrence's *Lady Chatterley's Lover*): "*I* won't allow such *filth* brought into my *house!*" (29).

8   Context: Amanda has just had a fight with Tom: "*I* make *myself* hateful to my *children!*" (36).

In sentences 1 and 2 Amanda is referring to Laura; in sentences 3, 4, 5, and 6 she is referring to Tom; in sentence 7 she refers to an object ("filth"); and in sentence 8 she is talking about herself. We see clearly that these triadic relations are indicative of Amanda's I_R and her relations with her children. In other words, the matrix of triadic relations woven around Amanda's I is indicative of her "self" and her self's positioning toward her children.

Amanda's predominant attitude toward Laura is disappointment ("I thought that you were an adult") and an expectation that she will fulfill her mother's fantasy of the gentleman caller, the knight on the white horse, the ideal man, the father, the phallus that will support her separation/individuation process (Benjamin 1988).

Sentences 1 and 2 are deeply connected. Blaming Laura for being a child is blaming her for failing to separate from her mother, while Amanda fails to separate from Laura too. Amanda's disappointment in Laura is primarily her disappointment in herself, the young, promising Southern girl who found herself deserted and alone, without the "capacity to be alone" (Winnicott 1965a).

The solution to this separation problem is the "gentleman caller." According to this gender perspective, powerfully articulated by Benjamin (1988), a woman can achieve this separation only by being "fresh and pretty" (sentence 2) for a "gentleman caller." However, the separation problem cannot be solved if the "gentleman caller" is either unavailable or not fully trustworthy. This point becomes clear when we analyze Amanda's positioning with regard to Tom.

It is clear that, as the male representative of the family and the substitute for the missing father ("I would like you to emulate your father"), Amanda's predominant relationship with Tom is one of *mistrust* and *suspicion*. Amanda does not "believe" Tom (sentence 4), does not "trust" him (sentence 5), and "suspect[s]" him (sentence 6). Men – whether husbands, gentlemen callers, or sons – are untrustworthy. They are untrustworthy because the woman free to choose her gentleman in the modern free market of relations faces a conflict and tension between choosing her genuine love regardless of the man's status and choosing a man based on his wealth per se. Amanda made the wrong choice. She chose the wrong man and fell into poverty and despair. This relational conflict is possible only in a free society and becomes interwoven in the representation of love only in societies in which this conflict has turned into an object of reflection. Later we will read together an excerpt from *When Harry Met Sally* and will see the same theme evident in a discussion of whether in *Casablanca* Ingrid Bergman should have chosen the sexy Humphrey Bogart regardless of his status as a bar manager in a French colony. This discussion between Harry and Sally is a wonderful instance of intertextuality. Within a movie dealing with the possibility of "friendship" between men and woman, the heroes bring in another text, which is the scene from *Casablanca*, reflecting in a fractal kind of nature the same relational theme.

Back to the Wingfields. The inevitable conclusion is that in Amanda's world a woman is caught in a paradox of being unable to live with men or without men. She can constitute her relational matrix only through the "gentleman caller," who is on the one hand a must and on the other hand someone who can never be trusted. In this context, it is not hard to understand Laura's hysterical resistance to developing an independent and separate identity and her pathological withdrawal to the womb of the "glass menagerie" where she is an object among other fragile objects.

DISCUSSION

As Mitchell (1988, 18) argues: "Once a semiotic matrix is established, both pre-verbal and non-verbal dimensions of experience can be restricted, experienced, and expressed only within a socially shaped system of linguistic meanings. The relational model within psychoanalysis is a social theory of mind in a similar sense." If we follow this statement, the theorization and technique proposed in this chapter give us possible coordinates for understanding the subject's semiotic matrix of relations.

First, by identifying triadic relations in which the I functions as an argument, we restrict our analysis to the informative essence that is the skeleton of the semiotic matrix.

Second, by grouping the objects and relations in which the I is embedded in triadic relations, we may uncover patterns and regularities that can be used diagnostically to understand the I_R as coming into being in relation to others.

Finally, by analyzing the use of hypostatic abstraction we can better understand how basic feelings are transformed into reified objects used as bricks to constitute the semiotic matrix.

The theoretical issues and the technique discussed above may also suggest a way of approaching the intrinsic tension of language in psychology. On one hand, we definitely reject the naive position that language is a representation of human experience and a mirror of (human) nature. On the other hand, we also reject the deconstructivist caricature that portrays human language as an autonomous system that is free to create realities regardless of the "true nature" of the realities (natural, personal, or interpersonal).

The position implied by the above theorization is that by listening to the subject's or subjects' language we can discover hidden patterns. However, as Mey (1998, 161) argues: "Linguistic techniques, however, even though often a necessary condition for interpretation, are never sufficient by themselves."

The psychological reality does not reveal itself through linguistic analysis per se but from the *emerging patterns of meaning* associated with "languaging" activity in context. In contrast to the "anything goes" stance, researchers have to validate their interpretations by carefully weaving the "semiotic matrix" of their subjects in a way that can be communicated to the interpreter and others, and in a way that allows for critical reflection and self-correction.

The "true nature" of the semiotic matrix is "true" as long as it presents a distinctive pattern of meaning supported and validated by the researcher's close examination of the data. Here, Peirce's theory of relations may be indispensable for uncovering these patterns.

One of the challenges facing computational cultural psychology is to develop new tools in order to represent the semiotic matrix, which is the focus of our interest, and through this semiotic matrix to better understand cultural dynamics. Again, the computational tools do not aim to replace the interpreter but to support her with a powerful methodology of analysis. This argument is further illustrated in Chapter 9, where our opening point is the study of group dynamics and the way we can identify themes in the dynamics. Chapter 9 presents a theme-excavating methodology that has been presented before. I present the methodology and explain how to use it for understanding group dynamics. The analysis of the Wingfields' dynamics will expose some interesting themes. The methodology will be further illustrated with regard to the analysis of real-world dynamics. To close our discussion of relational love and Dolly Parton's song, I will present an analysis of *Emma* by Jane Austen and *When Harry Met Sally*.

9

Identifying themes: from the Wingfield family to Harry and Sally

INTRODUCTION

The Glass Menagerie illustrated family dynamics in action. Family dynamics is only one instance of small-group dynamics. The study of small-group dynamics has long been of interest to psychologists and psychiatrists. From Bion (1961) to Foulkes (1964; see also Pines 2000), Yalom (1995), and others, the dynamics of small groups, such as the Wingfield family, have been carefully studied and mapped.

However, despite the rich insights gained into group dynamics, the techniques through which we can identify structural units of meaning (i.e., themes) emerging at the group level of analysis have remained largely unstructured. This observation is evident, for instance, in a wide range of the publications dealing with group psychotherapy from different theoretical and practical perspectives (e.g., Barnes *et al.* 1999; Berg-Cross 2000; Christner *et al.* 2007; Goldenberg and Goldenberg 2004; Rutan and Stone 2001).

We should remember here that in practice the therapist or group mediator observes the group dynamics in real time, and therefore the cognitive load under which s/he works impedes his/her ability to identify themes in a valid and empirically grounded way. Moreover, as the dynamics unfold, a complex network of signs is generated by the group. The complexity of this network imposes significant constraints on the ability of the group mediator to identify themes emerging from the discussion.

While there is no substitute for human intuition, experience, and professional knowledge, state-of-the-art advancements in science and information technology are providing us with powerful tools to *support* the interpretation of group dynamics. In this context, the aim of this chapter is to introduce a novel methodology for identifying themes in small-group dynamics, which is applicable, as I have shown earlier, both to the analysis of single texts (e.g., a political speech) and to small groups.

The methodology is illustrated in two cases: family dynamics as it appears in the literary piece previously discussed, Tennessee Williams's *The Glass Menagerie*, and the real group dynamics of Israeli and Palestinian subjects discussing the notion of forgiveness. Later, I will return to *Emma* and to Dolly Parton to apply the methodology in order to better understand modern love.

THE GROUP MATRIX

The "input" data of a researcher studying group dynamics mainly comprise the verbal utterances produced by the group members. Although nonverbal cues are of significant importance for understanding group dynamics, it is the verbal data that are the focus of our current study. In this limited context of interpretation, seeking themes is therefore *seeking structures in the textual data.*

It should be noted that the group constitutes a whole that is different from the sum of its parts. This emerging whole has been described by Foulkes (1964, 292) as a "matrix" comprising a hypothetical web of communication and relationships in the group and the common shared ground, which ultimately determines the meaning and significance of all events and upon which all communication and interpretations, verbal and nonverbal, rest.

What is the nature of this matrix? When producing utterances, the participants together construct a web or a matrix of linguistic and nonlinguistic signs. On the most basic level, some of those linguistic signs *represent* the speakers ("*I* wish you were more emphatic") and others the *objects* emerging in the dynamics ("The *dinner* you have previously mentioned ...") and their *relations.*

This matrix of signs has been described in the context of relational psychoanalysis as the "semiotic matrix" (Mitchell 1988). Let us remind ourselves of the quote from Mitchell in Chapter 8: "Once a semiotic matrix is established, both pre-verbal and non-verbal dimensions of experience can be restricted, experienced, and expressed only within a socially shaped system of linguistic meanings" (Mitchell 1988, 18). In other words, the semiotic/group matrix both emerges from the group dynamics in a bottom-up manner and guides the dynamics in a top-down manner. If we adopt this theoretical perspective, according to which the emerging whole is a "semiotic matrix," then the researcher seeking to understand the group should

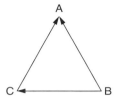

FIGURE 9.1 Illustration of a three-node sub-graph.

reconstruct this matrix/network of signs and identify themes within it. In this context, the study of "network motifs" may be of great relevance.

NETWORK MOTIFS AS UNITS OF MEANING

One of the major advancements in network analysis is the idea of "network motifs" (Alon 2007; Frankenstein *et al.* 2006; Kashtan and Alon 2005; Milo *et al.* 2004). A network is composed of nodes and edges. The nodes are the objects comprising the network, and the edges are the connections between the objects. A real network may be a vast forest of nodes and edges. However, within this forest, we can identify sub-graphs with well-defined configurations. For instance, one possible sub-graph comprising three nodes is described in Figure 9.1.

We can see that this sub-graph comprises three nodes – A, B, and C – connected by three edges. One edge is directed from B to A, a second edge from B to C, and a third edge from C to A. In textual data, the nodes can represent words and the edges the relations between them. For instance, A, B, and C could be three different people, and the edges could represent the relation FRIEND_OF. Therefore, B is a friend of A and C, and C is a friend of A.

A network may be broken down into a variety of sub-graphs. Breaking the network into all of its possible sub-graphs is of no interest to us, but finding sub-graphs that appear in a frequency significantly deviating from chance (i.e., a network motif) may well be of interest.

A network motif is thus a particular pattern of connections – edges and nodes – that occurs in an actual network at an observed frequency that is significantly greater than the estimated frequency of the same pattern of connections obtained randomly (Frankenstein *et al.* 2006, 32). Motifs are identified by comparing the observed frequency of that particular set of nodes and edges with the estimated frequency of the particular set (Frankenstein *et al.* 2006).

One of the main reasons for the importance of identifying network motifs is the "modularity" of naturally designed networks. Modularity is the "separability of the design into units that perform independently at least to a first approximation" (Kashtan and Alon 2005). The implication of this definition is that, through the analysis of "motifs" as *building blocks* of a system, we may better understand the behavior of the complex *as a whole*.

This is an interesting suggestion. We are aware that every complex system is built from simpler units. We may try to approach the system as a whole but it is unnecessary to repeat that this holistic approach leads nowhere as we are unable to "digest" the whole. Instead of reducing the systems to atoms, whether individuals or words, the network-motifs approach directs us to choose a more complex level of reductionism, which is the motifs level of analysis. These motifs are not isolated atoms but minimal building blocks of relational configurations.

While the idea of motifs has been intensively studied in the natural sciences, specifically in biology, I believe that I was the first to use this methodology for the study of psychological and linguistic data. First let me illustrate the way we may analyze the Wingfield family through this methodology.

CASE 1: ANALYZING THE FAMILY DYNAMICS
OF THE WINGFIELDS

The network construction

To identify motifs in the family dynamics, my colleagues and I first had to convert the text into a semiotic matrix. The first problem that we had to address was pronoun resolution (e.g., to which of the play's characters to attribute "I"). We manually annotated the entire text for pronoun resolution. For the first-person-singular pronoun (i.e., "I"), we replaced the pronoun with the proper name of the speaker (e.g., Amanda), but in other cases we resolved the pronouns only when we considered doing so possible, relevant, and appropriate for the analysis.

Following the pronoun-resolution procedure, we automatically analyzed each utterance produced by all the characters and created, through the Stanford Parser (de Marneffe and Manning 2008), a "dependency representation" that aimed to identify relations between pairs of words.

A dependency representation of a sentence consists of words linked by binary asymmetrical relations. The relation holds between a word described as a *parent* or *governor* and another word described as a *child* or *dependent*. Graphically, this relation appears as an arrow from the parent to the child.

FIGURE 9.2   A dependency representation of "depressed" and "person."

The relation is labeled according to the dependency type. For instance, the word pair "depressed person" is represented as shown in Figure 9.2. In this representation, "ATT" is the "attribute relation" of "person" to the adjective "depressed."

After we automatically analyzed the utterances and constructed a dependency representation for each utterance, we used several rules to construct a network of signs out of these representations. The aim of the rules was to identify the subjects and the objects of the sentences and to relate them to each other. In other words, we built the semiotic matrix by identifying, through our rules, words associated with each other through subject–object relations. Using this procedure, we produced a directed graph of signs at the group level of analysis (i.e., the semiotic matrix).

To identify the motifs in the network, we used FANMOD software for the fast detection of network motifs (Wernicke and Rasche 2006). We limited our analysis to three- and four-node sub-graphs.

Results and interpretation

The generated network included 864 nodes and 1,391 edges (1,364 single and 27 bidirectional). We ignored sub-graphs for which the Z-score was ≤ 2 and the p-value was ≥ 0.05 and that were found fewer than five times. The analysis identified four three-node motifs, and thirty-four four-node motifs.

In itself, the identification of the network motifs is of minor relevance to the psychologist, whose interest is in understanding the *meaning* of the motifs. However, identification of the motifs is the first step in the process. Let us examine the three-node motif with the highest Z-score (Z = 8.4982, $p < 0.001$, frequency 0.799%). This motif (ID = 38) in shown in Figure 9.3. It is constructed along the line of the diagonal link, which means that, if there is a link from B to C and a link from C to A, then a link is established from B to A.

When examining the motif for the character most frequently located at the B node, we found that it is Amanda (N = 356), followed by Laura (N = 278) and Tom (N = 258). Amanda is related mainly to Tom (38), Laura (29), and Jim (28) as C nodes. These are trivial findings that can easily be deduced from the simple frequency of the words in the text. However,

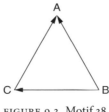

FIGURE 9.3 Motif 38.

when Amanda is related to Tom, what kinds of objects occupy the A node? What kinds of objects *mediate their relation*? Interestingly, there is no single object that is more frequent than the others as an A node in the relation of Amanda to Tom. However, the objects occupying the A node revealed an interesting pattern, which we exposed by using the LIWC software.

Using LIWC, we found an important difference with regard to two main categories, "family" and "work": in comparison with Laura, when relating to Tom, Amanda uses more family words (7.89% vs. 3.45%, respectively), and when relating to Laura more words concerning work (6.9% vs. 2.63%, respectively). A trivial finding was that Amanda relates to Laura, her crippled daughter, by using "health" words (Laura = 3.45% vs. Tom = 0%).

Our interpretation of the finding that when Amanda is the B node neither Tom nor Laura appears as the A node is that the A node constitutes the realm of objects to which Amanda relates in her interaction with Tom and Laura. In this context, the fact that "family," "work," and "health" are three important relational keywords may be of great importance for understanding the family dynamics. The meaning of these themes will be interpreted along the way.

The most frequent motif, which had the second highest Z-score, was Motif 6 ($Z = 5.58$, $p < 0.001$, frequency = 71.043%). This motif is shown in Figure 9.4. Amanda is also the most frequent B node in Motif 6 ($N = 20,880$), followed by Tom ($N = 18,906$) and Jim ($N = 13,340$). Despite the fact that Jim, the "gentleman caller," is a marginal figure in the play (in terms of number of appearances as a node), we see him repeatedly as a major component of the motifs. This finding indicates that the idea of a "gentleman caller" is highly important in the family dynamics. This is a point I emphasized in the previous chapter. *The gentleman (caller) is the woman's ultimate symbolic savior.*

The analysis uncovers more interesting themes. Amanda relates more than the other figures to words in the past tense. This finding is evident from her nostalgic approach to her past. In contrast, Tom, more than the other characters, relates to the present.

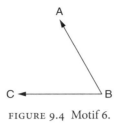

FIGURE 9.4 Motif 6.

This difference may be significant for a psychologist analyzing the family dynamics, and it indicates the difference between Amanda's nostalgic relation to the past and the need of Tom, as a young man, to live in the present. The characters live in two different time planes that simply do not intersect. Moreover, do you remember the "distrust" theme I proposed in the qualitative analysis? The idea that Amanda doesn't trust men? Her distrust is a worldview based on her painful past experience. When Amanda relates to Tom, she relates to him through her past.

While the above interpretations could clearly have resulted from the psychologist's intuition, the proposed methodology has the benefits of identifying themes through an economical and scientifically grounded process. In sum, the analysis of the above three-node motifs may help the psychologist to uncover hidden themes in family dynamics in a cognitively economical, fast, and valid way.

This process has clear practical implications. The identification of the three keywords "family," "work," and "health" in Motif 38, and the different relations to past and present in Motif 6, may provide psychologists with organizational concepts for examining matrixes that they strive to comprehend. For instance, psychologists may work along the lines of resolving the tension between Amanda's relation to her lost, cherished, and "sacred" past, and the poor present in which she is living, a present that is the most important dimension for her son. Psychologists may also examine Amanda's relation to Tom through the keyword of "family." Amanda probably regards Tom as the father or the male substitute in the house, and therefore she discusses with him family matters in a way that puts a heavy burden on the shoulders of a young man who strives for autonomy and to live in the present rather than living the role of the father who abandoned the family years ago.

Again, it is clear that interpretation is necessary to make sense out of the motifs, but that the motifs provide *empirically grounded anchors for interpretation.*

The above explanation is supported by the interpretation of the four-node motif number 2,190 (Z = 3.74, p = 0.001, frequency = 0.0005%). The

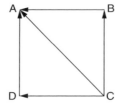

FIGURE 9.5 Motif 2,190.

motif is shown in Figure 9.5. We selected Motif 2,190 for analysis because it is of theoretical interest in that it is <u>a relational structure</u> composed of two triadic units (CDA and CBA) that converge on their initial object (node C) and terminal object (node A), and may therefore offer us a closed unit of meaning.

Let us explain the importance of this motif. In a nutshell, the motif involves a relation between the C node and the A node through the mediation of the B and D nodes. If we examine the characters that occupy the C and the A nodes, we may learn something about their relationship through the B and D objects that mediate their dyadic relations. In other words, this motif is highly important for identifying the relational "triangles" that have been considered as the building blocks of family dynamics.

When analyzing the nodes constituting the above motif, we found that Amanda is the character most frequently occupying node C, which is the origin of the above motif. She relates to two characters most frequently occupying the A node: Tom and Laura.

When Amanda relates to Tom, the most frequent object occupying both the B and the D nodes is "father." In other words, Amanda's dyadic relation with Tom is mediated by "father," thereby constructing the triangle Amanda–father–Tom. In contrast, when Amanda relates to Laura the most frequent mediator is "sister."

These triangles have an interesting interpretation perfectly converging with the qualitative analysis that precedes them: Amanda's wish that Tom take the role of the missing father is evident from a close analysis of the play and dynamics. Tom does not only have to function as a father, except for the sexual aspect, but is also the representative of the "symbolic father" associated with the law. We will touch on the idea of a symbolic father more deeply when discussing revenge and the novel *Michael Kohlhaas*. The fact that Amanda mediates her relation with her son through the concept of "father" further supports our previous interpretation. Men cannot be trusted even as sons. On the one hand they have the potential of saving the woman by being "gentlemen," but on the other hand there is always the danger of the gentleman enjoying the woman sexually only to move on to another woman. In traditional societies this conflict would probably be minor as the woman was an integral part of a larger group. However, the rise of the middle class and the modern family, together with the demand for free choice, has sharpened this conflict inbuilt in the relationships between men and women.

In contrast with her relation to Tom, Amanda's relation to Laura is mediated through a concept used by Tom: "sister." In this sense, Laura has no existence as an independent human being but exists only as the sister of Tom and as a potential wife for a "gentleman caller." The fact that Laura has no autonomous existence in the relational matrix of the family and the emerging triangles is theoretically clinically important and may also explain significant portions of her pathology and her withdrawal from reality.

The analysis so far has been focused on a literary piece. However, to further illustrate our methodology, we also analyzed a real case of group dynamics.

CASE 2: ANALYZING THE DYNAMICS OF FORGIVENESS

The data

As a real-world example, we chose an intercultural group comprising Israeli and Palestinian subjects dealing with the notion of forgiveness. The members of the group were seven Jewish-Israeli and five Palestinian teachers. All the teachers but one were female.

The session that we analyzed formed part of a 120-hour in-service training workshop conducted as part of a larger research project that was initiated in the 2008–9 academic year. The head of the project was my colleague, the educational anthropologist Zvi Bekerman.

The specific discussion that we analyzed focused on the notion of forgiveness and was based on a mediator-guided program prepared in advance. The program included questions regarding the meaning the participants attach to forgiveness, their perceptions regarding this concept, and the potential applicability of this concept to the present situation in Israel. The session, which was guided by an expert group mediator, lasted for two hours, and was recorded and transcribed. The transcript, which was analyzed by us, produced 1,502 line codes.

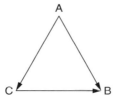

FIGURE 9.6 Motif 38 for *When Harry Met Sally.*

Results and interpretation

The analysis was conducted along the lines described previously. As a part of the manual pronoun resolution, the category "J" was used to describe cases in which a pronoun (e.g., "you" or "we") concerned the Israeli group, and the category "P" was used to denote reference to the Palestinian group.

The analysis produced a network with 535 nodes and 1,204 edges (single = 1,181, double = 23). The most statistically significant three-node motif was Motif 38 ($Z = 8.61$, $p < 0.001$, frequency = 2.38%) (see Figure 9.6).

Category J appeared 125 times in the discussion (0.007%) and category P appeared 65 times (0.004%). However, in Motif 38, J appeared 23 times (0.05%) as node A and P appeared 65 times (0.04%) as node A – that is, the categorization of the group's members as J or P appeared in the motif in a frequency that was approximately seven to ten times greater than their frequency in the overall discussion!

We can learn from this result that, despite the mediator's attempt to focus the discussion on the idea of forgiveness and to transcend ethnic boundaries, the motif as a unit of meaning had amplified by a factor of seven to ten the sharp division between the two groups, the "we" and the "they."

In other words, the motif and its components revealed the significance of ethnic boundaries in the group dynamics. It would have been difficult for the group moderator to have revealed this powerful amplification of the ethnic boundaries without the proposed methodology.

N, a Palestinian teacher, was the participant who appeared most frequently as node A in the motif ($N = 53$). She was connected mostly with three concepts located at node B: violence, forgiveness, and opposition.

When related to violence as the B node, the left node C was usually Y, an Israeli participant. Therefore, this triadic unit of meaning associated N, Y, and violence. A close reading of the text reveals the meaning of this motif: despite the fact that N was the most common speaker among the Palestinian teachers, she was positioned by Y as "different" in that she was opposed to violence. For example, Y said:

We should forgive her for having solidarity with her people, among other things, because she is fighting against violence, and she raises her children to support peace and oppose violence as a means to end the conflict.

This analysis reveals an important rhetorical *move* in the sense that, despite the fact that N was the most important speaker among the Palestinians and attempted to represent the Palestinian group, her positioning by Y as opposing violence and therefore being "different" from the other Palestinians weakened her role as the group "representative" and hence undermined her role in the group dynamics.

In practical terms, the group mediator could use this conclusion derived from the motif analysis to try to question this otherwise unnoticed exclusion of N from her representative role.

Another example indicating the benefits of motif identification derives from examining the role of Y. This person, who was the second most frequent figure in the upper node A (N = 28), was associated with two terms as a B node: state and exam. Exam was associated with Arabs as the C node. What was the story linking Y, exam, and Arabs? The association was presented by Y as follows:

I just did a week ago the final exam for my MA degree; for those who don't know, you have a certain topic, and you have a supervisor; he [the supervisor] gives you a bibliography to read and you meet and do the exam; my topic was the Israeli–Arab conflict as it is mirrored in the Jewish textbooks.

The books up until the seventies were very unbalanced and told only the Zionist narrative; later on the books became more balanced and in the nineties they are much more balanced.

This statement triggered a discussion, which was stopped by the mediator saying, "Sorry, it's very easy to deviate from the issue."

Our analysis suggests that, rather than deviating from the issue, Y's exam and the way the Arab–Israeli conflict is represented in the "official" textbooks of both Israelis and Palestinians is a point of interest in the discussion. To understand why, let us analyze the short discussion triggered by Y's critical comments. As a response to Y's reflection, S, a Palestinian, said: "We had to celebrate Independence Day and raise the flag."

S said that, as a Palestinian educated in the Israeli system, she had to celebrate Independence Day despite the fact that it is not *her* Independence Day but the Independence Day of the Zionist state. In other words, Y's critical reflection on the unbalanced representation of the conflict in the Israeli textbooks was picked up by S, who provided another instance of the "injustice" inflicted by the Israeli education system.

This move was responded to by the Israeli participants and summed up by Y, who "corrected" the consequences of his critical reflection by saying: "By the way, in the same research they also mentioned the Palestinian textbooks in which *the situation is much worse*" (my emphasis).

This short exchange, considered by the group mediator as a "deviation," is highly important, as it teaches us that self-criticism by one of the opposing sides should not be supported and encouraged by members of the other side, as it is then *considered as a threat to the self-criticizing party.*

This insight, gained through the analysis of the motif, has clear practical implications. In sum, by identifying the motif and its components, we have drawn attention to important phases of the discussion that would otherwise not have been noticed by the group mediator or by a researcher studying the group's dynamics.

The lack of a structured methodology for analyzing the group matrix probably results from the lack of appropriate tools rather than from an ideological or methodological bias. In this context, the current chapter constitutes the first stage in enriching the toolkit of researchers seeking to better understand the semiotic matrix. As I clearly argue, there is no substitute for the human interpreter, just as there is no substitute for the human painter, musician, or carpenter. However, just as the painter cannot paint without the appropriate brush and colors, just as music could not have been developed without the invention of musical instruments, and just as a carpenter needs a hammer, the therapist or group mediator seeking to understand group dynamics will surely benefit from new technological tools. The methodology presented here is novel but clearly constitutes the first steps in enriching the toolkit of those striving to understand group dynamics.

BACK TO LOVE

At this point let us return to the place we left, which is a better understanding of love. To try to better understand romantic love, I have analyzed Jane Austen's *Emma*. *Emma* is described in Wikipedia as a novel about "youthful hubris and the perils of misconstrued romance." Emma the heroine is a young, beautiful, and privileged woman who lives in the country with her wealthy and hypochondriac father, who seems to be characterized by weakness of the ego. Emma is the typical spoiled child who uses her beauty,

FIGURE 9.7 Motif 38 for *Emma.*

wit, and social status to manipulate and control the lives of other people, specifically by being involved in matching couples according to her childish and rigid view of relationships.

Her friend, the gentleman George Knightley, is the only responsible adult who challenges her childish and narcissistic behavior. The plot becomes complicated when Emma's attempts don't work according to her plan, but there is a happy ending (to be later detailed).

When analyzing *Emma* through the methodology presented before, I found Motif 38 (see Figure 9.7). Motif 38 has a very low prevalence of 0.50% ($Z = 3.55$, $p < 0.001$). The question of course is what this motif actually means. When Emma is the B node it is Mr. Knightley and Mr. Elton who are the A and C nodes. This finding is interesting as it reflects the two most significant relations of Emma's. Let me explain why. As I have outlined, George Knightley is Emma's older friend and her only critic. Emma, who is clearly a spoiled narcissist, considers Knightley to be her critical and rational friend, only to find out at the end of the story that he is in love with her. Friendship between men and woman, as Emma comes to know, is a tricky issue. The gentleman seems to have other intentions than playing the role of the rational superego …

Mr. Elton, on the other hand, is a good-looking young man whom Emma, in her urge to fully control her surroundings, tries to match to Harriet, her young, unsophisticated friend who is from a lower social class.

It is Emma, though, whom Elton wishes to marry, for practical economic reasons. It seems that the triangle we identify in the motif is the triangle of Emma's misunderstanding. In both cases, she fails to understand the men's intentions. Both men want her. One of them as a practical means to climb the social ladder and the other from true love. In other words, love, as implied from the motif, is about relations and the conflict they evoke. If we would like to better understand the nature of romantic love then we should do it by paying close attention to triadic relations constituting love and to the tricky and loaded "Romantic" tension between men and women trying to establish relations. As we will see, this theme is evident not only in Austen's *Emma* but also in one of the most successful romantic comedies, *When Harry Met Sally.*

When Harry Met Sally is one of the most successful romantic comedies. Written by Nora Ephron and directed by Rob Reiner in 1989, it follows the relationships between Harry, played by Billy Crystal, and Sally, played by Meg Ryan.

The comedy's success doesn't only result from its humorous aspect but also from its unique ability to reflect and discuss deep layers of romantic love and the possibility of *friendship* between men and women. Friendship as an asexual relation between heterosexual men and women is an intriguing social category of relations (O'Meara 1989). We will first present it and then discuss it by relating it to deep layers of love as a cultural construct.

The seed of this theme appears at the beginning of the movie, when Harry and Sally, two young and unrelated people, share a cross-country drive to New York. One of the first episodes is an argument about *Casablanca*, another great romantic movie, with Humphrey Bogart and Ingrid Bergman. Here is the episode:

> (a while later, still in the car)
> SALLY: You're wrong.
> HARRY: I'm not wrong, he wants …
> SALLY: You're wrong.
> HARRY: … he wants her to leave that's why he puts her on the plane.

The first few lines are indicative of Harry and Sally's discursive pattern, which is *argumentative*. They argue all the time. Argumentation is a sign of relatively symmetrical gender relations. In traditional societies, in which women have been subordinated to male dominance, there was no place for arguments. Some of the arguments could have been ended with authorized violence. For instance, the phrase "rule of thumb" originated from a verdict that allowed men to club their wives with a stick whose diameter should not be larger than the man's thumb. Now think about the unfortunate destiny of women who had husbands with a wide thumb.

In the above scene Harry argues that, in the final scene of *Casablanca*, Rick (played by Bogart) puts his love on the plane because he wants her to leave.

> SALLY: I don't think she wants to stay.
> HARRY: Of course she wants to stay. Wouldn't you rather be with Humphrey Bogart than the other guy?

Sally argues that Ilsa (played by Bergman) doesn't want to stay either, and Harry immediately tries to refute Sally's thesis by putting her in Ilsa's shoes, suggesting that Rick (Bogart) is the clear choice between Rick and Victor Lazlo, who is Ilsa's husband (i.e., "the other guy") and the resistance leader, and is the less sexy figure. Sally responds to Harry's thesis:

SALLY: I don't want to spend the rest of my life in Casablanca married to a man who runs a bar. I probably sound very snobbish to you but I don't.

Her rebutting defeater doesn't concern Rick's sex appeal but his occupation as a bar manager. That is, she ignores Harry's emphasis on the passionate aspect of relations and prefers to discuss a more rational issue. In fact, her thesis represents the same theme found in *Emma*: a woman in between the ultimate gentleman, whose social status and power may provide her with wealth and security, and a fellow who is less attractive from an economic point of view but much more attractive from other perspectives, such as the sexual one.

In one of my classes one of my students described this tension as the tension between the sexy motorcyclist and the nerd engineer. What I would like to argue later is that the conscious tension between the two is an interesting cultural theme.

Back to the scene. In a psychologically minded interpretation, Harry exposes this tension in Sally's perspective (my emphasis):

HARRY: You'd rather be in a passionless marriage.
SALLY: And be the first lady of Czechoslovakia.
HARRY: Than live with the man you've had the greatest sex of your life with, and just because he owns a bar and that is all he does.
SALLY: Yes. And so had any woman in her right mind, *women are very practical*, even Ingrid Bergman, which is why she gets on the plane at the end of the movie.

Interestingly, it is Harry, the man, who takes the more passionate, "romantic," and feminine perspective, while Sally is the one making the more "masculine" rational calculations of marriage. This clash of perspectives is only the first among many to come and to be surprisingly resolved when they fall in love with each other.

What can we learn about Harry and Sally when we use our methodology of motif analysis? First let's see the most common words in the movie script. Figure 9.8 shows a Wordle (www.wordle.net/create) visual representation of the script, limited to a hundred words. When we analyze *When Harry Met Sally*, we get the three-node motifs shown in Table 9.1.

TABLE 9.1 *Three-node motifs in* When Harry Met Sally.

Motif ID	Frequency (%)	Mean Frequency (%)	Standard Deviation	Z-score	*p*-value
46	0.41614	0.20669	0.00022865	9.1603	0
238	0.032188	0.0079163	2.9326e-005	8.2763	0.001
6	77.117	76.728	0.00060176	6.4712	0

FIGURE 9.8 Wordle visual representation of the script of *When Harry Met Sally*, limited to a hundred words.

Let's start our analysis with Motif 238, which is the least common among the three. When we examine the most common words occupying the three nodes we find two triads. The first triad is Harry, Joe, and Sally, and the second triad is Marie, Harry, and Sally. Harry and Sally are trivially evident in the two triads but they are not alone. Marie is Sally's best girlfriend and Joe is Sally's mythological ex. What we have just revealed is that *relationships are always triads*, including romantic relationships. This is the point we have made before about the emerging recognition of love and romantic relationships as involving triads.

In our case, Harry and Sally do not see themselves *only* through the eyes of each other. Joe, the mythological ex, and Marie, the best friend, are two perspectives necessary to understand the relationship between Harry and Sally.

When Joe first enters the plot it is in the airport when he is with Sally and they meet Harry. Sally recalls her old dispute with Harry and his attempt to make a pass at her:

JOE: So what happened?
SALLY: When?
JOE: When … when he made a pass at you and you said no and …
SALLY: Oh, oh. I said we could just be friends. And this part I can remember he said that men and women could never really be friends. Do you think that's true?
JOE: No.

In contrast with Harry, Joe believes in the possibility of friendship between men and women. This is the perspective he represents when he enters the plot. He is found to err, as Sally's friendship with Harry turns into a sexual affair and love. Therefore, his role in the triangle is to represent the perspective assuming friendship in cross-sexual relations is possible without being interrupted by the sexual desire of the man, as argued by Harry. Joe is the perfect "gentleman." Sex is not high on his priorities, as he epitomizes the ideal of the sublime, and the way the gentleman should transcend his animalistic feelings and urges.

Marie enters the plot when she shares with her friend Alice her spying on her married lover and her realization that her married man will not leave his wife for her. Alice tries to convince Marie that she should look for a single man, and her response is, "Sally got the last good one."

Marie is the mirror ideation of Joe, the "last good" (single) man on earth. The ultimate gentleman, the same type of gentleman admired by Jane Austen and Dolly Parton.

When Harry and Sally "gaze" at each other, to use Bakhtin's expression, it is not two different worlds that are reflected in the pupils of their eyes but the worlds reflected through Joe's perspective, which assumes the ability to neutralize the sexual aspect in cross-sexual friendship and the ideation of this highly self-controlled man through Marie's perspective.

Let's move to Motif 46 and check what the B and C nodes are. The B and C nodes factor through each other (i.e., they have arrows from B to C and from C to B, and both have arrows heading toward the A node). Broadly speaking, the B and C nodes are again Harry and Sally. What is interesting is the nodes to which they converge. The most salient node is "friends." It is of no surprise that the film is about friendship and the possibility of friendship between men and women and, more importantly, the way this possibility is evident through triadic relations. So let's return to Dolly Parton and the love lexicon.

WHAT WE TALK ABOUT WHEN WE TALK ABOUT LOVE

"What we talk about when we talk about love" is one of Raymond Carver's short stories and the title of his short-story collection (Carver 1989). In his rough and simple style, Carver describes an evening gathering of several people around a bottle of gin where the theme of love is discussed from various perspectives. For instance, did the ex-boyfriend of one of the characters really love her when his jealous envy turned into physical abuse and suicide?

This short story does not resolve the riddle of love, its universal core, or its cultural particularities. The aesthetic value of this short story is in providing us with a glance into the dissolving consciousness of ordinary human beings trying to *co*-nstruct the meaning of love.

In this chapter, I used computational thematic analysis in order to better understand the meaning of love as a cultural relational process.

In contrast with common psychological theories, I didn't try to identify the components of love nor to echo the ideas of love as a narcissistic mirroring. Starting with Dolly Parton, I proposed that, like Carver's characters, when we talk about love, our discourse echoes not only universal basic forms of attachment and embodiment but also cultural layers of meaning. Parton's love lexicon echoes romantic conceptions in their relational sense, the same relational patterns to be found in *Emma* and *When Harry Met Sally*. Women may want their love to be sweet and gentle and their loved one to be a gentleman, one whose kindness is an indicator of his social status and sublime character. However, in their relational conception of love, modern women would probably reflect the conflict between a longing for a man who has transcended his basic needs to turn into a gentleman and a man who is sexually attractive but less sublime. Friendship, as suggested by Harry, is a risky category as the cultural construct known as a "gentleman" is a social construct that covers other more carnal layers.

Civilization, as realized by Freud, is guided by striving toward the sublime, but this striving carries with it the seeds of annihilation. Dolly Parton, who longs for gentle love, is longing for the sublime, which is the imperative of cultural dynamics. She longs for the sublime both as a cultural ideal dating back to her cultural history and as a representation of the practical wealth that may assure her survival. Emma, who longs for the sublime as representing the *crème de la crème* of her social milieu, as well as for the passionate young gentleman caller, finds her love with a relatively old gentleman who is portrayed as the superego of the play. Sally chooses Harry over the gentleman caller but only years after meeting him for the first time. It is as if Ilsa would have finally chosen Rick, but many years later, after he had settled, maybe opening a respected business in New York. Life is guided by tensions and layers of meaning, and the more complex we become the more layers we have to examine. In this context, the computational methodology of theme identification is a way of handling this messy complexity. Have we learned something new through this methodology? It is for the reader to decide.

10

Eating and dining: studying the dynamics of dinner

Cultural psychology as the study of symbolic systems mediating the variety of human forms of thought and practice (Valsiner 2007) has always been interested in the symbolic value of food and food-related practices (Rozin 2007). Paraphrasing Freud, a food is never just food but always a psychocultural object loaded with meaning derived from associations, connotations, metaphors, and cultural practices in which those senses are embedded and materialized.

Despite the great interest in the symbolic value of food and its related practices, studies that use computational tools to examine the semiotics of food are rare. In this chapter I aim to address this challenge. The chapter is based on a paper I co-authored with my colleagues Daniel Unger, who is an art historian interested in the visual representation of food, and Norbert Marwan, a physicist who has developed sophisticated methods for analyzing dynamic processes. More specifically, we focused our study on one main practice of food consumption: dinner, the main meal of the day in the West.

DINNER AS A CULTURAL PRACTICE

The reason for studying dinner is that dinner is a highly contextual practice. As McMillan (2001) explains, in medieval England everyone knew when they should eat their breakfast. The food served at these meals was also quite standard. The English breakfast before 1800 was limited to toast. The differences in times of meals and variety of foods were evident between classes. Broadly speaking, the nobles ate more food with greater variety than the middle-class traders and merchants and the peasants of the lower class (Albala 2002, 184–216). Indeed, for the lower classes soup was the main dish of the day. After all what is soup? Just boiled water with minimally added ingredients. Prior to the French Revolution, the most common food in France was a soup that contained a piece of bread with small pieces of onion and garlic all covered by boiling water. This was the same soup that was consumed a hundred years later by French coal miners and that became a symbol of French poverty as Emile Zola describes it in his famous 1885 *Germinal*. Zola describes those poor miners coming back in the evening for a meal in which the soup is not only the main dish of the day but also the only thing they will eat after a long day's work. The French word for "supper" (*souper*) relates to this cultural – or should we say gastronomical – phenomenon.

In early-modern chronicles of the high social strata, the largest meal of the day was around noon because people went to sleep at sundown. The French King François I (1494–1547) used to wake up at five o'clock in the morning, dine at nine o'clock, have supper at five o'clock in the afternoon, and go to sleep at nine o'clock in the evening. The English King Henry VIII (1491–1547) dined at ten o'clock in the morning and had his supper at four o'clock in the afternoon. The French King Louis XIV used to dine (*déjeuner*) at twelve o'clock (Mallery 1888).

The development of factories and streetcars led the middle-class dining times in the same direction. McMillan (2001) emphasizes that these changes took place first in London and only then at the periphery, which lagged behind the big city. In contrast with the idea that innovations emerge from the periphery of the network, in the case of dinner the logic is reversed, with the changing patterns of dinner emerging from the hub, London, and moving to the periphery. Today, dinner time in North America is more fluid than it was in the past, a fact that reflects the variety of practices characterizing these societies.

In fact one may even infer the variety of practices in a given society by calculating the discrepancies in dinner time. Think about it: the more technological and variable is the society in terms of labor practices the more variety is allowed for dinner time. Some people may work from home, some are obliged to keep the late working hours of competitive high-tech companies, and some may work night shifts that oblige them to eat their main meal even earlier than their medieval compatriots.

EATING AND DINING

In many European languages there is a separation between "to eat" and "to dine." The first relates to sustenance. The second is connected with social and cultural experience. The one reflects a biological need; the other is related

to a more sophisticated practice that is connected with an established organized meal with no direct connection to the basic physical need. When
someone is hungry he will eat. Sitting around a dining table has nothing to
do with being hungry. In early-modern societies the poor would eat *anytime*
they came across food (Mallery 1888, 195). For the higher classes eating was
associated with social-political engagement. As we can see again, the higher
class is almost defined by its efforts to show how distant it is from its animalistic origins and by its investment of enormous efforts into distancing
itself from these origins and from the lower classes. The gentleman is too
satisfied to be excited by food. I learned this lesson many years ago when as
a very young researcher I participated in a conference in Amsterdam with
my friend Zvi Bekerman. We were invited to the conference dinner, which
was used by the organizers to celebrate the birthday of their dear professor.
When the courses started coming to our table I wondered how they could
satisfy even a short, thin guy like me. In the Mediterranean area, food is
usually served to guests generously as a way of showing respect and probably of emphasizing the host's wealth. However, my friend explained to me
that food is not served to satisfy the guests. The high class, he explained to
me, arrives satisfied for dinner. Dinner is not about eating at all.

The social aspect concerned such exterior elements as manners, table-
cloths, dressing properly, and so forth. *How* to eat became much more
important than *what* to eat. In this respect it is interesting to note the different presentations in early-modern painting between someone who is eating
and someone who is dining. Indeed, both actions reflect social standing.
Only people of low social standing or children are presented as actually eating; they are often depicted chewing. In contrast, dining is presented as an
activity of people of high social standing. Well-dressed men and women of
high social standing never appear in paintings in the act of taking a bite or
chewing. They never expose their teeth like animals.

Ken Albala (2007, 8) uses a quote from Ottaviano Rabasco's *Il Convito*
of 1615 that may relate to this concept: a civil man "does not devour like the
wolf, nor does he chomp vigorously like a goat, nor gnaw on bones like a
dog." In paintings, those of high standing hold a glass of wine, a knife, or a
napkin. As we can see, again, the high class is removing itself from its animalistic origin. Sublimation is at the heart of this process.

How should we study dinner? The distributional hypothesis of language
(Harris 1954) suggests that words sharing the same context share some
kind of semantic similarity or relatedness. Following this hypothesis, which
has proved to be extremely helpful in natural language processing, we first
decided to identify the words, more specifically the nouns, that exist in the

context of "dinner." The decision to choose nouns only is justified by the attempt to identify the objects that exist in the semantic field of "dinner." As the nouns that exist in the lexical surroundings of a target word are indicative of the "topic" (Turney 2012), we started our analysis simply by identifying the collocations of "dinner."

Therefore, we identified in COHA the nouns and more specifically their general forms – their lemmas – that are collocated with "dinner" in a window of plus or minus nine lexical units. This means that we look at a window of nine lexical units to the right and to the left of our target word. The thirty-eight most frequent collocations were selected for further analysis. These words had values for at least ten data points over the time series (the minimal number of data points we needed for the unique method of analysis we decided to apply).

We identified these collocations in twenty equally distributed time points, ranging from 1810 to 2000, and measured their relative frequency in the whole population of words (words per million). For instance, the words "table," "evening," and "guest" were most frequently collocated with "dinner." These are trivial findings but, as I will show, some nontrivial finding popped up along the way.

HOW DO WE ANALYZE A TIME SERIES?

A recurrence plot (RP) is a method of nonlinear data analysis for the investigation of dynamic systems. The basic logic behind RPs is of characterizing the dynamics of repetition, which is of great interest in Continental philosophy (Deleuze 1995). This dynamics may be informative by providing us with a unique "fingerprint" of the system.

An RP is a binary matrix with entries for all such time pairs expressing recurring states – that is, if a state at time i recurs at time j we have $R(i,j) = 1$. The fraction of recurrences in the RP (the recurrence rate [RR]) corresponds to the probability that the system will revert to a former state: $p = sum\_\{i,j\} R\_\{i,j\}$.

A joint recurrence plot (JRP) is an extension of an RP in order to study the simultaneous recurrence of the states of two dynamic systems. A JRP is the element-wise product of the two RPs of the single systems. The joint recurrence rate (JRR) of the JRP is an estimate of the average probability of simultaneous recurrence in the two systems. If the two systems are independent, then this JRR is simply the product of the RRs of the two single RPs. If, however, both systems have the same recurrence structure (as for generalized synchronization), the JRR will be equal to the RR of the single systems (Marwan *et al.* 2007). Therefore, the ratio JRR:RR is a measure of coupling. In order to consider only the significant couplings, we combine the joint recurrence analysis with a bootstrap test and report only statistically significant results.

In our case, the percentage of words over the two hundred years can be considered as a dynamic system and the JRR can be used to measure the degree to which two words have a similar pattern over the years. Therefore, the JRR is a way of measuring the words' *coupling* or *synchronization*. Synchronization is highly important in studying dynamic systems, from the synchronization of lightning bugs to the synchronization of audience applause. Here we are not discussing synchronization of words in the same way as physicists have formalized the synchronization of lightning bugs. Our analysis identified a softer version of coupling between words. It is important to understand that what we study is the coupling of the words' dynamics and the way they similarly repeat their appearance in the population of words *over 200 years*.

Now, our interest was not in identifying a simple linear relation between words. A linear relation means that the rate of change is constant. As we wanted to avoid the analysis of simple linear correlation between the words' appearance, our results present pairs of words whose dynamics are synchronized over the years but where no simple linear correlation was found between their appearances.

From dynamics to the social representation of dinner

In itself, the list of synchronized words does not allow us to grasp the full meaning of dinner as a holistic social representation (Rudolph and Valsiner 2012). To gain a better Gestalt form of understanding these couplings, we built a directed graph out of the coupled words by drawing directed edges from each word to all of the words that synchronized with it.

To gain a better understanding of the graph (produced using yEd: www.yworks.com), we used the *number of connected edges* of each word/node in the graph, and arranged the nodes in a five-layer hierarchy according to this centrality index (see Figure 10.1).

At the top of the hierarchy we find the word "soup." The second hierarchy includes "guest" and "gong," and in the third layer we find the following words in a descending order of importance (where the numbers in brackets indicate the normalized number of connected edges): "thanksgiving" (0.69), "jacket" (0.69), "menu" (0.62), "dessert" (0.62), "beef" (0.62), "table" (0.56), "restaurant" (0.50), and "salad" (0.50).

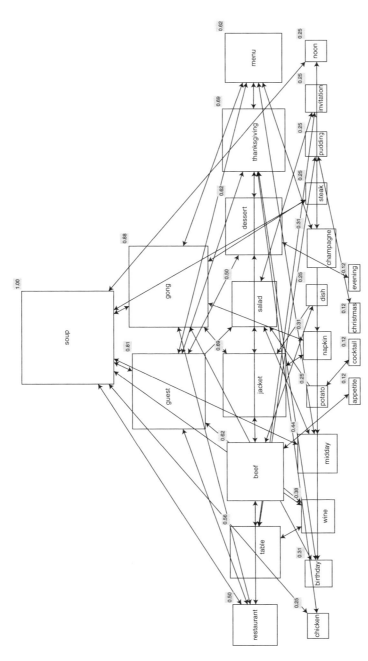

FIGURE 10.1 The graph of the coupled words organized according to the nodes' number of connected edges.

These results are far from intuitive or trivial. While "table" is the most salient noun associated with "dinner" in the corpus, when analyzing the dynamics of dinner-associated words over two hundred years we found that "soup" was the most central word!

This is a surprising result as, even among food objects, soup is not "quantitatively" the most salient. The probability of getting the word "wine" given the word "dinner" is four times higher than the probability of getting "soup" given "dinner" (0.004 vs. 0.001, respectively). Even the probability of getting "steak" given "dinner" is higher than getting "soup" given "dinner." At this point returning to in-depth interpretation is a must. The next section is an attempt to interpret the significance of "soup" in the dynamics of dinner.

Soup and restaurants

From the beginning of human history there have always been places where a person could eat, rest, sleep, and replace his horses. For those who were traveling, there were stalls of food waiting on the main roads. All nations have food stalls to this day. In towns there were always places that served meals, mainly those establishments that specialized in alcoholic beverages. Inns, taverns, pubs, bodegas, *weinstuben*, and *brauereien*, to name only a few, were very popular institutions populated by members of the lower class.

In this respect eighteenth-century London was different because it contained respectable taverns for the upper middle class and aristocracy. In eighteenth-century France inns had a terrible reputation for bad food. A person who wanted something to eat was offered the one dish that was served. Food was available all day long. Another kind of forerunner of the restaurant was the *table d'hôte*, French for "eating place." It served various kinds of courses but at a fixed hour. Guests paid in advance and could eat as much as they wanted (Ketcham 1983, 75–6).

Restaurants as we know them today have existed only since the second half of the eighteenth century. The restaurant was invented in Paris by Boulanger. They were also known as *Champ d'oiseaux*, meaning "to restore." Boulanger began by selling meat soups (*bouillons*). Later he added other kinds of meat such as mutton. Diderot complimented Boulanger's food: "I left to have dinner with the restaurateur on the rue des Poulies. One eats well there but pays dearly for the service" (Pitte 1999, 474). A famous eighteenth-century restaurant opened in 1786 in Paris – Les Trois Frères Provencaux. This restaurant was very well known for its fish soup (*bouillabaisse*). Therefore, soup has been a primary food and has acquired precedence over other meal types.

From a network perspective (Barabási 2003), this precedence is of great significance as it increases the probability that the node in the network will acquire the status of a hub (a well-connected node), precisely as revealed in our analysis. However, an etymological analysis of soup (www.etymonline. com) reveals another layer of its cultural significance.

The term "soup" originated in 1650 from French *soupe*, which originated from late-Latin "bread soaked in broth," which in itself emerged from a Germanic source that means "to take liquid." Soup is therefore not only a food that has precedence in the culinary history of Europe but is also associated with a symbolically loaded food – bread. Soup is also associated with symbolic redundancy. The broth is "hot" (the adjective mostly associated with "soup" in our corpus) and enriches the bread with taste, nutrition, and positive associations.

This redundancy is of significant importance and it is an additional aspect that separates the soup from other dinner-related ingredients such as "wine," while at the same time pointing to the cultural semiotic significant of dinner as a presentation of wealth (i.e., redundancy) for the establishment of social power. The "redundancy" of soup is further interpreted in the next section.

THE SURPLUS OF SOUP: INTEGRATIVE SEMIOTIC ANALYSIS AND DISCUSSION

The term "surplus value" is associated with Marx, who used it to denote the value created by workers in excess of their own labor cost. It is actually the "redundancy" created by the workers. In information theory, redundancy is a term used to denote the "number of bits used to transmit a message minus the number of bits of actual information in the message" (Wikipedia).

The surplus or redundancy is interpreted by Gregory Bateson (2000, 30) as "meaning": according to him, "meaning" may be regarded as an approximate synonym of pattern, redundancy, information, and "restraint." Bateson further discussed meaning and redundancy in the sense of a patterning (2000, 420), through which uncertainty is reduced. The idea of linking "meaning," "redundancy," and "patterning" is specifically interesting.

To understand this linking let us move to Saussure (1972, 113), who equated meaning with value. A value involves: "(1) something *dissimilar* which can be exchanged for the item whose value is under consideration, and (2) *similar* things which can be *compared* with the item whose value is under consideration."

For example, money is an abstract system of signs/values. In this system, like in the linguistic system, a one-dollar bill has no value/meaning in itself. The meaning of a one-dollar bill can be determined only in a closed system of values. To determine the value of a dollar we should know that a one-dollar bill can be exchanged for something different (e.g., a candy bar) and that its value can be compared to another value within the same system of currency (e.g., it may be exchanged for Euros). The language system is a system of pure values whose function is to combine the two orders of difference – phonic and conceptual – in the making of signs.

In *Capital*, Marx identified the "exchange of equivalents" as the "immanent" law of exchange. As suggested by Goux (1990, 9): "Metaphors, symptoms, signs, representations: it is always through replacement that values are created." As a sign is arbitrarily associated with the signified, the floating nature of value in its semiotic sense is inevitable. Value is implied in every replacement and therefore constituted by circulation.

How can surplus value be created in a semiotic system of exchange and replacement? My suggestion is that redundancy/surplus is produced when a signifier exceeds the limits of signification within a given system of exchange. Let me illustrate this point.

Let us assume that in an imaginary society a person earns a hundred coins per day. For simplicity let us also assume that he is a Robinson Crusoe kind of person who is not supported by others and does not have to support others. Fifty coins are used by our solitary figure to satisfy his basic needs, those that might result in death unless satisfied. The rest of the money has no clear signifier. The man is satisfied and therefore the money remaining in his pocket has no clear reference, neither food nor drink, for which it can be exchanged – not even savings. In this imaginary case, surplus seems like the redundancy discussed by information theory, a useless appendix that should be removed. However, as insightfully realized by Marx and elaborated by Goux, it is precisely this surplus that is responsible for the dynamic circulation of value.

The analogy we draw between money and language is deeply grounded in the European discourse. As argued by Gray (1996, 1): "The metaphorical field circumscribing analogies between language and money is undoubtedly one of the most productive in all Western culture." In fact, it is not a mere analogy but rather "a deep-seated isomorphism between the domains of money and language."

The isomorphism can be explained by the deep-seated nature of the semiotic system and its phase transition in the eighteenth century in Europe, where the desubstantiation of value became more radical than ever.

As argued by Goux (1997, 172),

> What matters is not what the value of some shared "really" is, at a certain moment, but what its value is going to be, later ... What the dealer desires is not to own, but to "make a difference." The whole game unfolds in the difference between value at time (t) and value at time (t').

Goux points out that the value originally associated with concrete goods has turned into a "difference that makes a difference," which is *precisely Bateson's definition of information*!

The value's fluctuating nature could not have emerged without a surplus or redundant meaning having no simple system of equivalents. That the nature of value changed during the eighteenth century through the logic of surplus into a floating signifier brings us back to our soup. However, before our soup, let us recall that the surplus of love has been discussed in the context of Dolly Parton's love lexicon. *This is not a coincidence!* In his insightful book *Signifying Nothing*, Brian Rottman (1993) has pointed at the way allegedly different cultural phenomena may be traced to the same semiotic origin emerging at a certain historical phase. The accommodation of wealth and the change in the value system identified by Marx and Goux still echoes in current Western culture. Now back to soup.

Originally soup was a symbolically loaded food (i.e., bread) soaked with enriching liquid. Bread of course has a loaded symbolic history, specifically for Christian Europe (Galavaris 1970), as illustrated by its major part in the Last Supper and in the two feeding miracles with loaves and fishes. In fact, the Last Supper was probably conducted in accordance with the Jewish religious tradition (Galavaris 1970). After all, Jesus was born, lived, and died as a Jew. According to this tradition the main course began with blessing God for providing the bread, a custom every practicing Jew still follows. Jesus's alleged use of the bread as symbolizing his body and therefore the son's body constituted the Eucharist.

From a psychological point of view, the sharing of the symbolic body by the father is of great importance. Years later another radical Jew by the name of Sigmund Freud developed a theory about the origins of human culture by inventing a mythological-psychological story about an ancient father who was murdered (and probably consumed) by his naughty sons. The symbolic act of consuming one's dead father is therefore of great significance to cultural psychologists. The bread therefore symbolizes the flesh of the father and his materialization in the son. In fact, the modern slang associating bread with money (i.e., "dough") preserves this deep-seated semiotic chain associating the corpus of the consumed father with the semiotic object epitomizing surplus. Money is therefore embedded in the body and mediated through the semiosis of bread.

Around 1850 in France, bread was eaten at all meals and in all forms (Drouard 2007, 285). It was the main food of the farmer. The fact that bread was enriched with liquid, which in itself has no substantive value (the liquid itself is not really food), turns the soup into a representative of the *floating value*, the *bread–body* enriched with *surplus–soul*. In contrast with wine or a steak, which have value but no clear redundancy, soup is by historical definition a value-laden food.

Here lies the explanation of why soup has turned into the first kind of food to be served to the higher class. To recall, dining, in contrast with eating, is a symbolically loaded activity and a display window of wealth (i.e., surplus value) functionally used to impress others and to constitute social status.

In this context, the *tertium comparationis* underlying soup and money is the surplus of meaning associated with the basic good. The eighteenth-century upper class was actually epitomizing the new zeitgeist of its time, a zeitgeist that echoes through the next two hundred years of textual history. *This is the same surplus that underlies the emergence of the gentleman and the rise of modern love.* Only through the nonlinear analysis we have used in this study could such a complex dynamic have been rigorously elucidated.

Rudolph and Valsiner (2012) ask: "What kind of mathematics is appropriate to use in modeling complex dynamical wholes?" Their discussion emphasizes the holistic, Gestalt notion of psychological wholes and their dynamic nature. Dinner as a situation is a Gestalt that has been transformed over the years. By identifying the nonlinear coupling of dinner's collocated objects we have studied the way dinner, as a Gestalt, has been transformed yet preserves its structure by moving in a psychological phase space (Valsiner and Rudolph 2008) of the studied culture. Moreover, by weaving dinner's coupled objects into a network we have been able to identify soup as a major component and to delve into its symbolic value.

11

Getting even: the cultural psychology of revenge and what computers can do about it

Sweeney Todd is a character who originated in the Victorian era and made his most recent appearance as the hero of a movie directed by Tim Burton in 2007. The hero is a barber and one may wonder how a barber, a profession without any sex appeal, could be turned into the hero of a movie. However, Sweeney Todd, played by Johnny Depp, isn't a typical barber. He is "the Demon Barber of Fleet Street," as indicated by the subtitle of the movie. Todd is a man on a mission, and the mission is to get even with Judge Turpin, who destroyed his life. Turpin lusted for Todd's wife and got rid of Todd with false allegations in order to satisfy his carnal lust.

On his way to achieving his goal to get even with the Judge, the bloody barber slices the throats of his clients, while his lover, played by the wonderful Helena Bonham Carter, disposes of the bodies by turning them into highly attractive meat pies. As we can see, the passion to annihilate others is deeply associated with what we might call "oral aggression."

Todd and his lover are not only serial murderers but cannibals too. This point is specifically interesting as it weaves psychoanalytic and psychocultural ideas. The European mind of this period, fascinated and horrified with cannibalism, was actually covering its own fondness for devouring the meat of its internal and external opponents, whether the lower class within Europe or the "primitives" of the colonies.

Burton's interpretation of an earlier musical presents nineteenth-century London in a demonic magical light and produces another instance of an artistic genre that is greatly enjoyed by audiences – revenge.

Revenge is one of the oldest cultural practices. The ancient biblical law demanding an eye for an eye is just one instance of vengeance. The Western ideas of revenge can be traced back to the Old Testament and then through the New Testament and Roman laws (Lord Smail and Gibson 2009) and up to modern times, when the nation state, as the extension of the subject's moral agency, has turned vengeance into a forbidden activity indicating a primitive and barbarian form of justice.

From a psychological point of view, it is extremely interesting that fantasies of revenge, as indicated by the popularity of the vengeance genre, flourish precisely in a period when the objective security of the individual has reached a peak. Why are we so excited by fantasies of revenge? Have we never been very modern or is it an indication of a narcissistic personality that cannot find justice in the impersonal law?

One recent answer is given from an evolutionary and functional perspective. McCullough *et al.* (2011) suggest that revenge is a "deterrence system designed to change others' incentives regarding the self and one's kin or allies." The idea is simple, as evolutionary ideas can be: "Revenge signals that subsequent acts will be subject to the same contingent response, thereby altering others' incentives." According to this functional explanation, revenge emerged from a more primitive retaliation system that is evident in nonhuman organisms too (Clutton-Brock and Parker 1995; Jensen *et al.* 2007).

Revenge discourages aggressors from harming the avenger a second time. If you hurt me once I will "get even," first to prevent you from repeating your aggression and second to establish my reputation as "nonprey." This idea is appealing in its simplicity but has its own problems. Retaliation may exist in nonhuman organisms but in these societies this form of punishment is used to establish dominance and so on. In a group of chimpanzees, the dominant male may punish a younger male who challenges him, but observing a low-status and weak avenger murdering the alpha male in a well-planned ambush, like the one planned for Julius Caesar, is not a reasonable scenario. Jensen *et al.* (2007, 13,046) suggest that, "Like humans, chimpanzees retaliate against personally harmful actions, but unlike humans, they are indifferent to simply personally disadvantageous outcomes and are therefore not spiteful." In other words, punishment and retaliation are not the same as revenge.

In the movie *Death Wish* (1974), Charles Bronson gets even with a gang that attacked his family. The chance of being attacked again by the same gang is extremely small, whereas the chance of risking his life and the lives of his potential next generation to come by confronting the criminals is extremely high. In addition, he doesn't have to solve any reputation issue. One look at the guy and you clearly understand that he is not potential prey. So how effective is revenge in producing direct deterrence? Assuming revenge to be an effective strategy would have led into a more stabilized world than we see. Genghis Khan, the bloody leader of the Mongol Empire, was probably well aware of the human wish to get even, but this didn't prevent him from performing his bloody deeds. Even in the most ancient documented history of human beings, in which people lived in small groups, revenge was not a highly effective mechanism.

Revenge can't simply restore a lost equilibrium, one that can be corrected by apology, for instance (Liebersohn *et al.* 2004). It can be a response to violating a code of honor. However, from a psychocultural perspective, revenge is specifically interesting as long as it involves the semiotically mediated nature of our harm and fantasies of retaliation. Indeed, and as taught by Luria and Vygotsky (1930), taking into account the evolutionary dimension of revenge is inevitable. Revenge has its roots in our ancestors' urge to punish those who harmed them or to restore their "face" when it had been degraded by others. However, revenge has a more complex aspect that I would like to further explore. The next section discusses the psychology of revenge by offering a novel interpretation of it.

My point of departure is the highly influential psychoanalytic interpretation of revenge as an expression of narcissistic rage. This interpretation will be presented, challenged, and elaborated. Following my interpretation, I will show how computers can help us to identify vengeful intentions.

REVENGE: A PSYCHOANALYTIC PERSPECTIVE

The ubiquity of revenge in human culture has not been proportionally addressed by the psychoanalytic literature. As Beattie argues (2005, 513), "The theme of revenge … has been relatively slow to engage the attention of psychoanalysis." Moreover, the study of revenge has been dominated by the seminal work of Kohut, who suggests in "Thoughts on narcissism and narcissistic rage" (1972) that revenge is the expression of narcissistic rage in response to narcissistic injury. This interpretation is clearly presented by Beattie (2005, 515), who argues: "The high-octane jet fuel of revenge is narcissistic rage, occasioned by humiliating attacks on the grandiose self with its idealized self-object, which result in a primitive drive for control and omnipotence through revenge."

This individual-centric explanation is as follows. All of us are to a certain extent narcissists as we must love ourselves. Otherwise we are doomed to misery. Some of us, however, have a distorted form of narcissism. They have a narcissistic personality disorder. These people are obsessively occupied with their self and its value. They are highly sensitive to their self-value and may respond to criticism with rage. Their self-occupation involves a sense of grandiosity that covers the painful truth, which is their deep sense of fragility. When a narcissist is degraded he or she cannot bear the pain. The resilience of the narcissist is actually zero. As a response to a degrading act the narcissist, with his or her fantasies of self-worth and deep fragility, may respond with rage, a rage that may lead to revenge.

As well as insightfully diagnosing the aggressive, archaic, and destructive aspects of revenge, Kohut paved the way to future generations of psychologists studying revenge in various settings, from the clinical to the cultural (e.g., Goldberg 2004; Goldwater 2004; Lane 1995; Lotto 2006; Werman 1993). However, there are at least two major difficulties with Kohut's interpretation.

The first is that narcissistic injury and rage cannot fully exhaust the complexity of revenge, and therefore the validity of Kohut's explanation is questionable. For example, in his classical paper on revenge, Kohut refers to the novel *Michael Kohlhaas* by von Kleist (1973) as a novel epitomizing revenge in response to narcissistic injury. Reading this novel I was shocked by the gap between the text and Kohut's interpretation. In his seminal paper "Interpretation and history," Umberto Eco (1992) warns us against using texts regardless of the texts' own logic. This kind of expletory reading is evident in Kohut's interpretation of *Michael Kohlhaas*. A close, critical, and respectful reading of *Michael Kohlhaas* does not fully support this interpretation or the possible attribution of Kohlhaas's vengeful activity to a narcissistic personality disorder. I will get into this point later, but reading *Michael Kohlhaas* I was personally shocked by the way Kohut's theorization guided and directed his reading of the text. Why destroy such a beautiful theory with the ugliness of reality …

Let's not forget that theories are like maps; they are never reality itself but a representation of reality only or representations of other maps. Some maps are better representations than others, and this statement is context-dependent of course. However, as Bateson (2000) has urged us to understand, we should not confuse the map with the territory. Kohut's theory is a map, but unfortunately it doesn't seem to represent the territory it wishes to describe. One may counterargue that Kohut failed to choose his example well but that his theory is still a valuable map. This counterargument will be challenged too. Here we move on to another line of critique.

The antiquity and prevalence of revenge at its various levels of intensity suggest that, similarly to apology (Liebersohn *et al.* 2004), revenge is primarily a basic psychosocial mechanism for repairing *face-threatening acts*. "Face," in the sense of prestige or honor, is an important sociological concept that points to the fact that our value and meaning among our group's members are semiotically and socially determined.

In contrast with old, anachronistic ideas, even the king isn't born with blue blood. His prestige is derived only from the social network of ideas to which he is born. According to this argument my positive public image may be threatened by others. Politeness is therefore a system of habits that aim to protect my face. If you were to enter into a traditional Arabic house and kiss the wife of your host as a friendly gesture, you would violate the norms of politeness, threaten the face of your male host, and probably have to run for your life.

Value, whether the value of a coin or of a human being, is determined only on the social-semiotic sphere, and when our value is threatened we may respond with anger and aggression. This is the bread and butter of social logic so why bother ourselves with a narcissistic interpretation of revenge?

When Beattie describes revenge in terms of narcissistic rage she probably addresses exceptional and theatrical acts of revenge such as those that constitute a unique genre in cinema, theater, and literature. From Bruce Lee's *Enter the Dragon* to Charles Bronson's *Death Wish*, from *The Count of Monte Cristo* to the murderous barber *Sweeney Todd*, vengeful personalities have been a source of artistic interest and pleasure. They are pleasurable not because they represent the well-established norms of society but because they go deeper into our innermost fantasies. However, it is questionable whether revenge can be clearly explained by "narcissistic rage" even in the dramatic cases presented by this artistic genre.

The problem with interpreting revenge in terms of narcissistic rage is closely associated with the second difficulty – the cultural one. Revenge is a common and sometimes obligatory social norm in many cultures. Is it justified to describe these cultures as suffering from narcissistic injury? Can we argue that the collective self of the group is responding with narcissistic rage to narcissistic injury?

Despite his deep interest in culture and historical processes, Kohut was clearly insensitive to the difference between the individual and collective levels of analysis, and easily – too easily, one may argue – applied his insights to the collective level. This insensitivity is evident in his reference to Benedict's naive diagnosis of Japanese culture as being inclined toward narcissistic rage due to parenting patterns involving mockery and shame (Benedict 1946, quoted in Kohut 1972). Reading Benedict, one might wonder whether she was familiar with Western Victorian patterns of parenting, such as those illustrated in *David Copperfield*, by Charles Dickens.

Today, based on our critical and reflective understanding of other cultures and our realization that shifting between the individual and cultural levels of analysis is not straightforward (Bateson 2000), one cannot naively accept the idea of a vengeful culture as suffering from some kind of "narcissistic disorder of the collective self."

In this chapter, I would like to present an alternative psychoanalytic reading of revenge that is applicable to both the individual and cultural levels of analysis. This reading, originally presented in Neuman (2012), is mainly based on ideas developed by the psychoanalyst Wilfred Bion. According to the interpretation I will present, a vengeful person cannot contain his painful experience. As a result he feels insecure and conceives the world as simultaneously and paradoxically existing in a state of *vicious order* and *monstrous disorder*. As a defensive act he develops a twisted form of superego and launches his revenge from the nonpersonal stance of "duty," "law," or "justice." This defensive act allows him to play the role of God in its most archaic, rigid, and punishing form. The biblical style of God, the same God who set Sodom and Gomorrah on fire. Fire, as we will see, is a repeated theme in revenge, and for good reasons.

As the world is conceived by the vengeful person to be in a state of monstrous disorder that threatens to annihilate him, the avenger takes the complementary form of annihilating the "external" order, what I metaphorically describe as "injecting disorder to order," and "ordering" the internal disorder.

Instead of presenting these ideas in a linear sequence I have chosen to present them through the interpretation of two novels epitomizing revenge: *Michael Kohlhaas* by Heinrich von Kleist and *V for Vendetta* by Alan Moore and David Lloyd. This presentation will be followed by the analysis of a murderous avenger and a link to the social-cultural level of analysis.

MICHAEL KOHLHAAS: THE BLOOD VENGEANCE OF THE HORSE DEALER

Kohlhaas, the horse dealer, is described by von Kleist as "one of the most upright," an "extraordinary man," "the very model of a good citizen," benevolent, fair-minded, yet at the same time "one of the most terrible men" whose "sense of justice turned him into a brigand and a murderer" (von Kleist 1973, 87).

The plot is rather simple. On his way to sell some of his horses, Kohlhaas passes through the castle of the Junker (a member of the Prussian nobility) Wenzel von Tronka. Using subterfuge, which Kohlhaas sees through, the Junker's knights ask him to leave two of his horses in the castle. Kohlhaas experiences this request as a "shameful demand" (von Kleist 1973). Trying to appeal to the Junker's sense of justice, the knights respond to Kohlhaas with humiliation, as the Junker calls him a "poor wretch" (Kleist 1973, 91). However, in contrast with our expectation, this act of theft and degradation *does not* lead to narcissistic rage, as Kohlhaas later returns to the castle "with no bitterness in his heart" beyond "the ordinary distress of the world" (von Kleist 1973, 43).

Now this is clearly not a response we could have expected from a person with a narcissistic personality disorder! Here you see why Kohut's interpretation is flawed. When examining your theory you can't use "true positives" only. You can't use only the examples that support your thesis.

Moreover, when he discovers the poor physical condition of his stolen horses, Kohlhaas feels helpless and is ready to give up. He is then degraded again, this time by the castellan. While wondering what to do next, Kohlhaas absorbs another insult from the Junker, who dismisses his complaint and calls him a "son of a bitch." At this point there is an emerging recognition in Kohlhaas's mind that "it was his duty to the world to do everything in his power to get satisfaction for himself for the wrong done him, and a guarantee against future ones for his fellow citizens" (von Kleist 1973, 95).

The reader is probably curious to know whether at this point Kohlhaas – the "mad narcissist" – is going to purchase an arsenal of automatic weapons and start a bloody trail of retaliation. The reader will probably be disappointed, as even at this phase our hero is holding himself tight.

However, there is another significant point in the above quote. Kohlhaas seems to respond scrupulously to the situation by including his "fellow citizens." From Jesus to Gandhi, history provides admirable instances of people who have transformed their personal painful experience into a quest for social justice. Apparently, Kohlhaas's "emerging recognition" follows the same path. However, an appeal to a transcendental sense of "duty" may indicate something quite different from a quest for justice. To explain this point and to question Kohlhaas's motives, I turn to Bakhtin.

As Bakhtin (1999) insightfully argues, *there is no alibi in existence*. I have no alibi in existence because I cannot claim to have been elsewhere than in the concrete and actual place where a deed was performed. In other words, I cannot *observe* my existence from a transcendental or theoretical standpoint, but only from my own particular and singular place. I emphasize the notion of observation because this is one of the superego's main functions and because the emergence of a unique form of the superego characterizes revenge in its most extreme form.

According to Bakhtin's moral/epistemological stance, an individual can never escape from his responsibility and has no "alibi" to justify an immoral deed. It goes without saying that transcending the personal perspective is the hallmark of ethics, empathy, and altruism. However, this is not the case for Kohlhaas. As implied by Bakhtin, we should suspect even a moral deed launched from a purely transcendental perspective.

As we quickly learn from the story, Kohlhaas is not a social reformer. His appeal to "duty" is the appeal of a person who cannot contain his personal and painful experience and seeks for an alibi while the seeds of his bloody deeds start germinating in his mind.

Kohlhaas's appeal to duty represents a process of *depersonification* of the painful experience and a *split* in which an internal object (Ogden 1983) representing the law or the superego starts functioning in a rigid and detached form. All of us have some kind of internalized regulatory functions. When we were children and were told by our parents "No!" our mind internalized these interactions in our episodic memory and learned from them norms to represent these interactions in our semantic memory.

In our mind the "law" is intermingled with relationships with significant others – the father who said "No!" but in other cases said "Yes!" My first argument is that vengeful activities as epitomized by Kohlhaas involve a process of depersonification and withdrawal to a rigid form of the superego (Holmes 2011) that functions as the alibi for justifying the destructiveness of the bloody deed. The reason for this process will be elaborated later.

Nevertheless, even at this point of our story, Kohlhaas does not express the intention to get even. His groom, Herse, who was beaten and expelled from the castle, is the one who seeks revenge and wants "to burn down the robber's nest" (von Kleist 1973, 96). Giving up his fantasy, the groom decides to "let God lay it [the Junker's castle] in ashes." Who is going to take the role of God? As will be argued below, the withdrawal to a transcendental perspective represents a split and the emergence of a superego, turning the vengeful person into a God-like figure.

For now, however, Kohlhaas is still seeking justice. He appeals to the court, which dismisses his suit out of hand. He then appeals to another representative of the law – the Governor of Brandenburg – and feels "more confident than ever before about the outcome of his case" (von Kleist 1973, 103). Unfortunately, his naive trust in the law and its representative has no ground; this appeal is dismissed too and Kohlhaas feels "consumed with rage" (104). This is when his vengeance starts crystallizing: "Through the pain he felt seeing the world in such a state of *monstrous disorder* flashed a thrill of inward satisfaction at knowing that henceforth he would be at peace with himself" (104, my emphasis).

This is a turning point in the novel, where the call for justice starts crystallizing into bloody deeds. Kohlhaas realizes that he is alone in his "struggle for justice" and that he must deal with the pain of observing the world in a state of monstrous disorder. Loneliness, as will be further argued, is a disease, and a crucial factor in the emergence of revenge.

In contrast with Kohlhaas's view, the "world" is highly ordered as it defends authorities such as the Junker. One may disagree with this order but cannot deny that it *is* order – a very simple and basic form of order, justifying those who are in power simply because they are in power. Like in a group of chimpanzees, justice stands to the right of the dominant male.

It is not the world that is in a state of "monstrous disorder" but Kohlhaas himself. Why is the world conceived by Kohlhaas to be in a state of "monstrous disorder," and why does he feel alone in the face of this monstrous disorder?

Who contains the pain?

In Bion's theory, the primitive experience of monstrous disorder facing each and every individual throughout life is chaotic and threatening. We live in a world in which order is not given for free but constructed through efforts. In order to digest the disorder one faces, one needs the mediation of containing others (Bion 1962a), whether "real" others in the early phase of development or their representative internalized function as one turns into an adult. Think about suffering pain as a child. Our basic fear is that such pain might signal our annihilation. Ashes to ashes, the second law of thermodynamics is always present, threatening to return us into the disorganized form of matter from which we emerged.

In this context, maternal reverie functions to patch fragmented aspects of the "rudimentary conscious" (López-Corvo 2003), the fragmented elements of experience, into a digestible form. It contains and "digests" the pain. As the term "maternal" has been established in the literature as being associated with containment and reverie, I will use it, assuming the reader understands the concept "maternal" as indicating a function that can be performed by both the mother and the father. In this context, the superego as both the observing and regulatory function plays an important role. As proposed by Holmes (2011), in the absence of a guiding internalized parent, the individual is on its own, doing its best to achieve its security.

Loneliness is therefore a lack of relationships through which we may transform fragmented, disorganized, and painful experience into a meaningful pattern. When the containment fails to properly function, two things can happen. First, the individual may respond by developing a twisted form of superego that appears as a transcendental and emotionally detached perspective, like the one structured by Kohlhaas. In other words, the absence of a guiding and containing other who may digest one's pain might lead to the "invention" of an imaginary transcendental observation and regulatory perspective that may be used as an alibi and an omnipotent fantasy for transforming the painful experience through a bloody deed.

Second, as the outside world cannot be digested, it may be experienced as a chaos (monstrous disorder) that threatens to annihilate the individual. This world is paradoxically conceived as *viciously ordered* and *monstrously disordered* at the same time. The result is a defensive attack on the vicious order in an attempt to annihilate it and by doing so avoid the monstrous disorder. At the same time there is an attempt to transform the internal chaos by ordering it from the outside. These ideas are elaborated in the following sections.

I am the law

According to Lacan (1977), the symbolic father is not a subject but a position in the symbolic order. The symbolic function identifies the father with "the figure of the law" (Lacan 1977, 67). This symbolic father may be discussed in terms of a modern relational perspective of the superego (Holmes 2011).

As insightfully argued by Freud (1964, 136): "A child's superego is constructed not on the model of the parent, but the parent's superego." The parent's superego is an internalized form of the society's observing and regulatory functions. Therefore, the *superego is constituted through parental and institutional practices of observation and regulation*. This is a crucial point in my thesis as it explains the relevance of the analysis at the individual level to the cultural level of analysis.

The regulatory function of the superego primarily aims to defend the individual against danger (Holmes 2011). As the symbolic father, the law (the external order) fails in defending Kohlhaas, and, as there is no containing function, the superego turns into an omnipotent, defensive, and destructive force. The reason is simple. As the symbolic father/the law/ vicious order does not protect his son, and as the maternal reverie does not digest the monstrous disorder, the son turns into his own father and feels free to ignore external regulatory constraints and to target his aggression against the law.

The process of a person facing "monstrous disorder" that threatens to annihilate him or her in the absence of a defending symbolic father can turn the individual into his or her own father. The idea of a person turning into his or her own father is poetically illustrated in Robert Pinsky's poem "Samurai song," here partially presented:

> When I had no roof I made
> Audacity my roof. When I had
> No supper my eyes dined.
>
> When I had no eyes I listened.
> When I had no ears I thought.
> When I had no thought I waited.
>
> *When I had no father I made*
> *Care my father. When I had*
> *No mother I embraced order.*
>
> (Lehman 2006, 951, my emphasis)

Reading this poem from a psychoanalytic perspective, one may interpret it as a poem dealing with absence and compensation. The poet describes his self-sufficiency as compensating for various absences. When he "had no father" he "made," all by himself, "care" be his father.

In the real world, however, we cannot "make" our own fathers. Our fathers are gradually internalized and woven into the emerging self, what I have elsewhere described as the "I-to-be-formed" (Neuman 2009c), through a delicate, constructive, and conflictual process. I can never be *my* real father or the symbolic father. When one turns into one's own father, a symmetrical pathological equation is created.

As Matte-Blanco (1975) insightfully suggests, our mind is governed by two complementary forms of logic (i.e., bi-logic): symmetrical and asymmetrical. Parent–child relationships are never symmetrical. I am the son of my father but my father can never be my son. The same is true for the collective. We are symbolic sons of our ancestors but we can never be the ancestors of our ancestors. Pathology becomes evident when a group believes in its superior God-like status, the Nazi *Übermensch* or *Übervolk*.

Asymmetry is the logic that governs our conscious life. When symmetry is established, the separation of consciousness from unconsciousness, which is governed by symmetrical logic, is violated. The "contact barrier" (Bion 1962b), the function that serves as a boundary between the conscious and the unconscious, is broken, and pathology prevails.

This idea is in line with the function of the superego. "A key part of the superego's role is to manage boundaries" (Holmes 2011, 1238). When a containing function does not exist and a detached superego emerges to defend the individual, it is characterized with an omnipotent nature that indicates the collapse of boundaries and the symmetrization of father and son. Therefore, when Kohlhaas turns into *The Father*, he expresses a pathological dynamic that when inseminated into the world can give birth only to bloody consequences.

The plot continues when Lisbeth, Kohlhaas's wife, senses the emerging catastrophe. She convinces him to let her bring his petition to the elector, whom she used to know. Lisbeth symbolizes the containing mother unsuccessfully, as she is unable to prevent the catastrophe. Stabbed by the elector's brutal bodyguards, she returns severely wounded and dies.

At this point Kohlhaas's emerging revenge fantasy takes the form of a bloody deed. His previous pain conflates with his unbearable grief and he chases the Junker and sets fire to his castles – once in Leipzig and three times in Wittenberg. Fire is an important aspect of his revenge as it is the ultimate annihilating process that restores the state of the world to its symmetric origin, to maximum entropy: "ashes to ashes, dust to dust." As we can see, the act of revenge does not really aim to bring justice but to annihilate what Kohlhaas conceives as monstrous disorder.

Knowledge and revenge

The plot of *Kohlhaas* continues to unfold as the reader is introduced to a mysterious gypsy fortune-teller in the marketplace. The elector, who is in the market, is astonished by the fortune-teller's prophetic ability, and his curiosity is evoked when she writes down his future and puts her prediction in a capsule. However, she refuses to give the capsule to the elector and surprisingly gives it instead to an anonymous person in the audience, saying, "Take good care of it and some day it will save your life!" (von Kleist 1973, 163). This person is … Kohlhaas.

The elector is obsessed with the capsule. Kohlhaas refuses to deliver the prophecy to him because he feels the elector to be responsible for Lisbeth's death and the injustice done to Kohlhaas.

The gypsy fortune-teller looks like "Lisbeth's mother" and "reminds him vividly of Lisbeth" (von Kleist 1973, 176). The fortune-teller is therefore equated with both the mother and the wife. Condensation has been identified by Freud as one of the mechanisms constituting the unconscious and the dream work. The story uses this mechanism to create an artistic impact on our mind by symmetrizing the mother and the wife. This condensed object represents one of Bion's three basic relations: knowledge, the function that translates fragmented experience into a digestible form.

As the plot unfolds, Kohlhaas seemingly innocently turns himself in to the authorities. He is incarcerated and falsely led to believe that justice will be done to him as promised. Conceiving the world as a "monstrous disorder," Kohlhaas's move is probably not an act of innocence but a suicidal act, a death wish (underlying the vengeful personality) to annihilate both the world and himself. Kohlhaas is executed. The elector attends the execution in order to get the capsule and the prophecy. But, as a final act of revenge, Kohlhaas swallows the capsule just before dying, literally assimilating knowledge into himself and so turning the vicious order – or, more precisely, its representative, the elector of Saxony – into a man "shattered in body and soul" (von Kleist 1973, 121).

Following Bion, I contend that knowledge emerges as a primitive form of relation in the mirroring phase, when projected beta-elements are transformed and reflected back to the infant, and a correspondence is established between the projected elements and their transformed image (Neuman 2009a).

In this process, we can see how primitive knowledge involves a *symmetry* established between the "I-to-be-formed" and the "other-to-become"; I know you because I know what is in you. I further argue that the interpretation of this basic form of knowledge resonates with the most basic sense of knowledge in our culture as an organic act of incorporation through eating or sexual intercourse.

Indeed, the knowledge given by the gypsy/Lisbeth to Kohlhaas is *literally* incorporated, like food, into his body. Kohlhaas "knows" through the "knowledge" contained in his body. In this sense, the female figure (Lisbeth?) is a dual representative of knowing. As her husband, Kohlhaas "knows" her in the biblical, sexual sense: he is "inside her." On the other hand, he knows her by letting her get "inside him" (i.e., by swallowing the capsule). *He is contained in the container that he recursively contains.*

This symmetrical, mutual knowledge can be understood as a form of reverie, for the chaotic beta-elements have now found their containing figure. Indeed, the gypsy is right, though not literally, when she says, "It [the prophecy] will save your life." Kohlhaas is executed but finds rest for his tormented soul in "knowing" and being "known." He gains knowledge of that which is beyond our grasp by containing an organized portion of the transformed monstrous disorder within his corpse.

There is another aspect to this knowledge. Bion argues that starvation of truth (i.e., knowing the real) is analogous to physical starvation (Bion 1962b, 310; see also Fisher 2006). The elector is actually starved of knowledge by

Kohlhaas as an act of revenge, and Kohlhaas himself is satisfied by consuming the capsule.

Weineck maintains that von Kleist's literary work expresses an "intense engagement with the question of (patriarchal) law" and involves a "systematic project to undermine all forms of fatherhood" (2003, 70, 83–4). She further argues that "it seems as if Kleist's fathers win all the battles" (84). However, in *Michael Kohlhaas* this is a limited victory. By injecting disorder into order and order into disorder (Kohlhaas's fragmented mind), Kohlhaas loses the battle but shatters the monstrous symbolic father for "generations to come." Rendering the unknown known through ingestion, and the known (vicious order) unknown through chaos, Michael Kohlhaas's vengeance is now complete.

In sum, the dynamics of revenge, as evident in *Michael Kohlhaas*, involves a painful experience of monstrous disorder that threatens to annihilate the individual. This painful experience is accompanied by an intense sense of *loneliness*, as there is no significant other to contain the threatening chaos. The expression of revenge is a twofold process in which the person injects disorder into (vicious) order and (good) order into (monstrous) disorder. I shall now illustrate my interpretation of revenge by looking at another novel.

V FOR VENDETTA: THE BLOOD VENGEANCE OF ANONYMOUS

V for Vendetta (Moore and Lloyd 1988) has become a cult classic among readers of graphic novels. It is a dystopia that describes a future England ruled by a fascist regime after a world catastrophe in which Europe and Africa have been destroyed. V – the hero – is a mysterious man on a mission: to get even with the regime. Wearing a mask with the face of Guy Fawkes (a historical figure who was involved in a conspiracy to blow up the Houses of Parliament), V inseminates terror and death.

Like that of Kohlhaas, V's vengeance seems impersonal in a very deep sense: it has no individualistic voice but rather the voice of "duty." Indeed, it is a moral duty to fight against the fascist regime, but a duty detached from the individuality of the moral agent can always be suspected of representing a psychological split.

In the novel, this impersonal aspect of revenge has two manifestations associated with "face" and "name." First, V hides behind a mask and thus has no face but that of a historical figure. The face is a mark of individuality. We are hardwired from birth to identify faces, and the frozen expression of the mask represents a twisted form of the face devoid of humanity and individuality. The mask hiding the individuality of the vengeful person is a theme that recurrs in several novels, such as *Watchmen* (Moore and Gibbons 1995), in which a central vengeful character hidden behind the name "Rorschach" also hides behind a mask covered by Rorschach-style inkblots.

As the plot unfolds, we learn that V was a victim and the sole survivor of a diabolic medical experiment conducted on prisoners in a concentration camp. His room number was 5-V. Another aspect, then, of his lack of individuality is *the absence of a name*. Even the sign "V" is polysemous, indicating his cell number in the concentration camp as well as the title of a novel by Thomas Pynchon. Again the lack of a real name is the lack of individuality.

V enters the stage when he saves a young woman from agents of the regime, who try to rape and murder her. When she asks about the identity of her savior, the girl – Evey Hammond – gets the following answer: "I'm the *king* of the twentieth century. I'm the bogeyman … The villain … The black sheep of the family" (Moore and Lloyd 1988, 13, my emphasis).

V's description of himself as a "king" (law?) recalls Lacan's insightful comment, "The madman is not only a beggar who thinks he is a king, but also a king who thinks he is a king" (quoted in Žižek 2006, 1,556). As Žižek goes on to interpret: "Madness designates the collapse of the distance between the Symbolic and the Real, an immediate identification with the symbolic mandate." This interpretation echoes the symmetrization process between the father and son that we identified in *Michael Kohlhaas*. The sense of loneliness painfully experienced by both V and Kohlhaas reflects their feeling of disconnection.

In his paper on revenge, Eugene Goldwater reminds us that "*love* (or a feeling of connection) and *esteem* (or a feeling of worth) are our two most basic emotional needs" and that the negation of these are the "experiences of *abandonment and humiliation*" (Goldwater 2004, 25), two basic injuries that might lead to a wish for revenge. The impersonal stance of both Kohlhaas and V, who regard their vengeance as a "duty" and not a personal matter, is a response to their abandonment and humiliation. Their response is therefore launched from the place of an impersonal perspective held only by those whose individuality has been brutally dismissed by others.

V's revenge targets the representative of the vicious order – the fascist leader known as "Adam" (the first man?), who broadcasts to the people of London through the "Voice of Fate" (actually a computer program heading the regime).

Fate is "God-like in its scale" (Moore and Lloyd 2008, 38), the master plan, and the ultimate expression of order and knowledge that is indifferent to human suffering. "Fate" has the maternal aspect of knowing, but in the monstrous sense, as "she" lacks the containing function. However, Adam adores her, consults her as a source of knowledge, and even falls in love with her in an act of perversion.

There is another important female figure in the novel: "Madam Justice" (as V calls her), who is actually "Lady Justice" – Justitia, the Roman goddess of Justice, familiar as the statue of a blindfolded woman holding a sword and scales. Lady Justice is blind, like fate. Both are blind to human suffering and represent the vicious face of knowledge and order. In a soliloquy delivered in front of the sculpture, V accuses her of treason and argues that he prefers anarchy, who "taught me more as a mistress than you ever did!" (Moore and Lloyd 1988, 41). Anarchy and mistress are therefore compared and contrasted with Lady Justice as a symbol of <u>order</u> and as the wife (of Adam) and mother of V.

This childish allegation of treason turns into the rage of bombing and destroying "Madam Justice." What is Lady Justice guilty of? After all, it is the fascist regime that should be blamed.

Reading along the lines previously presented, we can speculate that V interprets that the "mother," as represented by Lady Justice and fate, betrayed her son by depriving him of knowledge and giving it to the symbolic father – the vicious order. She didn't fulfill her maternal duty of providing "reverie-knowledge."

This interpretation is supported by V's dialogue with one of his victims, a woman scientist who was responsible for the experiments in the camp. Before letting her know that he injected her with cyanide while she was sleeping, he says: "There is no coincidence, Delia, only the illusion of coincidence" (Moore and Lloyd 1988, 74). This formulation echoes precisely the modern mathematical definition of chaos (Peitgen *et al.* 1992). Chaos is not equated with disorder. It is a hidden deterministic order that appears random.

Here we may expose another layer of revenge. Injecting disorder (i.e., anarchy) into apparent disorder (i.e., chaos) has the therapeutic aim of exposing the "good" order. The injection of disorder is meant to dismiss the apparent chaos and to reveal the hidden, true layer of reality. As V argues: "Anarchy wears two faces, both creator and destroyer. Thus destroyers topple empires, make a canvas of clean rubble where creators can then build a better world" (Moore and Lloyd 1988, 222).

As with Kohlhaas, V's rebellion against the law fails. When he is being shot by the agent who has been chasing him, V says: "Did you think to kill me? There's no flesh and blood within this cloak to kill. There's only an idea" (Moore and Lloyd 1988, 236). What kind of a human being can deny its embodiment in flesh and blood? Despite his death, which is experienced from an impersonal perspective as it is not *his* death, V gets his final revenge, which is closely associated with a woman and the knowledge she carries like a fetus. Evey, who under his paternal guidance has turned into a vengeful persona, wears V's mask and continues on his mission. Like the fortune-teller in *Kohlhaas*, Evey is a carrier of knowledge projected into posterity. Unlike V, however, Evey is motivated to take revenge by her *love* for V. V's final achievement is to be loved by a woman. Knowledge is conditioned by love (Neuman 2009a), even in the case of deadly knowledge such as that carried and delivered by Evey. Evey, the daughter/wife/mother, *knows* V better than everyone else, as she is the one he adopted and educated. Through her name, she also represents the first, archetypical wife and mother Eve (the biblical Adam's wife), who tasted from the Tree of Knowledge and delivered her knowledge to the generations to come at the price of mortal life. Eve is therefore the archetypical mother as she should have been, loving and containing.

WHAT HAVE WE LEARNED ABOUT REVENGE?

In *David Copperfield*, Charles Dickens insightfully presents the solitary nature of the young, abandoned David by describing him as "more solitary than Robinson Crusoe, who had nobody to look at him and see that he was solitary" (1996, 70).

This poetic description of "solitary" teaches us that we need others even in order to be alone. We need others because our status as symbolic creatures is interwoven with the lives of others. We need others in order to be recognized. The need for recognition is a constitutive aspect of revenge, as the theatrical act of vengeance desperately needs an audience. As LaFarge (2006, 449) suggests, the desire for revenge reflects the revenger's efforts to construct a story from this experience of felt disruption and anger and, linked to this, to reestablish the sense of an audience to whom the story can be told. This theme will be evident in the next section in an analysis of "Cho's manifesto."

Kohlhaas's spectacular show of fire and V's astounding, orchestrated bombing of the Old Bailey and the Tower are two expressions of this theatrical aspect of vengeance: the need for recognition from an audience, from others. The terrorist attack of September 11, 2001 is another manifestation of the bloody theater of revenge. The theory I have outlined suggests that

Muslim terrorists conceive of the Western world as introducing a "monstrous disorder" that threatens their collective self. The same dimensions of revenge evident in *Michael Kohlhaas* and *V for Vendetta* are evident here. Thus, I would argue that my interpretation of revenge is applicable at the cultural level, as its key concepts are not grounded solely in the individual level of analysis.

The inevitable question is whether we can use the above theorization and a computational methodology to "diagnose" and analyze vengeful intentions both at the personal and collective levels of analysis.

CAN COMPUTERS IDENTIFY VENGEFUL INTENTIONS?

The difficulty in applying the above theorization may be made clear through the analysis of a case study. The case is the "manifesto" of the Virginia Tech murderer, Seung-Hui Cho, whose personality has been intensively studied by my colleague, the forensic psychiatrist James Knoll.

Cho, who was well known for his mental disturbance, murdered thirty-two people in a massacre he conducted in April 2007 when he was twenty-three years old and at that time a student at this institution. He committed suicide shortly after the massacre, but had already sent to the media his "manifesto" in which he had explained his motives.

If we analyze Cho's manifesto by using several dimensions of LIWC software and comparing them to a baseline of personal texts, we get the results shown in Table 11.1.

In contrast with a possible hypothesis to be derived from the narcissist explanation, the percentage of self-reference words does not exceed the baseline of personal texts. While negative words are more frequent than positive words, the meaning of this finding combined with a high percentage of social words cannot testify regarding the pathology involved in the text.

As I previously argued, vengeful activity cannot simply be attributed to a narcissistic personality. As an alternative I proposed a different theorization applicable to both the individual and the cultural levels. According to this theorization, revenge emerges from a sense of disorder that threatens to annihilate the individual/group. This conception suggests that the avenger experiences the pain and horror of annihilation while having no others to contain his pain. Therefore, he experiences a painful realm of helplessness and loneliness in the face of a vicious and annihilating intruder that might disintegrate him.

From this conceptualization we can deduce that the first-person pronoun in avengers' texts should be associated with loneliness and pain. These

TABLE 11.1 *LIWC analysis of Cho's manifesto.*

LIWC Dimension	Cho's Manifesto (%)	Personal Texts (%)
Self-reference	5.21	11.4
Social words	15.19	9.5
Positive emotion	1.36	2.7
Negative emotion	6.13	2.6

feelings are associated with a *split* in which the avenger considers himself an innocent victim facing the evil of others. Following a modern attachment-based conception of the superego (Holmes 2011), I further suggest that, as a response to his feelings of threatening annihilation, the avenger regresses to an archaic form of regulatory and monitoring functions (i.e., the superego) and adopts a God-like position that attempts to annihilate the threatening object from a detached perspective. Following this conception, we should expect that the avenger would appeal to a God-like perspective representing a process of depersonification accompanied by a split of the world into good and bad objects. Therefore, we should expect that the first-person pronoun "I" will be associated with painful experience and with the God-like perspective, being identified with a God-like persona such as Jesus, while the second- and third-person pronouns will be identified with highly negative value judgments. A brief analysis of Cho's manifesto clearly adheres to this theorization.

Analyzing Cho's manifesto

Analyzing Cho's manifesto clearly supports the above theorization and paves the way for automatic screening for vengeful intentions. If we analyze the adjectives associated with the second-person pronoun ("you") and contrast them with those asociated with the first-person pronoun ("I"), we can easily identify the psychological split of the world into good and bad objects.

The opening paragraph of the manifesto is highly informative, in the same way as the titles of news articles. The first thing you choose to say or write, the first thing that comes to your mind, is a kind of mental fingerprint or identity card. It is the "who" you are. Cho opens by blaming his audience: "Oh the happiness I could have had mingling among you hedonists, being counted as one of you, only if you didn't fuck the living shit out of me."

This paragraph first indicates his loneliness. He could have been "one of you." He could have found his place among these "hedonists." The reason for not finding his place is that "they," the "hedonists," have "fucked" the "living shit out" of him. The expression "fuck the living shit" involves pornographic associations but points to the manifesto's recurrent theme of sodomization.

The others are described as "apostles of sin," "sadistic snobs," "descendants of Satan," "spillers of blood," and so on. Identifying these patterns automatically can be conducted through dependency parsing of the text (de Marneffe and Manning 2008) and the identification of modifiers/adjectives associated with the relevant pronouns.

In contrast to his description of the "others," the "I" is portrayed in the manifesto as a helpless and innocent victim who has been the passive subject of brutalization and who has been killed, raped, fucked, and sodomized by the "others" (all of these are direct quotes from the manifesto). As a short play written by Cho during his studies (titled *Richard McBeef*) involves a theme of sexual abuse of a child by his stepfather, it may be interesting to examine whether a background of sexual abuse was evident in his biography.

The split between good and bad objects is associated with Cho's God-like perspective in which he equates himself with Moses and Jesus. The short manifesto also involves interesting intertexuality, as it mentions many famous people, from Osama bin Laden to Kim Jong-il, Christ, George W. Bush, Moses, and the couple who inspired Cho by conducting the Columbine Massacre.

In sum, Cho presents himself as a passive, helpless subject of aggression, a sexually abused child. He is in pain, helpless, and lonely, and "pushed to the corner" by the unidentified "sadistic snobs." This aggressive and humiliating penetration threatens to disintegrate him. Destruction by the external bad object is unavoidable, and therefore the bad object should be destroyed in the name of Jesus and other God-like figures and by using a variety of weapons, whether a knife or a hammer; these are just two of the weapons mentioned in the manifesto.

This short analysis calls for several textual dimensions of revenge to include the experience of unbearable mental pain, the horror of being destroyed by the "bad object," and the explicit intentions to annihilate it; the call for revenge in order to restore order and justice to the world; deep helplessness and loneliness; the split of the world into good and bad objects; and the God-like perspective of the avenger and Cho's intertextual reference to "celebrities" of violence, politics, or religion.

What can computers do about it? There is one major application that pops into my mind, and it is the identification of vengeful intentions in a given population. Think about the benefits to strategic intelligence of identifying vengeful intentions in a given population.

In the violent neighborhood in which the state of Israel is located as the only democracy, bloodshed is inevitable. However, the consequences of certain military actions are not always expected. For example, in 1992 Israeli Defense Forces killed Abbas al-Musawi, who was the leader of Hezbollah, the Shia terrorist organization. In retaliation, the organization launched a bombing attack on the Argentine Israelite Mutual Association in Buenos Aires, killing eighty-five people and injuring many more. The anger following the killing of Abbas al-Musawi could have been expected, but was it possible to measure the level of vengeful intentions? Al-Musawi was one of the founders of Hezbollah and a symbolic father of the organization. The violent and nonproportional response of the organization taught us in retrospect about the deep emotional turmoil his targeted killing created.

It is not my aim to discuss targeted killing as a strategy or its ethical aspects. However, monitoring vengeful intentions in a target population that has experienced a targeted killing may be of some value to intelligence agencies and decision makers. In the discussion of whether anthropologists and cultural psychologists should serve the establishment I have a clear stance. The open democratic society, with all of its known problems, is a cherished institution that has no known substitute. Reading Reid's (2012) shocking story of Leningrad during the Second World War, one may better appreciate the benefits in living in a free society and the full justification of fighting for its survival and prosperity, to include the fight for a continuous critical reflection on its behavior and caution concerning guarding against its slip into decadence. In this context, computational cultural psychology, beyond its academic niche, is a tool that may be justifiably used in the hands of those who seek good.

Epilogue: on generals and mail coach drivers

The only people who believe in straight roads are generals & mail coach drivers.

(Flanagan 2001, 164)

Those who are interested in cultural psychology cannot follow the world-view of generals and mail coach drivers. The complexity of the cultural arena is such that "straight roads" are impossible. The context of culture, as the Latin origin of the word teaches us, is the context of interwoven threads in which evolutionary, ontogenetic, and social-symbolic layers obscure any straight road to understanding. Acknowledging the complexity of the cultural realm does not imply a depressive stance, at least not in the negative sense of the word. The psychoanalyst Melanie Klein has suggested that a depressive stance may be a sign and a phase of mental maturity. As suggested in the introduction, the world doesn't necessarily adhere to our fantasies. Our wishful thinking is such that we may expect the complexity of the world to be shrunken into very simple models, into straight roads.

The situation of a person seeking understanding reminds me of an insightful lesson taught by the philosopher Alfred North Whitehead (described in Avital 2012). Whitehead describes the case of a person who has lost his way in the wilderness. The question the person asks himself is, "Where am I?" However, this is the wrong question, says Whitehead. The real question is, "Where are they?" That is, the person should try to find those who look for him instead of trying to understand his absolute location on the manifold. This story should be qualified, of course. Knowing his location, the person may seek the shortest way to the closest village. However, this is not the point Whitehead is trying to make. The point is about the appropriate frame of reference.

In *Logic in Action*, Doron Avital (2012), a former commander of one of the Israeli Defense Forces' elite units, who received his Ph.D. in logic from Columbia University, uses Whitehead's story to explain that the meaning of the question "Where are they?" is "Where is my meeting point with reality?" for the specific action context in which we operate. On the one hand an absolute decontextualized point on the manifold is of minor and trivial value. Understanding a complex situation is understanding in context. On the other hand, giving in to the complexity of the situation is giving up the possibility of understanding complex situations.

Facing the complexity of the world while lacking any straight roads might lead to depression. As a consequence, one may withdraw from the world as an act of depression and reach a nihilistic stance (if the world is too complex to understand, let's avoid any attempt to understand it). The problem is that this depressive form is of minor constructive value. Once I saw an amusing slogan tacked to the door of a university professor's office: "If you think education is expensive try ignorance." As you can see it is all about alternatives.

One may use the same depressive stance described above as a springboard for mental or scientific growth. Unfortunately, psychology has been misled by a simple functional model of the mind. The dominance of simple functional analysis or group differences has encountered sharp criticism. For instance, the idea that we may learn about the individual, who is the ultimate subject of psychological research, through aggregates has been under heavy attack. In a highly influential paper, Peter Molenaar (2004, 201) writes: "Psychology is focused on variation between cases (interindividual variation). Results thus obtained are considered to be generalizable to the understanding and explanation of variation within single cases (intraindividual variation)." However, as he empirically proves, this generalization is shockingly invalid. One cannot simply confuse levels of analysis, as argued long ago by Bateson and others.

The same conclusion, regarding the levels of analysis, is evident in cultural psychology, where Matsumoto (2003, 92) writes: "Researchers have equated the two, suggesting or implying that their individual-level measurements of culture are in fact representative of group – and consensual-level – culture."

The conflation of levels of analysis may be addressed by paying close attention to the multi-scales of complex systems. As argued by Valsiner (2004, 12), "Multi-level hierarchically ordered processes are likely to be a part of any theoretical elaboration in cultural psychology." Shifting between levels of analysis is crucial for understanding a complex system, whether

biological or cultural-psychological. In the biological realm, it has been critically shown that brute reductionism is extremely limited (Cohen and Atlan
2006). Despite the enthusiasm for the Genome Project, it is now clear that
the role of genes, in understanding complex behavior for instance, is comprehensible only if we can understand the complex causal chain stretching over several levels of analysis/interaction. To understand the role of a
gene we must understand its complex interactions with various agents and
environments, such as the cellular environment, and the way it is translated
to proteins as well as the way its products themselves interact with other
top-down, bottom-up, and "horizontal" signals. What is true for biology is
probably true for psychology too.

While the methods for appropriately understanding the complexity of
the realm of psychology may vary, there is probably one theoretical stance
that is the most relevant and that may do justice to this complexity and
nurture the development of research methodologies and questions. This
theoretical stance is semiotics. Semiotics is not a theory but a perspective
(Deely 2009) urging us to examine processes of signification and the way
these processes turn us into the "meaning-making" creatures we are. Taking
the sign as a basic unit of analysis allows us to transcend the dichotomy of
language and thought and to naturally move between different scales of the
system, from the subject to the culture.

The sign is not a "magic bullet" for research, and there are too many
instances of poor research that believe that magic can be done by using the
sign only. However, as Voloshinov has insightfully proposed, the sign exists
at what I elsewhere describe (Neuman 2003) as the "interface" between the
subject and the society. Understanding culture, according to the semiotic
approach, is therefore understanding the way symbolic activity constitutes the meaning of human beings from more of a general universal and
embodied meaning to more local habitats of cultural senses and practices,
and down (or up) to the subject's contemplating mind with its unique first-
person perspective on the world.

Given that the sign is the ultimate subject in cultural psychology, the
complexity cascade is inevitable, as in itself the sign is devoid of meaning. A sign is meaningful only as a point in a high-dimensional manifold
of signs. It becomes comprehensible when projected into lower dimensionality and interpreted in the appropriate context. Interpretation has no
substitute, but on the other hand it cannot be a substitute for a systematic
analysis. In this context, the venture of computational cultural psychology
is an attempt to introduce powerful tools into the systematic analysis of
signification.

Our minds are both cognitively limited and cognitively unlimited. The cognitive load in analyzing a massive amount of data is such that human beings use various heuristics to survive in their messy environment. The computer is a mind-extending tool, as it reduces this cognitive load in terms of memory and processing. By using computers, we can process a huge amount of information and apply sophisticated algorithms that may harvest this information landscape in processing time with which no human mind may compete. As suggested by Pierre Lévy (2001; 2012), a noted philosopher who has inquired into the meaning of emerging technologies for the human mind, the digital sphere is a kind of "hypercortext." Like previous tools that have been introduced into human civilization through history, the computer is a reality-transforming tool. As we are reflective symbolic creatures, extending our limit line through novel tools is extending our mind, both the collective and the individual.

In this book I have lengthily delved into the applications of computational cultural psychology, from a novel idea on how to study the way language abstracts our thoughts to the way computers can help us to identify and understand conceptual metaphors, and from cultural intelligence to the meaning of dinner in two hundred years of textual history. These cases were not simple instances of computational social sciences. They did not involve simulations but rather the analysis of massive data sets as guided by semiotic understanding, unique and novel algorithms, and careful interpretative analysis.

While I have focused on texts only, pervasive computing and emerging technologies for analyzing other forms of data may be used for gaining deeper insights into cultures. For instance, advances in visual processing allow us to develop similarity measures between pictures. These algorithms can be used to analyze similarity, difference, and change in cultural iconic images across time, and the visual representation of various concepts. Love, for instance. If we search Google Images for "love" we may find familiar clichés such as red hearts. Searching Google Images allows us to constrain our search to various geographical and national locations. Can we use this option to analyze the differences and similarities in love images? While the computational analysis of sound signals is too trivial to be mentioned, the analysis of body movement is not. Cheap and light movement sensors may be used to follow the movements of subjects in various settings and to fuse this information with textual, vocal, and visual signals.

This brave new world might turn into a nightmare if managed inappropriately. Power has the Janus face of using and misusing, and therefore the ethical imperative of technology entrepreneurs is such that technologies should be carefully examined, and their use should not be considered apart from an ongoing ethical discussion. Those of us who are scared by the power of emerging technologies should realize that the Promethean nature of human beings cannot be blocked but only constrained and channeled for good. In addition, such people should avoid any form of false nostalgia, cherishing a wonderful past that probably never existed. There is "no alibi in existence," Bakhtin reminds us, and this wisdom should accompany any reflective individual.

Let me now return to the current book and to the only legitimate justification for publishing it. Valsiner suggests that there are two implicit functions of theories in psychology. The first is to consider the theory as a tool for "taking a new look at the phenomena we want to understand" (Valsiner 2004, 18). I warmly embrace this suggestion and apply it to the idea of computational cultural psychology, which may give us a new look at issues that have long bothered researchers in the field. However, a new tool never ends with a "new look" only. In her poem "Microcosmos," Wisława Szymborska writes:

> When they first started looking through microscopes
> a cold fear blew and it is still blowing.
> Life hitherto had been frantic enough
> in all its shapes and dimensions.
> Which is why it is created small-scale creatures,
> assorted tiny worms and flies,
> but at least the naked human eye
> could see them.
>
> (Szymborska 2010, 23)

A microscope, like any other scientific strategic tool, does not only give us a new look but also opens for us a window into another realm. Life is frantic enough but it is more frantic as we observe it through powerful tools.

This is probably an inevitable aspect of human understanding, insightfully recognized by Socrates in antiquity. The more we learn and extend our knowledge, the more we realize how little we know. Socrates realized that our knowledge always exists within a frame of reference. The more we know, the more aware we become of this frame and its limited scope and embedded nature, a frame within a frame. Socrates was not a sophist cynically observing the limits of knowledge but a philosopher who deeply grasped the paradoxical nature of our knowledge. Anyone who reaches this phase of understanding must respect the "frantic" world in which we live and the necessary modesty of any human being who tries to understand it. It is my wish that with this conclusion the book should be read and evaluated.

BIBLIOGRAPHY

Albala, Ken. 2002. *Eating Right in the Renaissance*. Berkeley and Los Angeles: University of California Press.

2007. *The Banquet: Dining in the Great Courts of Late Renaissance Europe*. Urbana and Chicago: University of Illinois Press.

Allan, Keith. 2007. "The pragmatics of connotation." *Journal of Pragmatics* 39: 1,047–57.

Alon, Uri. 2007. "Network motifs: theory and experimental approaches." *Nature* 8: 450–61.

Aponte Moreno, Marco. 2008. "Metaphors in Hugo Chavez's political discourse: conceptualizing nation, revolution, and opposition." Ph.D. diss., City University of New York.

Arunachalam, Sudha and Sandra R. Waxman. 2011. "Language and conceptual development." *Wiley Interdisciplinary Reviews: Cognitive Science* 1: 548–58.

Ashby, W. Ross. 1958. "Requisite variety and its implications for the control of complex systems." *Cybernetica* 1.2: 83–99.

Assaf, Dan, Yair Neuman, Yochai Cohen, Shlomo Argamon, Howard Newton, Mark Last, Ophir Frieder, and Moshe Koppel. 2013. "Why 'dark thoughts' aren't really dark: a novel algorithm for metaphor identification." In *Proceedings of the IEEE Symposium Series on Computational Intelligence*, 60–5. Singapore: IEEE.

Asur, Sitaram and Bernardo A. Huberman. 2010. "Predicting the future with social media." *arXiv*: 1003.5699.

Avital, Doron. 2012. *Logic in Action*. Tel-Aviv: Kinneret, Zmora-Bitan, Dvir-Publishing House Ltd. [Hebrew].

Bainbridge, Simon, ed. 2008. *Romanticism: A Sourcebook*. Basingstoke: Palgrave MacMillan.

Bakhtin, Mikhail. 1973. *Problems of Dostoyevsky's poetics*. Ann Arbor: Ardis.

1990. *Art and Answerability*. Edited by Michael Holquist and Vadim Liapunov. Austin: University of Texas Press.

1999. *Toward a Philosophy of the Act*. Translated by Vadim Liapunov. Austin: University of Texas Press.

Barabási, Albert-László. 2003. *Linked*. New York: Plume.

Barnden, John A. 2008. "Metaphor and artificial intelligence: why they matter to each other." In *The Cambridge Handbook of Metaphor and Thought*, edited by Raymond W. Gibbs, Jr., 311–38. Cambridge University Press.

Barnes, Bill, Sheila Ernst, and Keith Hyde. 1999. *An Introduction to Groupwork: A Group Analytic Perspective*. London: Palgrave.

Barsalou, Lawrence W. 2005. "Continuity of the conceptual system across species." *Trends in Cognitive Sciences* 9: 309–11.

Bateson, Gregory. 2000. *Steps to an Ecology of Mind*. University of Chicago Press.

Baudrillard, Jean. 1981. *Simulacres et simulation*. Paris: Galilee.

Beattie, H. J. 2005. "Revenge." *Journal of the American Psychoanalytic Association* 53: 513–24.

Becker, Alton L. 2000. *Beyond Translation: Essays toward a Modern Philology*. Ann Arbor: University of Michigan Press.

Benjamin, Jessica. 1988. *The Bonds of Love*. New York: Pantheon.

2004. "Beyond doer and done to: an intersubjective view of thirdness." *Psychoanalytic Quarterly* 73: 5–46.

Berg-Cross, Linda. 2000. *Basic Concepts in Family Therapy*. London: Haworth Press.

Bergson, Henri L. 1946. *The Creative Mind*. New York: Wisdom Library.

Bhattacharjee, Yudhijit. 2009. "A new spy agency asks academics for help in meeting its mission." *Science* 323.5911: 194.

Bion, Wilfred R. 1956. "Development of schizophrenic thought." *International Journal of Psychoanalysis* 37: 344–6.

1961. *Experiences in Groups*. London: Tavistock.

1962a. "The psychoanalytic study of thinking." *International Journal of Psychoanalysis* 43: 306–10.

1962b. *Learning from Experience*. New York: Basic Books.

1965. *Transformations*. New York: Basic Books.

1989. *Learning from Experience*. London: Falmer Press.

Birke, Julia and Anoop Sarkar. 2006. "A clustering approach for the nearly unsupervised recognition of nonliteral language." In *Proceedings of the 11th Conference of the European Chapter of the Association for Computational Linguistics (EACL 2006)*, 329–36. Trento: ACL.

2007. "Active learning for the identification of nonliteral language." In *Proceedings of the Workshop on Computational Approaches to Figurative Language at HLT/NAACL-07*, 21–8. Rochester, NY: ACL.

Bohanon, Jack. 2010. "'Ig Nobel' awards praise research into slime, snot and swearing." *Washington Post*, October 11. www.washingtonpost.com/wp-dyn/content/article/2010/10/11/AR2010101104499.html.

Bollen, Johan, Huina Mao, and Xiaojun Zeng. 2011. "Twitter mood predicts the stock market." *Journal of Computational Sciences* 2: 1–8.

Borges, Jorge L. 1964. "Borges and I." In *Labyrinths: Selected Stories and Other Writings*, 246–7. New York: New Directions.

1974. *The Book of Imaginary Beings*. London: Penguin.

Bowdle, Brian F. and Dedre Gentner. 2005. "The career of metaphor." *Psychological Review* 112: 193–216.

Bringsjord, Selmer and Bettina Schimanski. 2003. "What is artificial intelligence? Psychometric AI as an answer." In *Proceedings of the 18th International Joint Conference on Artificial Intelligence (IJCAI-03)*, 887–93. Acapulco: AP Professional.

Buck, Linda and Richard Axel. 1991. "A novel multigene family may encode odorant receptors: a molecular basis for odor recognition." *Cell* 65: 175–87.

Caron, John. 2001. "Experiments with LSA scoring: optimal rank and basis." *Proceedings of the SIAM Computational Information Retrieval Workshop*, 157–69. Raleigh, NC: SIAM.

Carver, Raymond. 1989. *What We Talk about When We Talk about Love*. New York: Vintage.

Charteris-Black, Jonathan. 2004. *Corpus Approaches to Critical Metaphor Analysis*. Basingstoke: Palgrave MacMillan.

Christner, Ray W., Jessica Stewart, and Arthur Freeman, eds. 2007. *Handbook of Cognitive-Behavior Group Therapy with Children and Adolescents*. London: Routledge.

Church, Kenneth Ward and Patrick Hanks. 1989. "Word association norms, mutual information and lexicography." *Proceedings of the 27th Annual Conference of the Association for Computational Linguistics*, 76–83. New Brunswick: Association for Computational Linguistics.

Clark, Andy. 2006. "Language, embodiment, and the cognitive niche." *Trends in Cognitive Sciences* 10: 370–4.

Clutton-Brock, Timothy H. and Geoffrey A. Parker. 1995. "Punishment in animal societies." *Nature* 373: 209–16.

Cohen, Irun R. 2000. *Tending Adam's Garden: Evolving the Cognitive Immune Self*. London: Academic Press.

Cohen, Irun R. and Henri Atlan. 2006. "Genetics as explanation: limits to the human genome project." In *Encyclopedia of Life Sciences*, 1–7. New York: Wiley.

Coles, John P. 2005. "Cultural intelligence and joint intelligence doctrine." *Joint Operations Review* 1: 3.

Coltheart, Max. 1981. "The MRC psycholinguistic database." *Quarterly Journal of Experimental Psychology* 33A.4: 497–505.

Corrigan, Roberta. 2004. "The acquisition of word connotations: asking 'What happened?'" *Journal of Child Language* 31: 381–98.

Curioni, P. M. G. and J. O. Bosset. 2002. "Key odorants in various cheese types as determined by gas chromatography–olfactometry." *International Dairy Journal* 12: 959–84.

Danesi, Marcel. 2003. "Metaphorical 'networks' and verbal communication: a semiotic perspective on human discourse." *Sign Systems Studies* 31: 341–63.

Davies, Mark. 2008. "The corpus of contemporary American English (COCA): 410+ million words, 1990–present." www.americancorpus.org.

Deely, John. 2009. *Basics of Semiotics*. Estonia: Tartu University Press.

Deleuze, Giles. 1995. *Difference and Repetition*. Translated by Paul Patton. New York: Columbia University Press.

Delp, Benjamin T. 2008. "Ethnographic intelligence (ETHINT) and cultural intelligence (CULINT)." IIIA Technical Paper 08–02. Institute for Infrastructure and Information Assurance, James Madison University.

de Marneffe, Marie-Catherine and Christopher D. Manning. 2008. "The Stanford typed dependencies representation." Paper presented at the *COLING Workshop on Cross-framework and Cross-domain Parser Evaluation*, Manchester, UK, August.

Deutscher, Guy. 2010. "Does your language shape how you think?" *New York Times*, August 29. www.nytimes.com/2010/08/29/magazine/29language-t.html? pagewanted=all.

Dickens, Charles. 1996 [1850]. *David Copperfield*. London: Penguin.

Drouard, Alain. 2007. "Chefs, gourmets and gourmands." In *Food: The History of Taste*, edited by Paul H. Freedman, 263–301. Berkeley: University of California Press.

Eagleton, Terry. 2006. *How to Read a Poem*. Malden, MA: John Wiley & Sons.

Eco, Umberto. 1992. *Interpretation and Overinterpretation*. Cambridge University Press.

Ellenberg, Jordan. 2008. "This psychologist might outsmart the math brains competing for the Netflix prize." *Wired*, February 25. www.wired.com/techbiz/ media/magazine/16-03/mf_netflix?currentPage=all.

Fass, Dan. 1997. *Processing Metonymy and Metaphor*. Greenwich, CT: Ablex.

Feldman-Barrett, Lisa, Kristen A. Lindquist, and Maria Gendron. 2007. "Language as context for the perception of emotion." *Trends in Cognitive Sciences* 11: 327–32.

Fisher, James V. 2006. "The emotional experience of K." *International Journal of Psychoanalysis* 87.5: 1,221–37.

Flanagan, Richard. 2001. *Gould's Book of Fish*. New York: Grove Press.

Foulkes, Siegmund H. 1964. *Therapeutic Group Analysis*. London: Allen and Unwin.

Frankenstein, Ziv, Uri Alon, and Irun R. Cohen. 2006. "The immune-body cytokine network defines a social architecture of cell interactions." *Biology Direct* 1: 32.

Freud, Sigmund. 1964 [1933]. *New Introductory Lectures on Psychoanalysis*. Standard Edition 22, 1–182. London: Hogarth Press.

Galavaris, George. 1970. *Bread and Liturgy*. Madison: University of Wisconsin Press.

Gedigian, Matt, John Bryant, Srini Narayanan, and Branimir Ciric. 2006. "Catching metaphors." In *Proceedings of the 3rd Workshop on Scalable Natural Language Understanding*, 41–8. New York: ACL.

Gibbs, Raymond W. Jr. 2007. "Why cognitive linguists should care more about empirical methods." In *Methods in Cognitive Linguistics*, edited by Mónica Gonzáles-Márquez, Seana Coulson, Michael J. Spivey, and Irene Mittelberg, 2–19. Amsterdam and Philadelphia: John Benjamins.

Gibbs, Raymond W. Jr., Paula Lena Costa-Lima, and Edson Francozo. 2004. "Metaphor is grounded in embodied experience." *Journal of Pragmatics* 36: 1,189–210.

Goldberg, J. G. 2004. "Fantasies of revenge and the stabilization of the ego: acts of revenge and the ascension of Thanatos." *Modern Psychoanalysis* 29: 3–21.

Goldenberg, Irene and Herbert Goldenberg. 2004. *Family Therapy: An Overview*, 6th edn. Pacific Grove, CA: Brooks/Cole.

Goldwater, Eugene. 2004. "Getting mad and getting even." *Modern Psychoanalysis* 29: 23–36.

Goux, Jean-Joseph. 1990. *Symbolic Economies*. Ithaca, NY: Cornell University Press.

1997. "Values and speculations: the stock exchange paradigm." *Journal of Cultural Research* 1.2: 159–77.

Gray, Richard T. 1996. "Buying into signs: money and semiosis in eighteenth-century German language theory." *The German Quarterly* 69.1: 1–14.

Groeger, Lena. 2011. "Spies, meet Shakespeare: intel geeks build metaphor motherlode." *Wired*, May 25. www.wired.com/dangerroom/2011/05/spies-meet-shakcspeare-intel-geeks-build-metaphor-motherlode.

Gruber, Tom. 2008. "Collective knowledge systems: where the social web meets the semantic web." *Journal of Web Semantics* 6: 4–13.

Halford, Graeme S., William H. Wilson, and Steven Philips. 2010. "Relational knowledge: the foundation of higher cognition." *Trends in Cognitive Sciences* 14: 497–505.

Harnad, Stevan. 1990. "The symbol grounding problem." *Physica D* 42: 335–46.

2005. "To cognize is to categorize: cognition is categorization." In *Handbook of Categorization in Cognitive Science*, edited by Henri Cohen and Claire Lefebvre, 231–3. Amsterdam: Elsevier.

Harris, Zellig S. 1954. "Distributional structure." *Word* 10.23: 146–62.

Hegel, Georg W. F. 2004. *Introductory Lectures on Aesthetics*. Harmondsworth: Penguin.

Hoey, Michael. 1991. *Patterns of Lexis in Text*. Oxford University Press.

Holmes, Jeremy. 2011. "Superego: an attachment perspective." *International Journal of Psychoanalysis* 92.5: 1,221–40.

Holquist, Michael. 1990. *Dialogism*. London: Routledge.

Houellebecq, Michel. 2007. *The Possibility of an Island*. New York: Vintage International.

Jensen, Keith, Josep Call, and Michael Tomasello. 2007. "Chimpanzees are vengeful but not spiteful." *Proceedings of the National Academy of Sciences* 104: 13,046–50.

Johnson, Jeannie L. and Matthew T. Berrett. 2011. "Cultural topography: a new research tool for intelligence analysis." *Studies in Intelligence* 55: 1–22.

Just, Marcel Adam, Vladimir L. Cherkassky, Sandesh Aryal, and Tom M. Mitchell. 2010. "A neurosemantic theory of concrete noun representation based on the underlying brain codes." *PLoS ONE* 5.1: e8622.

Kashtan, Nadav and Uri Alon. 2005. "Spontaneous evolution of modularity and network motifs." *Proceedings of the National Academy of Sciences* 102: 13,773–8.

Katriel, Tamar. 1986. *Talking Straight: Dugri Speech in Israeli Sabra Culture*. Cambridge University Press.

Ketcham, Wheaton B. 1983. *Savoring the Past: The French Kitchen and Table from 1300–1789*. New York and London: Touchstone Books.

Kintsch, Walter. 2000. "Metaphor comprehension: a computational theory." *Psychonomic Bulletin & Review* 7: 257–66.

Kipp, Jacob, Lester Grau, Karl Prinslow, and Don Smith. 2006. "The human terrain system: a CORDS for the 21st century." *Military Review* Sept–Oct: 8–15.

Kit, Chunyu and Tak Ming Wong. 2008. "Comparative evaluation of online machine translation systems with legal texts." *Law Library Journal* 100.2: 299.

Koehn, Philipp. 2010. *Statistical Machine Translation*. Cambridge University Press.

Kohut, H. 1972. "Thoughts on narcissism and narcissistic rage." *Psychoanalytic Study of the Child* 27: 360–400.

Kovecses, Zoltan. 2002. *Metaphor: A Practical Introduction*. Oxford University Press.

2007. *Metaphor and Emotion: Language, Culture and Body in Human Feeling*. Cambridge University Press.

Krishnakumaran, Saisuresh and Xiaojin Zhu. 2007. "Hunting elusive metaphors using lexical resources." *Proceedings of the Workshop on Computational Approaches to Figurative Languages*, 13–20. New York: ACL.

Kundera, Milan. 1988. *The Art of the Novel*. London: Faber and Faber.

Lacan, Jacques. 1977. *Ecrits*. Translated by A. Sheridan. New York: W. W. Norton.

LaFarge, L. 2006. "The wish for revenge." *Psychoanalytic Quarterly* 75: 447–75.

Lakoff, George. 1994. "The master metaphor list." University of California, Berkeley. http://cogsci.berkeley.edu.

1999. "Metaphorical thought in foreign policy: why strategic framing matters." www.frameworksinstitute.org/assets/files/PDF_GII/metaphorical_thought.pdf.

2002. *Moral Politics: How Liberals and Conservatives Think*. University of Chicago Press.

Lakoff, George and M. Johnson. 1980. *Metaphors We Live By*. University of Chicago Press.

1999. *Philosophy in the Flesh*. New York: Basic Books.

Landauer, Thomas K. and Susan Dumais. 1997. "A solution to Plato's problem: the latent semantic analysis theory of the acquisition, induction, and representation of knowledge." *Psychological Review* 104: 211–40.

Lane, R. C. 1995. "The revenge motive: a developmental perspective on the life cycle and treatment process." *Psychoanalytic Review* 82: 41–64.

Lawrence, Jeanette A. and Jean Valsiner. 1993. "Conceptual roots of internalization: from transmission to transformation." *Human Development* 36: 150–67.

Lee, Penny. 1996. *The Whorf Theory Complex*. Amsterdam: John Benjamins.

Leetaru, Kalev H. 2011. "Culturomics 2.0: forecasting large-scale human behavior using global news media tone in time and space." *First Monday* 16. http://firstmonday.org/ojs/index.php/fm/article/view/3663/3040.

Lehman, David, ed. 2006. *The Oxford Book of American Poetry*. Oxford University Press.

Levinson, Stephen C. 1983. *Pragmatics*. Cambridge University Press.

Lévy, Pierre. 2001. *Cyberculture*. Minneapolis: University of Minnesota Press.

2012. *The Semantic Sphere: Computation, Cognition and Information Economy*. Chichester: Wiley.

Liebersohn, Yossi, Yair Neuman, and Zvi Bekerman. 2004. "Oh baby, it's hard for me to say I'm sorry: public apologetic speech and cultural rhetorical resources." *Journal of Pragmatics* 36: 921–44.

Light, Marc and Warren Greiff. 2002. "Statistical models for the induction and use of selectional preferences." *Cognitive Science* 26: 269–81.

Lin, Chi-San Althon and Tony C. Smith. 2006. "A tree-based algorithm for predicate–argument recognition." *Association for Computing Machinery New Zealand Bulletin* 2.1: 1–14.

Livshits, Danny, Howard Newton, and Yair Neuman. 2012. "Can computers help us to better understand different cultures? Toward a computer-based CULINT." In *European Intelligence and Security Informatics Conference (EISIC), 2012*, 172–9. Washington, DC: IEEE.

López-Corvo, Rafael E. 2003. *The Dictionary of the Work of W. R. Bion*. London: Karnac Books.

Lord, Thomas and Mary Kasprzak. 1989. "Identification of self through olfaction." *Perceptual and Motor Skills* 69: 219–24.

Lord Smail, Daniel and Kelly Gibson, eds. 2009. *Vengeance in Medieval Europe: A Reader*. University of Toronto Press.

Lotto, D. 2006. "The psychohistory of vengeance." *Journal of Psychohistory* 34.1: 43–59.

Low, K. E. Y. 2005. "Rumination on smell as a sociocultural phenomenon." *Current Sociology* 53: 397–417.

Luria, Aleksandr Rovanovich. 1976. *Cognitive Development: Its Cultural and Social Foundations*. Cambridge, MA: Harvard University Press.

Luria, Aleksandr Rovanovich and Lev Semenovich Vygotsky. 1930. *Ape, Primitive Man and Child*. London: Harvester Wheatsheaf.

1992. *Ape, Primitive Man and Child: Essays in the History of Behavior*. Orlando, FL: Paul M. Deutsch Press.

McCullough, Michael E., Robert Kurzban, and Benjamin A. Tabak. 2011. "Evolved mechanism for revenge and forgiveness." In *Understanding and Reducing Aggression, Violence and Their Consequences*, edited by Mario Mukulincer and Phillip R. Shaver, 221–39. Washington, DC: American Psychological Association.

McMillan, S. 2001. "What time is dinner?" *History Magazine* Oct/Nov. www.history-magazine.com/dinner2.html.

Mallery, Garrick. 1888. "Manners and meals." *American Anthropologist* 1: 193–208.

Mangel, Marc and Francisco Samaniego. 1984. "Abraham Wald's work on aircraft survivability." *Journal of the American Statistical Association* 79.386: 259–67.

Markoff, John. 2006. "Entrepreneurs see a Web guided by common sense." *New York Times*, November 12. www.nytimes.com/2006/11/12/business/12web.html?pagewanted=all.

Marwan, Norbert, M. Carmen Romano, Marco Thiel, and Jürgen Kurths. 2007. "Recurrence plots for the analysis of complex systems." *Physics Reports* 438.5–6: 237–329.

Matsumoto, David. 2003. "The discrepancy between consensual-level culture and individual-level culture." *Culture and Psychology* 9: 89–95.

Matt, Daniel C., ed. 2004. *The Zohar: Pritzker Edition*, vol. II. Stanford University Press.

Matte-Blanco, Ignacio. 1975. *The Unconscious as Infinite Sets: An Essay in Bi-logic*. London: Duckworth.

Mellor, Anne K. 1993. *Romanticism and Gender*. London: Routledge.

Merleau-Ponty, Maurice. 1996. *Phenomenology of Perception*. Paris: Motial Banarsidass.

Mesquita, Batja and Janxin Leu. 2007. "The cultural psychology of emotion." In *Handbook of Cultural Psychology*, edited by Shinobu Kitayama and Dov Cohen, 734–59. New York: Guilford Press.

Mey, Jacob L. 1998. *When Voices Clash: A Study in Literary Pragmatics (Trends in Linguistics. Studies and Monographs 115)*. Berlin and New York: Mouton de Gruyter.

Milo, Ron, Shalev Itzkovitz, Nadav Kashtan, Reuven Levitt, and Uri Alon. 2002. "Network motifs: simple building blocks." *Science* 298.5594: 824–7.

Milo, Ron, Shai Shen-Orr, Inbal Ayzenshtat, Michal Sheffer, and Uri Alon. 2004. "Superfamilies of evolved and designed networks." *Science* 303: 1,538–42.

Mitchell, Stephan A. 1988. *Relational Concepts in Psychoanalysis: An Integration*. Cambridge University Press.

Molenaar, Peter. 2004. "A manifesto on psychology as idiographic science: bringing the person back into scientific psychology, this time forever." *Measurement: Interdisciplinary Research and Perspectives* 2.4: 201–18.

Moore, Alan and Dave Gibbons. 1995. *Watchmen*. New York: DC Comics.

Moore, Alan and David Lloyd. 2008. *V for Vendetta*. New York: DC Comics.

Musolff, A. 2008. "What can critical metaphor analysis add to the understanding of racist ideology? Recent studies of Hitler's anti-Semitic metaphors." *Critical Approaches to Discourse Analysis across Disciplines* 2: 1–10.

Neuman, Yair. 2003. *Processes and Boundaries of the Mind: Extending the Limit Line*. New York: Springer.

2004a. "Mirrors mirrored: is that all there is?" Special issue, *Semiotics, Evolution, Energy, and Development* 4: 58–69.

2004b. "Meaning making in the immune system." *Perspectives in Biology and Medicine* 47: 317–28.

2008. *Reviving the Living: Meaning Making in Living Systems*. Oxford: Elsevier.

2009a. "On love, hate and knowledge." *International Journal of Psychoanalysis* 90: 697–712.

2009b. "Double binds, triadic binds." *Semiotica* 174: 227–40.

2009c. "Peter Pan's shadow and the relational matrix of the 'I'." *Semiotica* 176: 15–27.

2011. "A novel semio-mathematical technique for excavating themes out of group dynamics." *Semiotica* 187: 323–36.

2012. "On revenge." *Psychoanalysis, Culture & Society* 17: 1–15.

Neuman, Yair, Dan Assaf, and Yochai Cohen. 2012. "Automatic identification of themes in small group dynamics through the analysis of network motifs." *Bulletin of the Menninger Clinic* 76: 53–68.

2013. "Fusing distributional and experiential information for measuring semantic relatedness." *Information Fusion* 14.3: 281–7.

Neuman, Yair, Dan Assaf, Yochai Cohen, Mark Last, Shlomo Argamon, Newton Howard, and Ophir Frieder. 2013b. "Metaphor identification in large texts corpora." *PLoS ONE* 8.4: e62343.

Neuman, Yair, Dan Assaf, and Gabbi Kedman. 2012. "Proactive screening for depression through metaphorical and automatic text analysis." *Artificial Intelligence in Medicine* 56.1: 19–25.

Neuman, Yair, Zvi Bekerman, and Avi Kaplan. 2002. "Rhetoric as the contextual manipulation of self and non-self." *Research on Language and Social Interaction* 35: 93–112.

Neuman, Yair, Zvi Bekerman, and Ophir Nave. 2012. "A generic methodology for measuring the potential number of structure-preserving transformations." *Complexity* 18: 26–37.

Neuman, Yair, Yochai Cohen, and Dan Assaf. 2013a. "A cognitively inspired algorithm for word sense induction." In *Proceedings of the IEEE Symposium Series on Computational Intelligence*, 66–72. Singapore: IEEE.

In press. "How do we understand the connotations? A cognitive computational model." *Semiotica*.

Neuman, Yair and Mor Levi. 2003. "Blood and chocolate: a rhetorical approach to fear appeal." *Journal of Language and Social Psychology* 29: 29–46.

Neuman, Yair, Yotam Lurie, and Michele Rosental. 2001. "A watermelon without seeds: a case study in rhetorical rationality." *Text* 21: 543–65.

Neuman, Yair and Ophir Nave. 2009a. "Why the brain needs language in order to be self-conscious." *New Ideas in Psychology* 28: 37–48.

2009b. "Metaphor-based meaning excavation." *Information Sciences* 179: 2,719–28.

Neuman, Yair, Ophir Nave, and Gabbi Kedman. 2010. "Using web intelligence for excavating the emerging meaning of target-concepts." *IEEE/WIC/ACM International Conference on Web Intelligence and Intelligent Agent Technology*, 22–5. Toronto: IEEE.

Neuman, Yair, Peter Turney, and Yochai Cohen. 2012. "How language enables abstraction: a case study in computational cultural psychology." *Integrative Psychological and Behavioral Science* 46.2: 129–45.

Neuman, Yair and Erez Weitzman. 2003. "The role of text representation in students' ability to identify fallacious arguments." *Quarterly Journal of Experimental Psychology* 56: 849–65.

NIST. 2008. "NIST 2008 machine translation evaluation – (Open MT-08). Official evaluation results." Gaithersburg, MD: National Institute of Standards and Technology, Multimodal Information Group.

Novikov, Sergeï Petrovich and Anatoly Timofeevich Fomenko. 1990. *Basic Elements of Differential Geometry and Topology*. Translated by M. V. Tsaplina. New York: Kluwer Publishers.

O'Brien, Sean P. 2010. "Crisis early warning and decision support: contemporary approaches and thoughts on future research." *International Studies Review* 12: 87–104.

Ogden, Thomas. 1983. "The concept of internal object relations." *International Journal of Psychoanalysis* 64: 227–41.

1985. "On potential space." *International Journal of Psychoanalysis* 66: 129–41.

O'Meara, J. Donald. 1989. "Cross-sex friendship: four basic challenges of an ignored relationship." *Sex Roles* 21: 525–43.

O'Reilly, Tim. 2005. "What is Web 2.0?" www.oreillynet.com/lpt/a/6228.

Ortega y Gasset, José. 1959. "The difficulty of reading." *Diogenes* 28: 1–17.

Peirce, Charles S. 1931–1966. *The Collected Papers of Charles S. Peirce*, 8 vols. Edited by C. Hartshorne, P. Weiss, and A. W. Burks. Cambridge, MA: Harvard University Press.

1992. *Essential Peirce: Selected Philosophical Writings*, vol. ii. Edited by the Peirce Edition Project. Bloomington: Indiana University Press.

Peitgen, Heinz-Otto, Hartmut Jürgens, and Dietmar Saupe. 1992. *Chaos and Fractals*. New York: Springer.

Pennebaker, James W. and Martha E. Francis. 2001. *Linguistic Inquiry and Word Count*. Mahwah: Erlbaum Publishers.

Pines, Malcolm. 2000. "The contribution of S. H. Foulkes to group therapy." In *The Evolution of Group Analysis*, edited by Malcolm Pines, 265–86. London: Routledge & Kegan Paul.

Pitte, Jean-Robert. 1999. "The rise of the restaurant." In *Food: A Culinary History from Antiquity to the Present*, edited by Jean-Louis Flandrin and Massimo Montanari, 471–80. New York: Columbia University Press.

Pragglejaz Group. 2007. "MIP: a method for identifying metaphorically used words in discourse." *Metaphor and Symbol* 22: 1–39.

Rash, Felicity. 2005. "A database of metaphors in Adolf Hitler's *Mein Kampf*." http://webspace.qmul.ac.uk/fjrash/metaphors_mein_kampf.pdf.

Reid, Anna. 2012. *Leningrad: The Epic Siege of World War II, 1941–1944*. New York: Walker and Company.

Reips, Ulf-Dietrich and Pablo Garaizar. 2011. "Mining Twitter: a source for psychological wisdom of the crowds." *Behavioral Research Methods* 43: 635–42.

Renzi, Fred. 2006. "Networks: terra incognita and the case for ethnographic intelligence." *Military Review* Sept–Oct: 16–22.

Resnik, Philip. 1996. "Selectional constraints: an information-theoretic model and its computational realization." *Cognition* 61: 127–59.

R. L. G. 2011. "Metaphors we do everything by?" *The Economist*, May 26. www.economist.com/blogs/johnson/2011/05/metaphors.

Rosch, Eleanor H. 1973. "On the internal structure of perceptual and semantic categories." In *Cognitive Development and Acquisition of Language*, edited by Timothy E. Moore, 111–44. New York: Academic Press.

Roth, Philip. 1967. *Portnoy's Complaint*. New York: Bantam Books.

Rottman, Brian. 1993. *Signifying Nothing*. Stanford University Press.

Rozin, Paul. 2007. "Food and eating." In *Handbook of Cultural Psychology*, edited by Shinobu Kitayama and Dov Cohen, 391–416. New York: Guilford Press.

Rudolph, Lee and Jaan Valsiner. 2012. "Introduction: mathematical models of social representation." In *Qualitative Mathematics for the Social Sciences*, edited by Lee Rudolph and Jaan Valsiner, 1–39. London: Routledge.

Rutan, J. Scott and Walter N. Stone. 2001. *Psychodynamic Group Psychotherapy*, 3rd edn. New York: Guilford Press.

Sapir, Edward. 1949. *Culture, Language and Personality*. Berkeley: University of California Press.

Saussure, Ferdinand de. 1972. *Course in General Linguistics*. Translated by R. Harris. London: Duckworth.

Schweder, Richard A. and Maria A. Sullivan. 1990. "The semiotic subject of cultural psychology." In *Handbook of Personality: Theory and Research*, edited by Lawrence A. Pervin, 399–416. New York: Guilford Press.

Shepherd, Gordon M. 2004. "The human sense of smell: are we better than we think?" *PLoS Biology* 2: 572–5.

Shiff, Zeev and Ehud Ya'ari. 1985. *Israel's Lebanon War*. New York: Touchstone.

Shukman, Ann, ed. 1983. *Bakhtin School Papers*. Oxford: RPT Publications.

Shutova, Ekaterina. 2010. "Models of metaphor in NLP." In *Proceedings of the 48th Annual Meeting of the Association for Computational Linguistics*, 688–97. Uppsala: ACL.

Steen, Gerard J., Aletta G. Dporst, J. Berenike Herrmann, Anna A. Kaal, Tina Krennmayr, and Trijntje Pasma. 2010. *A Method for Linguistic Metaphor Identification*. Amsterdam: John Benjamins.

Szymborska, Wisława. 1995. *View with a Grain of Sand*. New York: Harcourt Brace.

2010. *Here*. Boston and New York: Houghton Mifflin Harcourt.

Tausczik, Yia R. and James W. Pennebaker. 2010. "The psychological meaning of words: LIWC and computerized text analysis method." *Journal of Language and Social Psychology* 29: 24–54.

Trim, Richard. 2007. *Metaphor Networks: The Comparative Evolution of Figurative Language*. Basingstoke: Palgrave MacMillan.

Turin, Luca. 2006. *The Secret of Scent: Adventures in Perfume and the Science of Smell*. London: Faber and Faber.

Turney, Peter D. 2008. "The latent relation mapping engine: algorithm and experiments." *Journal of Artificial Intelligence Research* 33: 615–55.

2012. "Domain and function: a dual-space model of semantic relations and compositions." *Journal of Artificial Intelligence Research* 44: 533–85.

Turney, Peter D. and M. L. Littman. 2003. "Measuring praise and criticism: inference of semantic orientation from association." *ACM Transactions on Information Systems* 21.4: 315–46.

Turney, Peter D. Yair Neuman, Dan Assaf, and Yochai Cohen. 2011. "Literal and metaphorical sense identification through concrete and abstract context." *Proceedings of the 2011 Conference on Empirical Methods in Natural Language Processing (EMNLP-2011)*, 680–90. Edinburgh: ACL.

Turney, Peter D. and Patrick Pantel. 2010. "From frequency to meaning: vector space models of semantics." *Journal of Artificial Intelligence Research* 37: 141–88.

Utsumi, Akira. 2006. "Computational exploration of metaphor comprehension processes." In *Proceedings of the 28th Annual Meeting of the Cognitive Science Society (CogSci2006)*, 2,281–6. Vancouver: Cognitive Science Society.

Valsiner, Jaan. 2004. "Three years later: culture in psychology – between social positioning and producing new knowledge." *Culture and Psychology* 10: 1–27.

2007. *Culture in Minds and Societies: Foundations of Cultural Psychology*. Thousand Oaks, CA: Sage.

Valsiner, Jaan and Lee Rudolph. 2008. "Who shall survive? Psychology that replaces quantification with qualitative mathematics." Paper presented at the *29th International Congress of Psychology*, Berlin, Germany, July 20–25.

Vauclair, Jacques. 2003. "Would humans without language be apes?" In *Cultural Guidance in the Development of the Human Mind*, vol. II: *Advances in Child Development within Culturally Structured Environments*, edited by Jaan Valsiner and Aaro Toomela, 9–26. New York: Ablex.

Veale, Tony. 2011. "Creative language retrieval: a robust hybrid of information retrieval and linguistic creativity." In *Proceedings of the 49th Annual Meeting of the Association for Computational Linguistics*, 278–87. Portland: ACL.

Veale, Tony and Yanfen Hao. 2008. "A fluid knowledge representation for understanding and generating creative metaphors." In *Proceedings of COLING, the 22nd International Conference on Computational Linguistics*. Manchester: ACL.

Volosinov, V. N. 1986. *Marxism and the Philosophy of Language*. Translated by Ladislav Matejka and I. R. Titunik. Cambridge, MA: Harvard University Press.

von Kleist, Heinrich. 1973. *The Marquise of O – and Other Stories*. Translated by M. Greenberg. New York: Frederick Ungar.

Vygotsky, Lev S. 1962. *Thought and Language*. Cambridge, MA: MIT Press. Electronic source: "Thinking and speaking," www.marxists.org/archive/vygotsky/works/words/index.htm.

Wainer, Howard. 1990. "Graphical visions from William Playfair to John Tukey." *Statistical Science* 5: 340–6.

Waxman, Sandra R. and R. Klibanoff. 2000. "The role of comparison in the extension of novel adjectives." *Developmental Psychology* 36: 571–81.

Waxman, Sandra R. and Jeffrey Lidz. 2006. "Early word learning." In *Handbook of Child Psychology 6*, vol. II, edited by Deanna Kuhn and Robert S. Siegler, 299–335. Hoboken, NJ: Wiley.

Weineck, Silke-Maria. 2003. "Kleist and the resurrection of the father." *Eighteenth-Century Studies* 37: 69–89.

Wells, Herbert George. 1947. *The Country of the Blind and Other Stories*. London: Longman Green.

Werman, D. S. 1993. "Edgar Allan Poe, James Ensor, and the psychology of revenge." *Annual of Psychoanalysis* 21: 301–15.

Wernicke, Sebastian and Florian Rasche. 2006. "FANMOD: a tool for fast network motif detection." *Bioinformatics* 22: 1,152–3.

Whorf, Benjamin Lee. 1956. *Language, Thought and Reality*. Cambridge, MA: MIT Press.

Wilks, Yorick. 1975. "A preferential pattern-seeking semantics for natural language inference." *Artificial Intelligence* 9: 53–74.

Williams, Tennessee. 1988 [1945]. *The Glass Menagerie*. Harmondsworth: Penguin.

Winnicott, Donald. W. 1965a. "The capacity to be alone." In *The Maturational Processes and the Facilitating Environment*, 29–37. New York: International Universities Press.

    1965b. "Communicating and not communicating leading to a study of certain opposites." In *The Maturational Processes and the Facilitating Environment*, 179–93. New York: International Universities Press.

    1971. *Playing and Reality*. New York: Psychology Press.

Yalom, Irvin D. 1995. *The Theory and Practice of Group Psychotherapy*. New York: Basic Books.

Yeshurun, Yaara and Noam Sobel. 2010. "An odor is not worth a thousand words: from multidimensional odors to unidimensional odor objects." *Annual Review of Psychology* 61: 219–41.

Žižek, Slavoj. 2006. "The matrix, or, the two sides of perversion." In *International Handbook of Virtual Learning Environments*, edited by Joel Weiss, Jason Nolan, and Peter Trifonas, 1,549–69. New York: Springer.

AUTHOR INDEX

SUBJECT INDEX